Sandra S

PRIMARY
FIRST

A Handbook for Primary Teachers

Oxford University Press 1987

Oxford University Press, Walton Street, Oxford OX2 6DP

Oxford New York Toronto
Delhi Bombay Calcutta Madras Karachi
Petaling Jaya Singapore Hong Kong Tokyo
Nairobi Dar es Salaam Cape Town
Melbourne Auckland

and associated companies in
Beirut Berlin Ibadan Nicosia

Oxford is a trade mark of Oxford University Press

© Sandra Soper 1987
ISBN 0 19 918149 7

Front cover illustration by Mark Rowney; book illustrations by Trevor Mason
Set by Christie Typeset (UK) Limited, Bristol
Printed in Great Britain

Contents

This book is dedicated to my parents

Introduction

This book is intended to help new primary school teachers, and to complement the teaching which you received in college. It is based on experience gained over ten years teaching in various schools around the country. It would be impossible and unwise to try to write a book which dealt with the specific needs of every kind of primary school — they are so many and so various. And yet, although there is this great diversity in the size, location and circumstances of our primary schools, there is also a central concern which they all share. The central concern of the primary school is the growing child. This raises many questions, how and what things stimulate and encourage growth, to what extent can and should the growth be directed, how best can detrimental influences be counteracted, and so on. These questions are as relevant to the multi-racial school as to the rural school, to the inner city blackboard jungle as to the serene village idyll. It is with these questions that this book is chiefly concerned.

Nothing in the book is being said for the first time. Most of it has been said long ago and many times since. Nevertheless time and attitudes change. The book has been written in the belief that a new way of saying the same thing is sometimes necessary and can often be helpful.

Inevitably there is a great divide between actual practice and talking about it. The last thing I wish to do is to make it all sound too easy. Feelings of inadequacy, discouragement, irritation, frustration and exhaustion are no strangers to me. There seemed to be no good reason for discussing such things since this book is intended to encourage you and not to help you to despair.

Finally it is acknowledged that the views expressed here will inevitably be somewhat idiosyncratic. But I think that probably most valuable points of view must be idiosyncratic, and further that it is by constantly reshaping (however infinitesimally) our own point of view in the light of the idiosyncratic view of others, that thought remains alive.

1. Looking ahead

When your final term at college comes to an end, your feelings will probably be rather mixed. Partly you will want to forget all about college as quickly as possible but partly you will want to look ahead and plan for the coming session and the new job. There is some point at this stage in casting a backward glance over your college career. Have some questions in mind such as:

- which parts of your college course did you think were most valuable?
- which parts did you think were least valuable?
- do you have reasons for your answers to the above two questions?
- did you disagree with any of the points put across at college?
- do you have alternative suggestions for the points with which you disagreed?
- for which areas of your work in the classroom do you feel least prepared?
- how could you find out more about these areas for yourself? (e.g. in service courses, private reading)
- do you have a contact at college from whom you could seek advice if necessary?
- did you encounter any first rate teachers during teaching practice to whom you could return for help and advice?
- have you checked out all possible facilities available to you as a teacher? (e.g. teachers centre, library, dept. of Education, college of Education.)

The point of this backward glance is not to catalogue a list of shortcomings of your college course but to put it into some kind of perspective. Also it is to set about making the most of what you have received from college.

An important part of your preparation for your new job will be to take a holiday of some kind. There is nothing to be gained by spending the entire summer worrying about school and the term ahead. A complete break during which you forget about all things educational will do you more good and enable you to come to school with a freshness of approach which you will not have if you spend the whole summer thinking about school.

Nevertheless, some part of the summer vacation can and perhaps should, be spent on forward planning. This could include a visit to your new school. Those of you who know which school you will join can make an appointment to visit the school by ringing or going to see the head. The end of term is an extremely busy time for all schools. It would be helpful therefore if you could offer a choice of dates and times for your appointment.

During the visit to the school there will be: Things to see

a) Staff room; cloakroom, caretaker's room, first aid post (this is very often a tin box in the secretary's drawer), offices of the head and secretary. Knowing the location of such places will increase your sense of security during the first week.

b) Playground; have a walk round during playtime if possible. Notice the play equipment if any and how the children use it. Are the children mixed or segregated in some way? Are there areas which will be 'out of bounds' to your children?

c) Try to see your classroom and children if possible though these may not be decided upon yet. You will not be able to take in a great deal nor should you attempt to, but even a brief glance will give you something concrete around which you can plan. You will also be able to find out basic details like whether or not your classroom has a sink, how far the lavatories are from the classroom and so on. Do not attempt to take in too many details or the whole exercise will become counter productive. The important thing at this stage is to take in a general impression of the school, its surroundings and the people with whom you will be working.

d) Library/resources room; again do not try to take in everything but try to get a general picture of the kinds of books/resources which are available, and in some cases not available.

Things to do and questions to ask

a) At some point during the visit, have a general walk round the school, not to look for anything in particular but more to try and sense something of the atmosphere of the place. You may not notice but a lot will go in.

Is the work of the school going on totally behind closed doors? how do children conduct themselves as they go about the school? How do the teachers talk to the children and each other? How do the staff react to the head? Are there signs of care for persons and property or signs of lack of care? The point of these questions is not to make premature value judgements it is simply to build up as accurate a picture as possible of the school as it is.

b) If time allows and it is appropriate i.e. where the school serves the streets in the immediate vicinity, walk up and down the neighbouring streets. This will help you to understand something of the kind of homes from which your children will most likely come. The more the two influences of home and school can be in harmony the better for the child. And, unless you have some understanding of what the home background is you will not be able to make any attempt to harmonise with it.

c) Have some questions ready for when you are given the opportunity to ask. If you are not given the opportunity you must take the initiative yourself. The questions will be specific e.g.

- starting time: at what time are you expected to be in school/classroom before the morning and afternoon sessions begin?
- lunch duty: are you expected to participate?
- playtime: are the children allowed to stay indoors?
- toys: are the children allowed to bring toys from home?

They will also be of a more general nature e.g.

- does the school encourage the children to go on trips?
- what is the buying policy of the school i.e. will you have any money to spend, any say in what is bought?

Be careful not to sound too much like the Grand Inquisitor. These questions at this stage are only to help you to get to know the school better. Cast your mind over the first week of term — if anything comes to mind about which you are not clear, ask while you have the chance. Do not ask questions for the sake of asking and do not ask too many questions. You will only become muddled and unnecessarily burdened. Much of the daily detail of organisation will be easily assimilated in the first few weeks of term.

Finally a word about the other members of staff. When you are introduced to them be friendly but not too overbearingly eager. Remember this visit will probably be taking place at the end of a very busy term. Consequently most members of staff will probably be tired and not at their best. Mostly they will be very willing to offer guidance and lend a helping hand, but give them time to get to know you. Observe and listen but above all reserve judgement. It is possible that you will hear a remark expressed against college and 'new fangled ideas' which could give you the wrong impression. Do not take such remarks too seriously. It would be a pity if you were to enter your first teaching post bearing a negative attitude towards future colleagues. Especially one which is based on nothing more than a few chance remarks made at the end of term. There are many excellent and kindly teachers who could be thought of as absolute dragons, if some of their words were to be taken literally.

For many of you it will be impossible to make a school visit before term actually starts. Your first encounter with the school therefore will be on the first day of term.

Although this arrangement is perhaps less than ideal it need not be a cause of too much concern. There are even some positive advantages. For instance, you will not be expected to know anything about the school and it's organisation. You will therefore probably receive more help during the first few days than you would do otherwise. Also, your mind will be free of details like where to put the empty milk crates or how to mark the dinner register etc. While details of this sort must be known, they will be easier to pick up in the context of the classroom where they naturally fit into the scheme of things. Certainly there is no point in worrying over such details throughout the summer holidays. Far better that your energies be directed towards the working out of strategies which will be of positive use to you during your first term.

Things to prepare

Whether or not you see your school before the beginning of term, there are useful preparations which can be made. These will serve to ward off any panic you may feel and also to increase your confidence generally.
 • Buy some paperback books, short stories, nursery rhymes, songs, poetry, 'things to do' etc. They are relatively cheap and are usually very good value. Take the time to browse through a book shop or attend a publisher's exhibition. It is easy to get bogged down in such places though, so stop if you begin to feel overwhelmed. Keep your eyes open for jumble sales/second hand book sales. Some of my best 'finds' have been at these. Don't bury yourself in a mound of books, your main aim in the first weeks is to make contact with the children and books can get in the way of this. Also it is only by *using* books *with* children that you will learn what sort of books work best for you. So, half a dozen

or so 'helpers' of the kind outlined above will be enough to begin with. You may hardly ever use them but the knowledge that they are there if you need them will be a comfort.

• Ask in travel agencies for old or spare holiday posters. These can be used simply to brighten the classroom and create a welcoming atmosphere for the children. They will of course be replaced by the children's work as the term progresses and may even be the starting point for some post holiday project by the children.

• Equip yourself with a wadge of scrap paper. Computer print out sheets are relatively easy to come by, ask in offices or other premises where such sheets are likely to be used. Those of you who plan to teach in the more remote parts of the country (i.e. where offices etc. are in short supply) should stock up before you leave college. Dustbins from offices and shops are an excellent source of scrap paper and card, so are publishers and printers. Often you can obtain such materials before they reach the dustbin simply by asking. Spare paper is in short supply in some schools. To have your own will mean that you can use as much as you like without having to worry.

• Buy a decent set of broad felt markers. You will use them constantly in school and you may well want to use them before terms starts. It is a great treat for children to be allowed to use 'your set' occasionally. If you keep up the image of your markers being 'special' the work produced is usually of a 'special' standard. You cannot rely on being issued with a set. Schools vary in the quantity and quality of markers which are issued per term. To begin the term with your own set will get you off to a good start.

This is not supposed to be an exhaustive list of a 'basic kit' for teachers but it will be relatively easy and inexpensive to gather these things together and they will almost certainly be useful during that first term. The rest of your own particular 'basic kit' (things like, a Bible, dictionary, atlas etc.) you can gather as you go along and as your needs develop in the light of experience. Finally for that first morning it would be as well to take a

pencil	small stapler and some staples
pencil sharpener	roll of Sellotape
rubber	lump of Blu-tak
pair of scissors	ruler
red and blue ball-point pen	
note pad	

Unlikely as it may sound, there may be the odd situation where these things are not supplied, and you may find yourself in it.

So much then for what you can do outside the classroom before terms starts. Here are one or two reminders for you to think about, which will help you once term has actually started.

- Give the children something to do once they have finished a piece of work. Whether you are working with the whole class or in groups some children will inevitably finish before others. A common mistake at first is to over estimate the time needed for a piece of work. Order will quickly turn to chaos if children finish a task in half the time you have allowed and you have nothing for them to do. Eventually you want to aim for a working atmosphere in the classroom in which the children are rarely at a loss for what to do. In the meantime it is enough to insist that whenever the children have finished a piece of work they do one of two activities. The choice can be as basic as say to read or draw. Limit the choice to two activities but give them two so that there *is* a choice. A choice however limited makes a vital difference to the attitude with which a child approaches an activity and often has a bearing on the depth of concentration given to a task and therefore on the quality of work which is produced. Remember to tell them at the beginning of a piece of work what to do when they have finished. Do not wait till they *have* finished or you will have to say the same thing a dozen times as each child finishes and comes to ask what to do next. There is an added bonus when you give instructions like this to cover more than one activity, you give the child a greater sense of responsibility over its own actions. Children can only learn to be responsible if they are allowed to be so.

- Do all you can to make the transition from one activity to another happen with the minimum of fuss. Look round the classroom to visualize how a child is to put her book on your table and gather what she needs for her next activity. If the drawing paper is in a cupboard under a pile of books she will have to cause unnecessary disruption. Are the crayons easily accessible to all the children, and do they know where and how they are stored? It is necessary to tell them these things. Do the children know what to do when a pencil breaks? Unless you want to hear about every single breakage (and I suggest you do not), then tell them what to do. Have a pot for broken pencils alongside a pot of ready sharpened ones. If a pencil breaks the aim is to exchange it as quickly and sensibly as possible. It is not to use the broken pencil as an excuse for a hue and cry and general interruption of work. The children will take their cue from you here. If you seem to think that a broken pencil is worth an interruption in work so too will they. Attention to minute detail like this will stand you in good stead when you come to apply it to more complicated activities.

• Do not be too ambitious about work projects. It is enough for you to successfully manage each school day, every one of which will uncover some new aspect of school life. If you do feel that things are running away from you and that you are losing control, have no hesitation about stopping and starting again. In a specific lesson if things get out of hand simply stop the lesson and set the children to quiet work. You can resume the lesson later when you have a chance to do some re-planning. Do not be afraid to change course like this because of losing face in front of the children. You are not expected to be superhuman. The one thing the children will respect though is honesty. They will trust you more if you honestly admit your mistakes and keep them informed of your change of plans. If you keep them in the dark, or worse, blame *them* for your mistakes, you cannot expect trust or respect in return.

• Keep a tight rein on the children during the first few weeks. Be firmer than you would perhaps like to be. It will do no harm and you will feel much happier if you can relax at *your* pace. The children will be as unsure of you as you are of them and it will help if they know exactly where they stand. Show them that you expect them to be sensible, responsible and interested, (it is important that you *do* expect them to be these things). Most of them will want to be these things but inevitably some of them will want to test you out. Some children cannot resist a chance to show off or to play the fool. It is often a cry for attention or it can be just plain clownishness. Do not allow such incidents to assume too much importance but do stamp on disruptive behaviour before it gets out of hand. To begin with do not allow any second chances. Move a disruptive child the moment something starts. Either bring him beside you or at any rate remove him from the scene of disruption. Give him plenty to do and make it as interesting as you can. So often the cause of inattention and bad behaviour is boredom.

Be firm certainly but do not forget to be fair. This is very important in the creation of a good working relationship. Children are more yet less vulnerable than we sometimes suppose. A cutting remark or unfair punishment can remain with a child for a very long time indeed, and you will not get co-operation from a child who is harbouring a grudge against you.

Above all avoid empty threats. If a child is causing a problem then take the initiative there and then and do something about it. Don't be afraid of becoming unpopular. Children will take a great deal of honest discipline, fairly administered and they will even grow to respect you for it.

• Make use of other members of staff. The help and support of colleagues will be a vital part of your development as a teacher. Tap this source of help from the start. Observe colleagues at work with the children. Spot their various strengths so that you know who to go to for what kind of help. Most will be delighted that you seek to enlist their help whether it is specific (to do with a particular project) or more general advice you are after. There could well be a fund of knowledge and experience on your classroom doorstep. Take advantage of it while you have the chance.

Take advantage also of the experience of the various non-teaching staff at school. If you can enlist the help of a sympathetic caretaker you can move mountains. Early on in my career I had reason to be grateful to one of the non-teaching members of staff. At the end of my probationary period I had to fill in 45 record cards which would accompany my class of the past two years up to the junior department in the Autumn term. So meticulous had the Infant mistress been, and so mindful of the reputation of 'her department' that she had filled in the fronts of all the cards herself (this meant 90 cards for two classes) leaving the other probationer and myself to fill in the relatively simple first page. To my abject horror I realized whilst filling in the 10th card that I had made the same glaring error on each card. I was frantic. After all we had heard about the importance of these cards and how painstakingly they had been filled in over several long evenings, the thought of going to confess my crime was out of the question. In my desperation I thought of the school secretary with whom I was reasonably friendly. I rang her up and asked if she could replace the 10 cards with 10 new ones from the stock room. She laughed at my plight but said she would see what she could do, and the next day she smuggled the cards to me when she brought round the registers. I had to forge the handwriting on the front of these replacement cards and lived under a cloud of fear for the next week or so in case the forgery would be spotted. It wasn't and as far as I know my crime remained undetected. I hope you will be able to use your good relations with the non-teaching staff for nobler ends than this. Nevertheless it is advisable to set about fostering these relationships with potentially co-operative and helpful colleagues.

Having done all you can outside the classroom and then thought about how to minimise problems inside the classroom there is one final device you could usefully have up your sleeve. It is always useful to be able to gather the children together to spend 10 minutes or so in fruitful and enjoyable activity. The following list of easy adaptable ideas is not for you to follow slavishly, but it is for you to think about in the light of how you personally would use them. Also it is to stimulate you to add your own ideas for suitable time fillers.

If you imbue these activities with the same importance that you give to other areas then the quality of the children's involvement will make it possible for the activities to be as enriching as anything else the children do. There is also the added bonus here that the children are usually so relaxed during these sessions that much learning goes on almost unwittingly. Many of these activities will be incorporated into your daily curriculum. The curriculum aspect is discussed in a later chapter.

Singing

Learn some songs by heart. If you cannot/will not sing in front of the children then at least know the words. Most children are quite happy to start after a count of two or whatever if the song is well enough known to them. Insist that they sing softly to begin with. It is much easier to keep in tune and you will have more control. Stop immediately anything goes wrong and start again. Singing is a useful way to calm the children down. It can also serve to bring them together after a period during which they have been working at various activities. 'Guess the tune' was a game which proved popular with me. Someone hums the first line of a well known tune and the others guess the title. You will be able to develop variations on this game as you go along.

Rhythm tapping

The rhythm of a well known song, rhyme, person's name etc. is tapped out with a pencil/ruler/drumstick on a desk/table/blackboard and children guess what it is. The categories are endless —

Vegetables	*cauliflower carrot*
Cities	*London Aberdeen*
Animals	*horse guinea-pig*

Besides being fun this activity is an excellent way to improve listening skills. These are so vital yet so often neglected.

Poetry

If you haven't already started a personal anthology *start one now.* Do not put poems in it simply to fill it up. Choose poems which please you in some way or poems which suggest good follow up work like painting or drama. Mark those poems you like in paperback books and jot down the page and title inside the front cover until you get round to entering them in your anthology. My anthology started off beautifully enough but soon became a collection of assorted shapes of paper on which I'd scribbled down poems and verses from various sources. Many poems still await inclusion. I do not recommend this as a way to compile an anthology or to store poens. Time is wasted each time you thumb through the unfiled poems looking for one in particular. Nevertheless a jumbled collection is better than none. You can read a poem to the children at any time during the day. Like singing it is a particularly useful activity to bring the children together. You could well end a noisy session on a more peaceful note by reading some poetry together. Present as wide a variety of poems as you can. You will soon see which sort of poems appeal to particular children. Encourage the children to read aloud to themselves and to each other. Poems which can be split into two or more parts are useful. The children can be divided into the appropriate number of groups for each part. All the children can then participate in the reading aloud of a single poem and also those children who are perhaps rather shy about reading aloud by themselves have the support of the others in the group. The rhythm and rhyme of simple poems are incidentally an aid to poor readers. Sometimes it will be necessary to make duplicated sheets of a poem so that every child can see the words clearly. Poetry, however, should not *always* be linked to reading. The effort to read the words can get in the way of the sheer enjoyment of listening to them.

Mime

This activity needs no equipment and is so adaptable that it can be used in practically any situation. Stick to individual mimes at first, group work can come later. Show the children a few simple examples (e.g. teeth brushing, needle threading, putting on a sock, etc.) then let them have turns. The others must *wait till the mime is finished* before they can put up their hands to guess the mime. This is usually an extremely absorbing activity and even after the excitement of guessing the children instantly settle to complete silence to watch the next mime, (if they don't, wait until they do before allowing the next mime to start). Impress upon the children the importance of quality of mime and the importance of detail. Allow the child miming to choose the next child. Lastly, to avoid unnecessary fidgeting and neck craning, make sure all the children are comfortable and can see easily.

Story

This is so obvious a time filler that it needs only to mention a successful variation called 'How will it be?' It needn't be called this, you could probably think up a better title of your own. These fanciful titles seem to appeal to the children. Somehow they enter more unreservedly into the spirit of the activity if they think it is a game. They forget that here for example they are doing aural composition and concentrate all their energies on keeping the story going. You start the ball rolling by saying something like 'This morning I forgot to . . . . . .' then point to a child at random who continues the narrative by any number of words, even one, so that the story line continues as smoothly as posible.

Performance

This is another fanciful title for an activity which is based on the fact that children love to perform and to watch others perform. Limit the choice at first to perhaps reading, reciting or singing. You can gradually extend the choice as the children become familiar with the activity. Stress that before something is offered for performance it must be worked out or rehearsed enough to be worth watching. Initially some items will not be worked out to a high enough standard. In this case do not hesitate to stop the performance. Explain that the thing is simply not ready to be performed and make some helpful comments if you can. With younger children you can help them there and then to speak out, hold the book down, face the audience or whatever. Gradually they will grasp the idea and you will see a steady increase in the quality of the items which are offered. Eventually there will be almost no limit to the choice of items e.g. joke telling, gymnastic display, creative movement, drama, dance etc. If you give the children the opportunity it will surprise you to note how much care and attention they will give to the preparation of these items. One of the values of this activity is that it can offer to every child, regardless of ability, the opportunity to make a contribution. Also, when the performance is a group item, it is a valuable exercise in learning to work together in a spirit of mutual co-operation.

I-spy

This traditional game is equally adaptable. If you add the words *in my mind's eye* you make the possibilities limitless.
e.g.
I spy in my mind's eye:

> a number which is three times eight
> a shape which has four equal sides
> the name we give to a baby cat
> the capital of Scotland
> an orange vegetable
> Mandy's favourite pudding

. . . and so on. The traditional *I spy with my little eye* is just as much fun and gives good practice in observation but there is no harm in a little variation from time to time.

Anecdote

You or one of the children may have something worthy of recounting. Say at the beginning of the morning 'remind me to tell you about my neighbour's cat when we have a minute to spare' or 'John's brother came back from Australia last night, he'll show us his present later'. An important element in these time fillers is that the children must be interested and enthusiastic about them. An element of anticipation is a good way to sharpen interest. Do tell the children of incidents and experiences in your daily life. The passing on of first hand experience is as educative a device as any I have witnessed apart from giving the children first hand experience for themselves. And since you, unlike Merlin will not be able to give them more than a few such first hand experiences, do the next best thing — tell them of yours. So, if you break a bottle, win a prize, visit the dentist, enjoy a film, fly in an aeroplane — tell them about it. Be assured, they will be interested.

These then are a few of the time fillers which I have found successful and more interesting than the standard spelling/arithmetic/general knowledge quizzes, though these too have their place.

The vital thing is to get the children enthusiastic and interested. It is important therefore to vary the activities and also to give them something of the aura of a treat, e.g. 'you've worked well this morning I think we might have time for 'How will it be?/I-spy' etc. or 'Katy has asked if she could read you her story, if you finish off now we could spare 10 minutes before playtime.'

Very often the children will come to you and ask 'When could we have a performance/mime session/poetry reading?' etc. This could lead to the creation of a waiting list — those children who are keen to do something enter themselves on the waiting list under

| Name | Item | Length of Time | etc. |

The problem, when you reach this stage, will be not how to fill the time but how to expand it so as to fit everything in.

Finally, to end this chapter, a brief glance at the first day. Try to be in school early enough to:

- put up a few pictures
- check you have enough pencils for each child (and spares)
- check that you have enough chairs for each child
- check if you do not already know, the location of the lavatories, staff room, head/secretary's office etc.
- ask when playtime is and jot this down on your note pad
- check milk and straws (if appropriate)
- put some work on the black-board (a piece of writing to copy will do) You may not use it but if you do then better that it is there ready than that you have to write it up one step ahead of the children.
- look at the registers (fill these in in pencil at first, you can go over them in ink later)
- find out where you are to meet your children (you may have to collect them from the playground or from another classroom)
- see that you can open the windows
- check that you have a black-board eraser
- see that you obtain keys for cupboards and drawers if necessary

Don't let this kind of detail get in the way of the main business of the day which is to meet and make contact with the children. Have some ideas jotted down on your note pad in case you have a mental block and cannot think of what to do next.

Soon after the children come in you can ask them to write their names on strips of paper (which you will have ready) and place these on their tables or desks. This will not only help you to learn their names more quickly but also allow you to address each child correctly from the start.

My recollection of the opening minutes in front of my first class (forty-six 5 year-olds) is of a sea of faces looking at me and a mounting inward scream of HELP. This only lasted a few seconds however before I introduced myself and let the children practise my surname a few times. I then told them to lift the lids of their desks so that we could explore and explain the contents; 'this is your tidy box and it will help you keep your desk tidy, and underneath is your blackboard, can you find your chalk tin?' etc. I had been in school the previous week to prepare the classroom and their desks and so was in a position to make the most of this desk exploration. I then told them to take out their name cards (which I had made in the holidays) and put them on top of their desks. Each child in turn then '*read*' his name aloud to 'check that I had got them right'. After this they were ready to be left to play with plasticine for a bit whilst I collected my thoughts and the dinner money. The rest of the day passed in a variety of activities alternating between gathering together for a story or song and going off to work unsupervised for short spells. No two first days will be alike of course and yours will have your own unique stamp upon it. Happily there is no one right way of going about it. Nevertheless everyone regardless of ability or inclination will undoubtedly be helped by some advance preparation and a little thought.

2. First Term

During your first term you will have a lot to learn about the running of the school and the personalities of the staff. You may also be anxious to try out ideas which until now you have only been able to think about. The amount of help you receive during your first term will of course vary from school to school. No one will expect you to know everything so for goodness' sake ask questions if you feel in the dark about something. This applies to questions about the running of the school as well as to those more particular to your classroom work like the teaching of reading. Throughout this term you will be feeling your way, getting to know your children and learning about what works and what doesn't work in the classroom. Take things slowly at first. Do not be in too much of a rush to carry out your ideas before you first establish a good working relationship with the children. Here are three ideas to help you to do this.

First expect respect from the children and work towards earning it, i.e. be on time to greet them coming into the classroom, take the trouble to prepare your work and take serious notice of theirs, listen to what they say and as far as possible be fair in your dealings with them.

Second, over simplify instructions. Breakdown in classroom order often happens simply because the children do not understand what they are supposed to be doing. When you give an instruction explain each stage carefully and make the stages as small as you can. This applies whether you are telling the children how to line up (see section on Infants) or whether you are explaining a piece of work (see section on Juniors). As you go along your ability to give clear concise instructions will improve, but in this first term you will learn largely by experience what to include/omit and how not to be vague or ambiguous.

Third, be prepared to be flexible in your plans, i.e. do not have too fixed an idea about the end of this or that project. Imagine this scenario — you have a vision for a display of some kind — the children do their parts and bring to you their efforts — the display looks nothing like you had imagined. Instead of just feeling depressed or frustrated about it you could try to improve the display. Try a few additions of your own (a thick black outline round a child's drawing can work wonders for a display) to make the most of what the children have offered. I remember things went haywire for me more than once in the gym. To give carefully prepared instructions to forty or so five-year olds, and then to see them get up and practically as a body do something completely different can be salutary as well as amusing.

When things go wrong or not as you had planned, it is not the end of the world. You can stop and start again as would be best in the gym, or make the best of things as they have turned out as would be best with the art work. You are the best judge of which course to take, but it will probably help you if at the beginning of a lesson or project you bear in mind that with children there is always an element of unpredictability.

This chapter is divided into two sections: *Infants*, and *Juniors*, i.e. children from 5–7 years and children from 8–11 years. You are urged to read both. It is vital to know and understand as much as possible about the kind of environment a child has come from/will go to when he/she reaches/leaves you. There is a lot to be earned by the Infant teacher from the Junior teacher and vice versa. Some schools (though not many) actively encourage internal exchanges so that staff can have the opportunity of teaching children at a different stage from their own. If you are not offered this direct opportunity perhaps you could acquaint yourself with older/younger children in an extra curricular club, (suggestions for these appear in chapter 6). Ask about the work of the class immediately above/below your own, and look at some samples of work not to learn details but more to develop a general feel for what is going on.

Each year an enormous amount of time and energy is completely wasted simply because teachers will not take account of the stages in a child's development other than those with which they are directly concerned. A teacher who understood the struggling efforts of a 5 year-old to hold a pencil and write her name legibly would perhaps be less impatient with her 7 year-old who was still struggling to write a sentence unaided. Similarly a teacher who understood that next year her ten-year-old would have to lead a much more independent school life, would perhaps be more inclined to give him the kind of responsibility for his own actions that will stand him in such good stead in his secondary school. The problem is indeed highlighted when the next stage involves a change of school. For example, many nursery schools proudly state that it is not their policy to teach reading, writing, number, etc. This is fine, but there are many specific pre-reading activities etc. which can and ought to be given to the children in their pre-school term at nursery, with a view towards what will be required of them next term. The attitude of *that's their job not ours* is at best unprofessional and at worst harmful to the children.

Naturally you are not expected to become familiar with all stages of development during your first term. It is right though that you should be aware of their existence so that when time and opportunity arise you can find out more about them. You are urged therefore not only to read both sections here but to go on 'reading both sections' that is to go on being prepared to learn from colleagues whose immediate objectives must necessarily be different from your own.

Infants

It seemed sensible to start at the beginning so this section is written from the perspective of the reception class. Those of you with older children can make the required shift in emphasis. For the first few weeks in a reception class much of your time will be taken up with basic training and getting to know the children. Basic training may sound dull or even worse but it is essential to the running of a well ordered and happy Infant room.

Your children should know: How to address you

Many children go to school for weeks without properly knowing their teacher's name. Make a point of checking that your children know your name and how to pronounce it. Later you can introduce them to the names of the other members of staff. It is preferable that members of staff be addressed by their proper names rather than by the anonymous Miss or Sir. First, it is not accurate, and second, it can cause confusion when there are several 'Misses' and 'Sirs'.

How the classroom is organised

Where the pencils/paper/crayons etc. are kept. What to do with broken pencils/scrap paper/finished work. All these things are a matter of individual choice based on pragmatic considerations, but however you decide to organise things make sure the children understand your organisation. They will need several carefully guided tours before they feel at home in the classroom. Make a game of it —

'John, run to the broken pencil pot, pick up a pencil in your left hand, put it back, walk here and sit down.'

'Mary, tip-toe to the boat picture, count the boats, read the title, sit on your chair.'

'Tom, hop to my table, pick up the drawing pin pot, carry it to the owl picture, put it on the floor, sit down beside it, fold your arms.'

It is surprising how often the childen do not know where the pencil pot or whatever is (despite countless tellings). This game can serve to teach you as much as it can teach the children. With older infants the title of the game can be changed to 'following instructions' — the sound of the words will have more appeal for them and they will often ask if they can have the 'following instructions' game.

How to dress and undress

For younger children this can be a major obstacle. Be patient with them and allow as much time for practice here as you can afford. The manipulation of buttons, zips, buckles, laces etc. serves to increase manual dexterity and the use of words like *too small, inside out, back to front, left, right, tight, slack* etc. will extend their experience of language. If you can look upon the periods of dressing and undressing as an opportunity to improve motor skills and extend language, you will be less likely to become impatient and rush the children through these sessions. Children will vary in speed and dexterity so have an activity (reading will do) available for those who are dressed first.

Where the lavatory is and how to use it

Young children are very often worried about asking to go to the lavatory. Make it as easy for them as possible. As a general rule, I would let them go as they asked. You will soon learn to distinguish the child who really does need to go from the one who doesn't. Initially though let the odd few go who may not need to, rather than risk an accident in the classroom. If an accident does occur deal with it as quickly and lightly as you can, that is make as little fuss as possible. Keep a box of spare clothes in the classroom and some plastic bags for wet or soiled clothes. Take the children TO the lavatory to demonstrate its use — how to flush clean water in, how to wash and dry hands, how to use a paper towel etc. A visit of this kind where you can actually SHOW the children what you mean will be much more effective than numerous explanations.

Something about the basic geography of the school

For many young children the school building is a vast and mysterious place. Help them to feel a little more at home by pointing out some appropriate landmarks — head's office, caretaker's room, hall, dining room, gym etc. Show them only as much as they can comfortably comprehend. Take them on a short guided tour from time to time but do not show them too much or they will become more baffled than ever. They will need to be shown where and how to hang their coats. Where possible, young children should have a coat peg of their own marked with their name and/or an easily identified picture or symbol. This helps the dressing and undressing to be more ordered and can save endless confusion.

People's names and jobs

Explain who the various people are who help to run the school and say a little about the work of each of these people. If you present the whole thing as a co-operative venture you will be in a strong position to ask for *their* co-operation when the time comes.

e.g. The school caretaker. You can say something like 'Mr Brown is our caretaker. He is called this because he helps take care of us and our school. He makes sure that our floor is swept every day, that our classroom is warm in Winter, that our school is safely locked up at night etc. Then, at some point when a complaint arises you can enlist the children's help — 'Mr Brown needs some help because some of us haven't been taking enough care of the school. He wonders whether we could remember to check under our table before we go home/wipe our muddy boots outside/put our litter in the litter bin etc.'

It is better for you to make a reasonable plea for co-operation than to demand dumb obedience. You will also then, when the time comes, have more right to take firmer measures with those children who appear not to be pulling their weight.

A great deal of your time will be taken up by giving instructions to the children. This in itself is quite an art and something in which you are well advised to become accomplished. Do not be afraid to over simplify things since this is almost impossible with Infant children. As I said at the beginning of the chapter make each step small, i.e. each step should contain no more than *one* thing to do. The children will learn to fit one step to another to see the sense of the whole instruction.

Assume to start with that the children know virtually nothing, e.g. even the seemingly self explanatory instruction 'line up at the door' will need initially to be broken into parts in order to minimise confusion. Tell the children that they are going to learn how to line up. The tone of your voice and your general attitude ought to convey the IMPOR-TANCE of the task. 'Mary come and stand in front of me. John come and stand behind Mary — there Mary is *in front* of John and John is *behind* Mary. Now Peter come and stand behind John, look at the back of John's head to make sure you are tucked in behind him. Now, Katy come and stand behind Peter, etc. All the while you will be explaining that they are making such a long line and such a straight one. Tell them how well they are doing and let half the class see how well the other half lines up and vice versa.

There is no shortage of learning in this kind of activity. The children learn how to follow instructions by fitting simple steps together. They are hearing words perhaps used in a new way or even hearing words for the first time. Besides, life will be much easier for you when the children can do routine things like lining up without fussing and squabbling.

Another important point to remember is to *wait* for attention before you dish out an instruction. This applies especially when the children are already working and you want to tell them something. If you start to tell them when they are only half listening they will only half hear. From time to time throughout the day you will need to have the atten-tion of the whole class. Indeed the ability to instantly command the atten-tion of a large group will be useful to you throughout your career. It is not one which comes naturally to most people but it can, to a certain extent be learned.

My first Infant mistress used three signals which would bring ins-tant attention from the children. The importance of these signals was of course stressed to the children and they worked so well for me that I pass them on to you for consideration, to take up, leave or adapt as you will.

Stop Working

At the sound of these words the children would 'down tools'; pencils, books, toys or whatever would be placed down quickly and quietly. All eyes would fasten on the teacher. Practice as a game to start with. It is a useful device for when the children are engaged in a variety of activities in various parts of the room. Be extreme in your standards when introducing the game — 'not quite right, John is still holding his pencil', 'Andrew's eyes are not on my face' etc. Make much of it when it is done properly, 'that was splendid, shall we see if we can do it again?' As a tool it can save a great deal of time throughout the year as well as wear and tear on your nerves.

Listen

This is a useful signal for those times when the children are not actually working yet their attention is elsewhere and you need it. Again it is a signal for instant attention. Stress the importance of LOOKING at the person who has given the signal or the person who is talking (a useful point for radio/television programmes, assemblies, visiting talkers. On such occasions you can signal by a nod of your head to an inattentive child to look at the person to whom she is supposed to be listening.) Reinforce the habit from time to time. Ask the children to chat quietly and at the sound of the word LISTEN they must whip their eyes around to your face. They love it and the habit is strengthened.

Three Claps

For the claps to be effective they must be clearly audible above a considerable amount of noise. Learn, if you do not already know, HOW to clap. Slightly cup the palm of one hand; with the fingers of your other hand firmly clap right over the rim of the cup making sure to completely cover it. Practise a little until you can make a resounding crack. It is a useful way to reduce noise level without interrupting the children's work. It can also be used effectively when someone comes into the room to talk to you. If noise starts to grow you can check it without taking your attention from your visitor. We used to say the claps meant please-be-quiet but the claps will probably mean more to the children if they can translate them themselves — less-noise-please/not-so-loud/shhhh-shhhhh-shhhhh, etc.

As with all tools regular maintenance will help to keep these functioning efficiently for you. The children's response will tail off from time to time. When this happens a short practice will soon sharpen things up.

Another detail of routine which will need your attention is the tucking in of chairs. Help the children to make a HABIT of tucking in their chairs each time they leave them. Again this will need practice, simply to tell them is not enough. Spend five minutes or so from time to time reinforcing the habit. Choose a group, call them to you ('all the people at Mark's table come and stand by me'), see how many chairs have been left out, repeat the process, how many this time etc. At a moment when the whole class is seated ask them to quickly stand behind their chairs. How many remembered to tuck chairs in? Make a game of this from time to time and the children will soon make a habit of it. It is a small detail but it can make the difference between an atmosphere of tolerable disorder and one of total chaos. It is also an important safety precaution.

It may seem that an inordinate amount of time has to be spent on these training games and devices. Be assured that by giving the children adequate training at the beginning you will save countless hours throughout the term. You will also save yourself needless nervous exhaustion. A vital part of your job is to create an atmosphere which is conducive to serious work and indeed serious enjoyment. If you get the details of organisation out of the way then you will be free to deal with more important matters. If you do not, these details will constantly interrupt and disturb your daily work. So the point of this initial training is to create as much time as possible for serious work so that the children make the most of their time in school with you.

Daily Activities

There are certain activities which have to be done every day. This does not mean that they have to be tedious because they are repeated each day. All children, but perhaps especially little children, enjoy a certain amount of repetition and routine. It can help to provide a reassuring framework on which to hang the events of each new day. How you focus your attention on your daily routines will depend on your particular circumstances and personal inclinations. However you decide to arrange things give some thought to these routines so that you can at least not waste the time they take up and at best take real advantage of it. The following are some of the things I did every day along with some personal thoughts about each.

Registration

This happens twice daily, once in the morning and once in the afternoon. It is helpful to have a similar routine every morning for when the children come into a classroom, e.g. to sit and read a book, or to choose from a number of activities which have been laid out for them. With one reception class I used to ask the children to come in and sit on the mat (a large rectangle of carpet in front of my table) and have a quiet chat until I was ready for them. Whatever your arrangements the children should be well acquainted with them so that they know exactly what to do when they come into the classroom. When the time comes to do the register the children can either go on working quietly or you may want to have their undivided attention. It is probably better to adopt the latter for the first few weeks. Explain to them the rudiments of registration that you have to count the number of children who are here and the number of children who are not here, and write the numbers down in this special book called a register etc. Explain lunch or dinner registration in a similar way so that the children understand something of what is happening at this time. Indeed a useful way to ensure daily concrete number experience, for all the children is to physically count the children who are staying to school dinner. The 'dinner children' stand in a line and a child counts the heads (you will quickly spot the child who cannot yet master one-to-one correspondence); another child touches the heads while the whole class count aloud, each dinner child takes a bead and threads it on to the 'dinner' string, (are there the same number of beads as children?); dinner children stand at one side of the room, home children at the other, count the two groups separately — then together, (is the total number the same as the attendance total?), and so on. Most mornings you will probably have time to do no more than simply count the dinner children. Occasionally it is possible to enjoy a whole morning's number work which has been generated by the dinner register.

A great treat (with a considerable advantage in phonetic work) and one which grew from a daily routine, was to occasionally read the children's names from the register with the initials of the first name and surname reversed so that

    Susan Roche became Rusan Soche
    John Ridgely became Rohn Jidgely

    but

    Murray MacMillan stayed Murray MacMillan and so on.

This never failed to cheer us up (me included) but of course such things can only be done now and then or the novelty appeal is lost.

Assembly

You may be expected to join the whole school in a morning assembly. This can be a weird and mystifying experience for small children. Tell them as much as you can to help them to understand something of what is going on — that the whole school is gathering together to think about the day ahead; to give thanks to God and ask for His help (the Christian emphasis on assembly will vary according to the religious standpoint of the person conducting it as well as to the ethnic mix of the children in the school); to hear important bits of information, etc. and that even though they are quite small they can still practise sitting still and listening well. When I went to one school I discovered that the Infant children did not have an opportunity to sing i.e. they had to struggle through picking out the odd word in junior hymns. I mentioned it to the head and we introduced a slot in assembly in which these children could sing a song/hymn that they knew and understood. Thereby they were able to contribute and participate more fully and therefore have a greater understanding of what was going on.

If there is no assembly it is a good idea to have a short together time of your own somewhere near the beginning of the day. A time for reflection, for some news to be shared, for a song or verse, for looking ahead, for a recap of the previous day. It need take no longer than 10 minutes or so but it allows you to approach the day as opposed to falling into it. Also you can direct the children to their various activities while they are together and calm.

Milk time

You may or may not be in a position to *have* a daily milk time. It seems rather a cheerless prospect for a child to go from breakfast till lunchtime without sustenance of any kind. If there is no physical need surely there is a psychological one. Some schools now run schemes whereby parents can pay for a daily third of a pint for their child, others again allow the children to bring a beaker of milk from home. You could initiate such a scheme yourself if you wanted to.

Mid-morning is widely accepted as the best time for milk. As a feature of the day to which the children look forward, you can use it to observe them while they relax as a group — who is friends with who and who is left out etc. I once spent a weary few weeks in an open plan set up where 'it had been decided' that the children could drink their milk at what *they* thought was an appropriate time. Each afternoon saw me chasing up children who had forgotten all about milk, and standing over them while they quickly drank it down. When *I* forgot, I had to empty the contents of several bottles down the sink. Very quickly we realized that this idea was not working and that the children had enough to think about and decide, without the added worry of when to drink their milk. In order for it to be an enjoyable time you will have to be precise in your organisation and take the children through the routine very slowly. Have some golden rules like sitting still whilst drinking and always holding the bottle with two hands. This will help to keep spilt milk and broken bottles to a minimum.

Some teachers think of milk time as a tiresome bother, an irksome interruption to the work schedule. They get rid of it as quickly as possible. How would they feel, I wonder, if their mid-morning coffee had to be rushed or even cancelled because it interrupted the work schedule. My own feeling is that the taking of refreshment together should be a pleasure. Yes, it will interrupt work but the effect on that work will, in the long run be more gain than loss.

Keep well loved tales and rhymes for these periods, and the children will *want* to sit quietly to drink and listen. They can quietly return empty milk bottles as they finish or leave them till you say. Do make sure that the tops are off, straws out and bottles empty before they are returned to the crate. It looks so bad to see milk crates stacked at a school gate with milk left in some of the bottles and tops/straws unremoved. Apart from being unsightly it is unhygienic. *Someone* has to empty the bottles and remove the tops and straws. It *ought* to be the children. Take advantage of the wealth of potential number experience embedded in a milk crate. Let two children pierce or remove the tops and put straws in the milk — it almost *always* generates a conversation on number. There are educational possibilities in practically everything — milk time is no exception.

Calendar

A simple seven day strip is preferable at the reception stage. The more complicated calendars say too much for a five-year-old to understand. You may be provided with a commercially produced one. If so put it away until at least next term. There is a point beyond which visual aids become too complicated to be of any real value. Give everyone a chance in turn to change the day. A week is a good time span for this

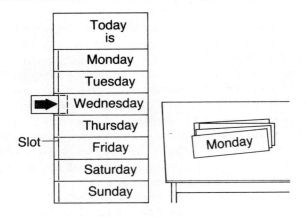

job. Do it at a fixed time each day (just before or after assembly is probably best) so that you are less likely to forget. Bring everyone's attention to the 'day changer' e.g. 'Listen, Polly is going to change the day — what day was yesterday Polly? — yes, Tuesday.' Now move on one day — 'What day is today? — yes Wednesday' — then again to everyone — 'What day is today? — Wed-nes-day.' Near the week strip you can position a set of cards on which the days are printed. The day changer can then (as well as changing the day and reading it aloud to the others), find the appropriate card and match it to the day on the calendar.

A very effective way to show how quickly the days go by in comparison to the months is to have a month strip in operation at the same time.

Animals/plants

Daily feeding may not be necessary but a daily check will be. Again set aside a specific time for this task each day so that there is less likelihood of forgetting it. On some days a daily check is all the attention these things will receive. At least if they have this you will avoid the depressing sight of parched plants, last months dusty old twigs and goldfish made invisible by algae. Make a rota for children who would like to be responsible for the welfare of the guinea pig, goldfish, snowdrops, cactii or whatever. If you see to it that enough importance is attached to these tasks the children will usually be very conscientious in carrying them out. The problem often is that the children become over zealous with their care and attention. You will have to keep an eye on things to make sure your plants and animals are not being killed by kindness.

Clearing up

This is as much a part of your daily routine as anything else. The easier you can make it the better. 'A place for everything and everything in its place' was an oft-repeated maxim by one of our teachers, and although it may have the ring of a sermon about it, it is in fact sound advice. Especially the bit about a place for everything. If the children know where things are stored the business of clearing up will be so much easier. Have a basket for lost lego/puzzle pieces/oddments. This can be gone through every few days to replace missing bits. I found that the children were amazingly clued up about what went where and very keen to replace missing bits or find a lost piece.

Have a quick tidy at the end of the morning when possible. You will tackle the afternoon with more energy when you have not got the remains of the morning's clutter to clear up first. Obviously this will not always be possible nor indeed desirable, for there will be days when you will want or need to continue the mornings activities straight on into the afternoon. When you can though it will probably be helpful to have a quick clear up at the end of the morning.

At the end of the day leave your desk-if you have one, in some kind of order rather than an assorted jumble sprawled over the whole surface. And, as a matter of course, check the floor. Make a daily point of it, set a few minutes aside at the end of each afternoon, appoint some children if need be to act as floor checkers. Make a game of it from time to time, count the number of articles found on the floor each day — keep a pictorial record of it etc. It is surprising how much equipment and debris finds its way to the floor by the end of the day. More surprising still is the number of teachers who simply leave it there for the cleaning staff to pick up. There will of course be times when you are so exhausted by the end of the day that you will be unable to summon up enough energy to stoop for a crayon or even to ask a child to do so. The odd crayon or piece of puzzle left lying about is understandable and perfectly acceptable. A floor which is littered with pencils, crayons, plasticine, etc. is not. It is sloppy, unprofessional, and inconsiderate to the cleaning staff, and unfair to the children. So, devise some method which ensures that clearing up becomes part of the daily routine, and one in which the children play an active part.

There we leave daily routines though there will be many more which apply only in particular situations. Whatever yours turns out to be, try to make them as pleasant as possible. Routine is by its very nature repetitive, this does not mean it must be tiresome. Nor does it mean that there is any excuse for a slipshod approach. These routines provide a framework for much of the rest of your work and deserve as much care and attention.

Before we leave this section, a final word about maintaining order. One of the main causes of chaos in an Infant room is that the teacher has not grasped the level of the children's thinking. Mentally they trail along behind picking up scraps of information here and there, trying to make sense of what to them seems to be a huge and bewildering puzzle. Naturally in your first term you will not be expected to key in at the right level all the time. It will be well to remember though that the children may not always understand what you say in the way you intend them to.

I once saw a child desperately try to work out what was going on by copying those around him. The children were seated on the floor and had been asked to move backwards. Some of them wriggled back others half got up, and so on. When an exasperated teacher asked 'Sancho what ARE you doing? I said move *backwards*' he was forced to ask 'Please miss, what is backwards?' We assume so much.

On another occasion I had an art student for a term. He started off miles above the children's heads — 'Today we are going to think about the 4 basic geometric shapes.' This was to second year infants! He might as well have been speaking Chinese.

Spoken explanation can be the key to clarity or confusion. A useful exercise during your first term and one which can be done on a car journey or in a bus queue, is to think of an instruction or explanation which you might want to give to the children, then break it down into as many simple stages as you can. You will quickly learn to key in at the right level, but at the beginning, if in doubt, it is always safer to pitch the level too low than too high.

Sometimes the signs that you have misjudged the level will be obvious. Often then will not, and so you must continually question and converse with the children with the specific intention of checking their level of understanding.

So much then for your first term with Infants. Now we turn our attention to Juniors.

Juniors

A first term with juniors will in some ways be more difficult than that of your colleagues in the Infant room. In other ways, it will be easier. For example, the children are more complex and therefore harder to get to know; you will have less of a 'clean slate' — the children will already have been taught a lot and will have learnt to do things in a certain way. The children's attitude to school and teachers will be more rigid and they will perhaps be more guarded towards you. But, in general, they will be able to concentrate for longer periods of time, they will be less dependent upon you, and you will be less taxed physically. There is little point in a book like this in dwelling on the differences between the two stages. More important is that you see the stages as different parts of the same thing. It is important too that you concentrate mainly on the age group with which you will be working, so that you can gear your work and approach to the appropriate level.

So, what will be your main concerns during your first term with juniors? The following section divides this question into three main areas:

1 Getting to know the children
2 Incorporating your ideas into existing systems, and
3 Record keeping

Getting to know the children

This is probably the single most important aim you can have. Do not assume to know the children's needs without first finding out something about the children themselves. The more you know about a child the better you are able to understand and therefore help him or her. As a new teacher what can you do to find out about the children in your care? There are several sources of information.

Reports

You may receive written reports from a previous teacher. Read these through and jot down information which seems to you important (e.g. left-handedness). After this put the reports away and forget about them. It is important that you create an atmosphere of acceptance and encouragement. You will not do this if you are seen to know about past faults and worse if you are seen to hold these as important. Some children get off to a bad start at school or hit a troubled patch. This need not be a permanent state of affairs. I used to reread the reports at the end of the year and was quite often surprised at the discrepancy between the report in front of me and my own assessment of the child.

If you show the child that you believe he or she is capable of making a fresh start then the child will be more likely to try to make one.

Medical reports are usually in the keeping of the head or secretary. Ask if you may have any medical information about your children, or look through any available reports themselves. Occasionally information of this kind (special dietary restrictions, allergies, asthmatic conditions, difficulties with sight or hearing) does not reach the class teacher until a dramatic event brings it to light. I once had rather an alarming experience when a ten-year-old in my class had a minor fit during a game of netball. Fortunately it passed quickly with no harm done but there were a few difficult moments. I later found out that this had happened once before in school and the child's condition though not at all serious, was known about yet I hadn't been told. Oversights like this can happen in even the most efficient set-ups, so do your part to reduce the risk of such a thing happening in your school.

Parents' evening

Some schools have a parents' evening near the beginning of term so that parents can report to teachers and offer information about their children. You might have to take the initiative and say that during this interview the emphasis is on the information coming from the parents to you and not the other way round. Parents are usually very happy to talk about their children and the fact that you are interested will in itself enlist their support.

I always found these occasions worthwhile especially with older children whose parents I did not see every day. A new dimension was added to my somewhat limited picture of the child. I almost always looked at each child in a more sympathetic light after a chat with his or her parents. If your school makes no provision for an early meeting with parents, ask the head if you could hold a meeting of your own. This could be a sensitive issue though so be careful not to unduly upset other members of staff.

Written work

Older children often show more of themelves in what they write than in what they say. On a surface level you will be able to spot the tidy child, the weak speller, the slow worker, the poor writer etc. Even details of information like this will help you to build a more complete picture of each child. On a deeper level you will be able to find out something of their thoughts and attitudes. Children, like icebergs, have large areas which are hidden beneath the surface and which their teachers seldom see. Devise specific strategies in their written work to shed light on their lives outside school, their interests, attitudes etc. e.g.

Essays — my home, room, family, pet, hobby, bike, garden, street, school, and so on. If you show that you are really interested in what the children write they will be more likely to *want* to write. Don't spoil this motivation by making too much of spelling or punctuation mistakes.

Lists — favourite/least favourite colours, cars, people, places, comics, food, music, dreams etc.

Pictures — dream house, toy, car, etc.

For those children with limited writing skill it is a good idea to form a group, each member of which contributes to a communal description of an ideal house, farm, factory or whatever. You act as scribe and write down the children's sentences on the blackboard (if they are to copy it later) or in a book which can be read back to them, then read by them etc. A relaxed atmosphere is important so that the children can offer contributions in a natural uninhibited way.

Drama

Sometimes more of a child's personality comes across while he or she is acting than is apparent in every day life. Use this activity to learn about your children. How they emulate people and which people are emulated, how they use words in certain situations, etc.

In a sense much of the work of the Primary school is dramatic activity. It is not so much a subject as a method. It is mentioned here to remind you that it is a good way to help you to get to know your children better. In your first term, be structured in your approach. Most children love drama and in their exuberance they can sometimes become difficult to handle. So, to begin with give precise instructions about what is wanted and if things start to get out of hand in any way then stop immediately. Tell the children why you have stopped and *don't* start again until you have gone over certain points (noise level, attention to the performers etc.), and things have settled down.

Listening in

Another way to get to know your children better is by unobtrusive eavesdropping while the children chat to each other over some model, painting or self-chosen work in which they are so involved that they can relax and chat naturally. I once overheard a conversation between a rather 'difficult' ten-year-old in my class and another boy. They were discussing the merits of Bing Crosby's singing voice, I had always placed A . . . . . in the aggressive/tough/cocky category and treated him accordingly with consequent limited results. The fact that he'd even heard of Bing Crosby was surprising enough let alone that he seemed to be so knowledgeable about the singer's repertoire. Now I do not claim a miraculous conversion on the basis of that one overheard conversation. I do claim though that it was a valuable insight into the child which helped me albeit in a very small way to have more fruitful and satisfactory dealings with him.

These then are some of the possiblities which could help you to get to know your children, I was once asked what a teacher should do with the information gathered about a child. This is a non-question because you *do* nothing with it; simply by having it your work will automatically be adjusted to fit the child. You will *know* when one explanation is enough, and when several are needed etc.

So, getting to know your children is a priority.

Incorporating your ideas into existing systems

What ideas? those about —
a) The Organisation of the Classroom
b) Ways of Working
c) Discipline

The Organisation of the Classroom

To begin with try not to be over ambitious. A colleague of mine moved all the desks out of her room into the corridor in the first week of term (she had decided that desks in the classroom were an unnecessary encumbrance). The experiment only lasted a few days and by the end of the second week of term the desks had been carried back inside the classroom again. Much time had been wasted and unnecessary distress caused to herself and the children in the process. This is rather an extreme example but the lesson is obvious. Do not rush to change things all at once.

You will probably have your own ideas about how you would like to see the classroom furniture arranged. If so, incorporate these ideas *gradually*. Try out one idea at a time. For instance you could rearrange the grouping of the tables/desks/cupboards in one fell swoop OR you could rearrange one section of a plan, see how it works then fit in the rest. With the latter you will quickly see what works and what doesn't work; it is easier to change one idea at a time than several. It will also be less disruptive to the children.

There are numerous ways to organise classroom furniture and happily, no ONE right way. This subject is expanded in a later chapter. For the moment, suffice it to say KEEP THINGS SIMPLE. An important aim during this first term is to make life relatively easy for yourself in order that the daily running of the classroom does not become an unmanageable burden. Elaborate arrangements will have to be masterminded and supervised if not *done* by you. All this is time consuming, exhausting and can even be disruptive especially when the finished plan does not 'work' as you had visualised.

Next term will be time enough to try out new ideas. For the moment keep things simple and easily workable. Leave things exactly as they are, if you like, for a week or two. The children may be used to the existing arrangement. This in itself can help to keep things running smoothly. Make sure though, that there are no serious flaws. CHECK for example that:

- no child's vision is obscured. I once watched a child bob back and forth from his seat to copy a Maths problem from the blackboard. His vision was obscured by the upper half of a book-case which had been place at right angles to the wall so as to create a book corner. We cannot rely on things that to us seem obvious, being so to a child. The seemingly 'obvious' remedy for this child's problem — to tell the teacher — was clearly not obvious to him, and so he struggled on with a task made needlessly laborious.

- left-handed children are catered for. Make sure that the arm of a left-handed child is not pinned up against the wall or another child. These children very often need more room when doing written work than right-handers. See that they are not therefore unnecessarily disadvantaged.
- children with poor hearing or eyesight are suitably positioned so that their particular handicap is minimised as much as possible.
- as far as possible, tables or desks and chairs 'fit' the children. A school day cannot be enhanced by having your knees scraped against the underside of a table or desk. Also a child will find it easier to produce neatly written work if his or her feet can comfortably reach the floor.
- movement in and out of seats is made as easy as possible. This will save time and reduce disruption throughout the day. (I have seen an arrangement where the child had to climb over his desk to get into his seat and one where a book case had to be slid aside each time the child left his seat.)
- potentially harmful, nails, sharp edges, wobbly chairs etc. are attended to. Don't wait for the cut finger or torn skirt, reduce possible accidents by a regular check throughout the term.

So, having sorted out any serious flaws in the existing arrangement you can then use it to see what works and what doesn't work for you. Possible arrangements of classroom furniture are discussed in the next chapter. During your first term, apart from anything you feel you absolutely must change, it is probably as well to leave things more or less as they are.

Ways of Working

These are many and various, e.g.

- do the children correct their own work always/sometimes/never?
- do they correct each others work?
- are they allowed to stay indoors at playtime?
- are they expected to line up before they leave the classroom?
- how do they answer questions? Do they put up hands or call out?

Ultimately your ideas about these things will decide what the children do, but at the beginning beware of banishing everything immediately. Naturally if the children come yelling and screaming into the classroom you will want to change this immediately. Don't put up with ridiculous practices. Don't be afraid to speak out against them either. In general though, during your first term you want to aim for a balance between discarding practices you don't like, and keeping some for the sake of continuity and reassurance to the children. For instance there may be a team system in operation. The children gain points for their team both collectively ('the 'Lions' were ready first 2 points to their team') and individually. At the end of a week or month the points are added up and prizes or praise is dished out accordingly.

Whatever your attitude to a team system in the classroom, find out what the children's attitude is first. They may be fiercely proud of such systems and could be hurt or offended to see them instantly discarded. Ask the children to explain a particular system to you. This can teach you a lot about the children's perception of a system, and will stand you in good stead when you come to put your own systems into operation.

While continuing with these past practices it is important not to appear to be slavishly following them for want of any ideas or confidence of your own. Otherwise the children may be constantly reminding you that Miss X did something *this* way or that Mr Y didn't allow such and such. Rather give the impression that you have chosen this or that practice to continue as you judge it to be the best thing to do for the moment.

There are some things of course which cannot be changed gradually. I once worked with a new Head who announced that he was going to gradually 'atrophy' the electric bells in the school. You can imagine the mirth in the staffroom over remarks about how we were going to do this. Was it going to ding ding/ding/di/d or brrr/brr/br/b etc.

Seriously though when you do have to discard something, tell the children why and if possible enlist their support by appealing to their better nature. I once worked in a school where the children who stayed to school lunch had been told to show their plates to the teacher on duty to show that they had 'eaten up' sufficiently well. Apart from the rather unappetising experience of having to look at sixty odd plates each containing varying remains of lunch, I found this practice demeaning to the children (especially the ten to twelve-year-olds). I had a word with the head who had no objection to giving the new system a try provided it did not lead to food being wasted. One day before lunch I explained to the children that we were going to dispense with the practice of plate showing, I was sure that they would eat as well as they could and that if there was a problem they could come to the teacher on duty. On the whole the new system worked and there was no visible increase in the amount of wasted food.

When my son was about eight he reported to me that they weren't going to line up anymore to go into school. Mrs K had said that she could see they were sensible children and so she didn't want to ask them to waddle in like a line of geese. He seemed to take a certain amount of pride in this announcement and as far as I could tell the changeover was smooth and untroubled.

So, cast a critical eye over the system you have inherited AND
Do get rid of ridiculous practices as soon as possible BUT
Don't replace everything immediately.

Discipline

This subject is dealt with in more detail in a later chapter. Here in the light of incorporating your ideas it may be useful to consider some of the following points.

Whatever else you hope to do, the better your discipline the better you will be able to put other plans into action. Discipline is not advocated for its own sake so much as a means to reasonable working conditions. If there is no good discipline then very often there is no good anything else. This doesn't mean you have to become a sergeant-major figure who barks orders and expects instant unquestioning obedience. The best and most effective discipline is that which comes from within the children themselves rather than that which is imposed from without (usually through fear). But, to help children towards self-discipline is a long term aim, and during your first term it is probably enough for you to concentrate on simply being able to maintain a reasonable amount of order i.e. to conduct most of your lessons without having to shout; to be able to command attention quickly; to have an idea of what most of the children are up to most of the time. These things can all be learned. First of all it is a good idea to *tell* the children what you expect in the way of reasonable behaviour. This may seem painfully obvious yet it is so often left undone. The child finds out what is expected through a cutting remark or an uncalled for telling off. The result is that anger and hostility build up in the child, and despair and weariness in the teacher.

I shall never forget the humiliation I suffered as a fifth former when I bent the covers of a new book back on themselves in an attempt to get the book to stay open on my desk. Suddenly I heard my name bellowed across the classroom S . . . . G . . . . don't *ever* let me see you doing that again. I couldn't think what on earth I'd done when, in the same loud tones came 'that is a *dreadful* thing to do to a new book etc.' The teacher let me (and everyone else in the building) know what my crime had been. This wasn't strictly speaking a question of discipline but it does illustrate how teachers assume that children will *know* what is and is not acceptable. Since this can vary from teacher to teacher it is no wonder children become confused. So, tell your children right at the beginning what is and is not acceptable to you in things like, dress, courtesy to others, conduct in the classroom etc., then at least they will be in the picture and have no excuse when something goes wrong for saying 'I didn't know'.

Secondly, show them by your example how you expect them to behave. It's no good telling them what you expect, then yourself *doing* the complete opposite. Words and action must match. I used to help out a junior teacher with sewing once a week. The overriding impression at the end of the afternoon was of the teacher's loud voice issuing a steady stream of largely pointless remarks — 'Edward your *voice*/is that you *again* Angela/ahem, *noise* children/can I hear somebody *humming*' etc. Half the time there was no need for any comment. The children themselves were quiet enough but the effect of the steady stream of loud comments from the teacher was to raise the noise level generally.

Thirdly, do not start off by having too romantic a view of children. You will be quickly and sadly disillusioned if you do. They are human beings with negative as well as positive potential. They will let you down and you will have to deal with the consequences. Don't duck out of difficult decisions because you are afraid of being unpopular. You will suffer much worse unpopularity if you cannot keep order. I had a voluntary helper for a spell in a class of top juniors. She was a qualified teacher and had great ideas about 'giving the kids fun'. The ideas themselves weren't all that bad, but the children rarely had the fun because order would often break down somewhere between the launching of the idea and its completion, with the result that they ended up doing routine work because 'they couldn't behave sensibly'. On one occasion she decided, after a request from one child, that each member of the class could change his or her first name if they so desired. (I could have said no at the outset but the idea was for her to be responsible for one or two hours each week and besides I did not want to pour cold water on all her plans). She started by giving a preamble about there being no reason to stick to our first names if we didn't like them, and went on to ask each child in turn to pick a new name. I was working outside the room and could hear things gradually disintegrate — one child chose the name 'Geronimo' which produced a roar from the others someone else chose 'Big Uggie' — more mirth, someone else wanted to change his mind etc. soon the children were calling out suggestions and Mrs R was trying to be heard above the growing din. In the end the children were told to take out their books and 'get on with some work'. The whole enterprise had been far from fun for anyone.

On another occasion I was filling in for a head of a nursery school when I heard an incredible tale of anarchy among four-year-olds. The Head had decided it was wrong for a child to be told to come and listen to a story so each one in turn (30 or so) was asked if he or she would like a story. Usually a handful said yes and the rest went on doing or not doing what they were supposed to. The story was constantly interrupted by children running in and out, calling to each other, throwing paper aeroplanes and the like across the room. Eventually the staff complained to such an extent that by the time I went there, 'story' had become an obligatory part of the timetable, and the children grew to enjoy it and learn from it quite willingly and naturally.

The point of these stories is to illustrate the outcome of an ill conceived, ill thought out approach — everyone loses. Children do not like shoddy treatment and if they receive it they reflect it in their behaviour and their work. They *expect* certain standards of honest dealing and are confused and troublesome when they do not get it. You have got to accept the responsibility of your position if you are to make the most of your job. That means making decisions for the children (not all decisions, and a decreasing number as you get to know them). At the beginning let the children know that the buck stops ultimately with you in classroom affairs and that, for the time being at least, you are in charge.

Fourthly, a useful (though *not* to be overworked) aid to discipline is to keep children busy, that is to have enough work which is easy enough for them to do without your help. Too much of this kind of work leads to problems of a different kind — a dullness of mind and deadness of thought. It stultifies the children's natural curiosity and is a pernicious evil. Many classes given too much of this kind of work may appear well disciplined and orderly but they actually display a lack of vitality. It is important for you to distinguish between the two. Nevertheless it is unrealistic to expect every particle of the child's work to be relevant, stimulating and of high educational value. When you *have* to use time-filling material make it as interesting as you can. To do the job well the child's work ought to be well within his or her range of ability. Work cards are a good idea. Text books can work but they are of course less tailor-made for your needs. Make your own cards if you can and keep the work straightforward and the instructions simple, e.g.

- Copy this poem in your best handwriting. Decorate the page when you have finished.
- Work out the answers to these problems.
- Write out the names of 6 girls and 6 boys in your class.
- Copy these sums into your book then work them out.
- Trace this picture then colour it.
- Fill in all the odd/even numbers in this hundred square (provide duplicated sheets of 'empty' hundred squares).
- Draw a triangle with sides of 2, 4 and 5 centimetres.

When the need arises you can simply tell a child or group of children to take a green card or number card or whatever. As long as this material is not the main body of your work it will fulfill its function efficiently and do no harm.

Finally, take account of the attitudes of the rest of the staff especially if you are trying to introduce a less formal approach. Your children won't benefit if they are known as 'that lot in Miss Y's class who do as they like'. Your first duty is to the children, but it is as well to try to make this compatible with good relations amongst the rest of the staff.

Two of my top juniors (eleven-year-olds) were working outside in the corridor when a younger child from the class next door came out to wash a cut finger. One of my children, M, helped to wash the finger, then went to the first aid cupboard for a plaster to cover the cut. The incident was related to me when M returned to the classroom just before playtime. It was mentioned again in the staffroom during break and to my surprise I realised that M's action, far from being praiseworthy as I had seen it, was seen as a breach of discipline, 'fancy going into the first aid cupboard without asking permision. . . .' Since there was nothing dangerous in the cupboard I couldn't see the harm. Still, different people have different ideas about what children will/will not, can/cannot, should/should not do. If I'd been more aware of the prevailing attitude of the other members of staff I could have explained to the children that to be absolutely safe, it was better to see a teacher before going to the first aid box (or whatever).

Record keeping

You won't have a lot of time during your first term to think about the keeping of records. Nevertheless you will have to do something about it and you cannot assume that the school will have a worked out policy on the subject. Since it is not the intention of this book to give a series of blueprints which are copied without question I shall simply give a possible model then some general points for you to think about before you devise your own system.

The model described here is where each child has a large folder containing a selection of work. The idea is to give a picture of the child's development throughout the year and to show the range of work covered. Material is selected to this end, but not too much, or the system becomes unwieldy. A particularly good, or for that matter bad, piece of work is dated and placed in the folder. Inside the cover a sheet or two of paper is pinned on which to jot down points about each piece of work. This is useful when Parents' Evening comes round or for when you have to do a written report on a child. It is also a useful source of reference if you have to deal with a parent who is anxious about the child's progress.

There is a tendency to put too much in these folders so it is a good idea to go through them at the end of each term and weed out unwanted material, while at the same time giving yourself a quick recap of the term's work. Large items of work (paintings, graphs, etc.) are stored separately in a suitable cupboard if you have one, or in extra large packets. These are made by stapling two large sheets of card round three sides and are useful where space is tight since they can be attached to the wall, back of a cupboard, side of a bookcase etc.

Alongside the children's work there is a record of what they have done (not all of which will be in their folder). This can be in an exercise book with 2 pages for each child. It is supposed to be more of a guide to the teacher then to anyone else, but the best examples are not overburdened with detail and are reasonably easy for others to understand at a glance. The time span varies for regular entries but once a fortnight is reasonable, with additional entries for activities requiring special comment.

General points

a) An efficient system of keeping records is necessary so that you can conduct your work in an orderly way rather than one which is random or haphazard. Concern was expressed in a recent H.M.I. report over the general lack of serious curriculum planning (apparently random choices of subject for topic work, and lack of continuity in topic planning). You cannot of course fully plan a topic based approach or you will contradict the ethos of topic based learning. Nevertheless efficient record keeping will help you to avoid the worst excesses of random selection.

b) The key to efficient record keeping is simplicity. Cut out unnecessary information. The aim is to keep yourself and others informed of each child's progress, and also to maintain a flow of work at the appropriate level. So, record information just often enough to enable you to feel confident about your knowledge of each child's progress.

c) Records are not an end in themselves. There are teachers who conscientiously compile a list of reading ages and enter these on carefully prepared progress charts then carry on as if nothing had happened. They do not go on to ask what can I do to *improve* this standard or that rate of progress.

d) There can be a false security in records where the keeping of them and the ticking of boxes takes over or at least becomes divorced from the teaching of children.

e) Two of the most valuable things you can give to the children are your time and attention. If records start to take these away from the children the balance is wrong. Records should help to ensure that the time and attention you give to the children are of maximum value. Without an analytical perspective your work could be rather a hit and miss affair. So, you have to devise a system which helps you to keep tabs on the children's progress but at the same time does not demand too much of your attention.

These then are some of the concerns you may have during your first term with juniors. Whether you are with Infants or Juniors, you will inevitably make some mistakes. Whatever you do, don't worry about them. Nothing worthwhile was ever learned without a few mistakes being made in the process. You may tip the balance too much in one direction but you have plenty of time to redress that balance next term. The important thing is to keep a constructive attitude. Look for successes on which to build, and use failures as a guide to what should be avoided in the future.

End of Term

Before we leave this chapter I shall say one or two things about the end of term. Since no useful purpose would be served by dividing this section into Infants and Juniors, we come together again to think about the end of your first term.

For many of you, your first term will be the one which leads up to Christmas. The end of this term is particularly hectic in a Primary school. The children are excited and excitable. There are decorations and presents to be made, words and music of carols to be learned. You may be involved in a play or concert etc. To help you avoid being caught out and yet to get the most out of this time, it might be useful to consider the following points.

Decorations

Before you start, make a list of all the things you hope to make. You don't have to stick to it and you can add to it as you go along but to have it will give you a framework round which to work. Collect the extra materials you need, glue, glitter, tissue paper etc. Put the small things in plastic tubs inside larger portable boxes, (plastic cutlery trays are useful here). Since there will be an extra demand for glue, paper fasteners etc., make extra pots using small yoghurt tubs to tide you over the Christmas period. Give the children a quick lesson on how to use and store these items and try to organise an even distribution of materials around the room so that there isn't a constant crush at one central point.

During my first Christmas with first year Infants, sellotape was in short supply. We were limited to one roll per class and I was rather too poor or too mean to buy more. I got round the problem by cutting lengths from the roll and sticking these to a suitable door/wall/chair near each group. When a child needed some tape he or she would walk to the nearest length, and cut off what was needed. I had to go over it with them once or twice but on the whole it worked well and released me from cutting hundreds of small pieces off the same roll and chewing my fingers and nerves to bits in the process.

As for the actual decorations it is quite helpful to work round a theme so that the whole classroom is given over to that theme. It is simpler and often more effective than a collection of all the various strands of Christmas lumped together without a connecting thread.
Examples of suitable themes are:

a) **Colour** All decoratons and art work fit into an overall theme of say red and green. Communal work can be a large Christmas or holly tree collage, with red decorations/berries. Individual items are mounted on a red or green background; paper hats for parties made in red with green trimmings or vice versa; words of poems and hymns are printed in red and green felt pens etc. Obviously colour combinations like red/green, blue/silver, red/white are more suitable than orange/brown, blue/yellow, or pink/green.

b) **Season** Everything connects with the theme of winter and snow. Communal work can be a large scene with the background painted first then individual efforts cut out and stuck on. Individual contributions — robins, snowmen, bare trees (black on white and vice versa), snowflake designs, 'frosty' pictures.

c) **Nativity** Everything ties in with the Nativity story. Divide the class into three groups, one to make large collage kings on one wall, one to do the shepherds on another wall and the third to do the stable scene. Individual items might be a silhouette of donkey and Mary, star designs, calendars displayed away from the walls, depicting the Nativity.

Keep things simple. If one group of children are working on a complicated decoration, make sure the others have less demanding work to be getting on with so that you can give help where it is most needed. It's a good idea to record some of the carols the children have to learn. Play these while they draw, paint, cut out etc. Some of the words and music will go in and your job of teaching them will be made a bit easier.

Do not undertake something unless you can see more or less how the end result is going to be, and more or less how to achieve it. There will be other times to undertake a project in a spirit of adventure, to 'see what happens' — your first Christmas in a school is *not* one of them. I once returned to school two weeks before the end of term after a spell in hospital. To decorate the classroom I used ancient tinsel and crêpe paper decorations from the school attic. The children made simple paper chains (which we had been told at college were *death* to artistic creativity). Though the classroom looked more garish than usual it was one of the happiest and least fraught Christmases I have ever spent in a school. This is not to say that you make little of the celebration, only that you do not spoil it for yourself and the children by trying to do too much. An atmosphere of peace and harmony is desirable at all times in the classroom but it is perhaps especially welcome at Christmas. If this can be gained only at the expense of elaborate decorations then so be it.

Christmas play/concert

If you are asked for (or want to offer) a little play or item for the school concert, choose something well within your children's range of ability. It is much better to offer something simple, done well and with *obvious enjoyment* than to cause stress to yourself and the children by choosing something too difficult. It is a cheerless yet common experience to see children performing well enough but without an ounce of zest or a spark of enjoyment.

I made the mistake of 'getting it wrong' with a class of nine and ten-year-olds. Members of staff had been asked to contribute a small play with a Christmas theme to be performed to the parents at the end of term. I had a class of nine and ten-year-olds and chose to do 'The Journey of the Magi'. The play opened with the first wise man looking through his telescope and perceiving the new star in the sky. On hearing the exclamation, the second wise man took up his telescope to have a look. Alas on the night this second wise man pointed his telescope in the *opposite* direction to the first. Consequently his 'ah yes it is surely the sign' was met with gales of laughter from the audience. During a later scene we were to use a tape recording of a new born baby's cry. On the night, the tape recorder had been used by another class just before our performance and when I switched it on, behind the scenes loud pop music was heard. I quickly switched the machine off again and got a child to imitate the baby's cry so that it would be heard 'out front'. Unfortunately the sound was greeted by more laughter from the audience. Before we reached the end of the play, two further hitches occurred. The outcome of this was that the children were hurt and indignant that the audience had laughed. 'They don't even know the meaning of Christmas', one nine-year-old exclaimed. I'm not sure whether I had chosen something with too many possible pitfalls or whether I hadn't rehearsed sufficiently. Probably it was a combination of both. At any rate the children were let down and I felt responsible.

For the same evening a colleague had simply dressed her seven and eight-year-olds in a variety of costumes — toy soldier, doll, monkey, clown, teddy bear, kitten etc. They were to be some of the toys which Father Christmas was to put in his sack. The children were assembled before the curtains were drawn. A Christmas fairy appeared and touched each toy to bring it to life. The toy did a little dance or tumble till Father Christmas appeared. At that point they again became lifeless and were each covered with a sack by Father Christmas. The whole thing was simple (the mothers had mostly provided the costumes) yet very effective, and obviously thoroughly enjoyed by the children.

It will help the children to enjoy the rehearsals if *you* appear to be enjoying them. Search hard for points of praise and work round these. If rehearsals consist of a steady stream of nagging the performance is unlikely to be lively.

Finally if you are watching the actual performance have the courtesy to at least look interested (even if you have seen it a dozen times before). You will be on show as much as the performers. To see teachers paying no attention to the performance or looking downright bored is not only a poor reflection on themselves but also on general standards of conduct in the school.

Work

Christmas lends itself naturally to the thematic approach to learning. If you can tap the central theme of Christmas for language and number work you will be able to sample the thematic approach at its best. There is no excuse for neglecting language and number during the Christmas period, but somehow to slog doggedly on with spelling lists and multiplication tables doesn't seem quite right. The best idea is to look at the material you are using for Christmas and find the number and language (and a lot else besides), in that. You won't have to look hard for:

- the maths in the making of a Christmas pudding
- the language in the Christmas carols and poems
- the geography and history in the Nativity
- the music in the radio/television play.

With infants I used to put ordinary sum books etc., away and make special Christmas sum and story books. These contained much the same work as earlier in the term but bells, crackers, holly etc. were used instead of cars, boats and balls.

Loose pages worked better for juniors. For the last weeks of term they did all their work on loose pages. Even pages of ordinary sums could be decorated with borders of Christmas motifs. At some point during the last week of term these pages were sorted and selected by the children themselves to make a book to take home.

Working in this way allows you to keep things on a reasonably even keel (through all the plays, parties and treats) to the very last day of term. After a visit to the theatre for example, you can come back to the classroom and ask the children to draw their favourite character and write a few sentences about it. So you extend the visit and at the same time encourage the children to practise language skills. The same effect could not be had if you returned from the theatre and asked them to take out their books and do page such and such. In the end, the keeping up of 'routine work' becomes so untenable that the children spend the end of term doing no work at all and become over excited and troublesome because of it. An element of routine work should be kept up and this will be easier to do if the work is linked to the rest of your activities.

Clearing up

There are so many last minute jobs to be done that it is difficult to fit them all in *and* maintain a harmonious atmosphere in the classroom. A little forethought could help you here. Make a list of jobs to be done before the last day of term, e.g. clearing art displays; reorganising art and craft materials (replacing special Christmas materials in central store, throwing out anything which cannot be re-used); sorting out things for the children to take home; finishing off calendars and presents; cleaning windows if these have been painted or decorated, and so on. You may hardly use the list at all but the actual making of it will help you to be aware of what actually has to be done before the last day of term.

During the periods of clearing up let the children bring in their own games from home. Explain that the games must be played with a minimum of supervision (e.g. draughts, snakes and ladders, lego etc.) and they should not bring in anything complicated. Choose a few responsible figures and give them specific tasks and tell them what to do when they have finished, e.g. take all the yellow stars down from the back wall, check that each star is named, put any un-named ones in that box and the rest on this shelf; when you have finished do a number card before you choose a game.

If your children are too young to be of real practical help you could perhaps borrow one or two children from an older class. Be methodical when you start to clear the walls; start with one wall or one kind of decoration and do not move on to something else until that has been completed. Keep a container for oddments, and anything which has no immediate 'home' can be put in that for the time being. You can sort through it with the children at a later date when you are less rushed. Put it on your list of jobs though, or the box could lie around till next Christmas waiting to be sorted.

Take *all* Christmas displays and decorations down. It will be a very bleak greeting for you to return to school on a cold January morning to a classroom showing the forlorn remnants of Christmas. If you have time, re-cover display areas with fresh paper; if not, then come in early enough next term to do this before the children arrive. Sometimes the Head will take the whole school for a film, or a sing song, or whatever to give the staff a chance to clear up without the children. You cannot count on this though so it's as well to think of strategies of your own. Co-operate with a colleague to give each other some free time. While one copes with two classes the other can get on with those jobs which are done so much more quickly without the children. Keep successful music/movement or story programmes you have taped. These can be used with more than one class and the children should be able to remember enough of them to be able to follow them easily.

Obviously you won't be able to escape a certain amount of 'frazzle' during these last days. This is almost inevitable so don't worry about it. Rather, accept it as part and parcel of the whole business. The aim is to keep the frazzle down to a minimum so that you can get on and achieve as much as possible with the children.

We can hardly leave the subject of Christmas without saying something about the religious aspect. That there is a religious aspect is unquestionable. You would be selling the children short if you did not fully explain this aspect as a Christian celebration of the birth of Jesus Christ, who came into the world as a sign of God's love for mankind, and who displayed that love in human terms and taught us how to live through loving in order to grow nearer to God. This is what Christians believe about the baby born in the stable and this should be explained as accurately as possible. So if you celebrate Christmas at all with the children, then whatever their racial mix they deserve to know about every aspect of what and why they are celebrating. (This applies to every religious festival you celebrate with the children whether Christian or non-Christian).

Christmas of course has many aspects. It means the middle of Winter (or summer in the Antipodes), the giving and receiving of gifts and greetings, the making and eating of special food, Father Christmas/Santa Claus, carols, cards, crackers, pantomimes, parties, and so on. But, to treat Christmas seriously it has to be put in a world wide context. This means thinking of the millions throughout the world who are suffering unimaginable deprivation. The children deserve to be made aware of the problem and to think about it in their terms. They may offer suggestions for active involvement, e.g. the organisation of a Bring and Buy Sale to raise money to give to the needy. You could invite them to write a Christmas letter to the homeless/jobless/foodless, or organise a class discussion/debate if the children are old enough. What you do is up to you, but Christmas must be placed in this wider context in order to rekindle and make sense of its message of eternal hope. The question 'Is hope a viable option in the late 20th Century?' receives answers of *no* from many quarters, but the Christian message of Christmas remains a resounding and indefatigable *yes* in answer to this question.

There is certainly much to hate about Christmas, the commercialism, hypocrisy, greed. Your job is to focus on the hopeful not the hateful aspects. If you adopt a cynical attitude towards Christmas you shouldn't really be in the Primary school since you will have nothing of real value to offer your children.

The challenge then of Christmas in the Primary school is to attempt to weave the various strands together for and with the children so that they and you are enriched by the fun, the thought and the fellowship which help make up its amazing tapestry.

3. In the swing

This chapter heading may or may not apply during your first year. Some of you will take longer than others to settle down, to feel 'at home' in the classroom and to lose that sense of unease which comes with being new. Take as long as you need to settle in and build up your confidence. When you do feel comfortable and completely at ease in the classroom enjoy the increased sense of security but do not come to a standstill. Use your increased confidence to advantage. Pleasant though it will be not to have to worry about the prospect of having to fill each day you should guard against complacency. So, as soon as you lose the feeling of being the 'new one' you can start to experiment. Covering the same ground in the same way year after year can lead to a staleness of approach, and this gradually develops into a vicious circle — new ideas will seem less and less attractive, and your confidence in trying anything new will gradually diminish. The end result of this is an approach so lacking in vitality that both you and the children are bored, fed up, dissatisfied, and you spend most of your time in school wishing that you were somewhere, anywhere rather that there.

Of course there is nothing new under the sun. But, there is always a fresh angle to be looked at a new slant on something which you haven't considered before. You could watch a thousand sunsets or pick as many ivy leaves and never find two the same. The children are not the same from one year to the next. Not, that is, if you take the trouble to get to know them properly. There are similarities of course. Many things look the same on the surface. You have to get beneath the surface to see the differences. It is the purpose of this chapter to suggest ways in which you can get beneath the surface of your job so that your approach can be fairly described to be 'new every morning'.

This chapter then, is really a plea for you to

a) keep your teaching alive and to find out for yourself (i.e. to learn by doing) what does and does not work well in the classroom;

b) to extend your teaching beyond the walls of the classroom.

It is so easy once you have got things running smoothly to keep on covering the same ground in the same way year in year out. The only difference is that each year you lose a little more enthusiasm. It is fatal. To maintain a high level of quality and enjoyment in your work it is a good idea to 'give yourself a shake' occasionally. Not to change for change's sake, but simply to question your assumptions so that you can exchange those found wanting for something better, or so that you can retain them but with a clearer understanding of why. For example, there is a common assumption that to work in groups is more progressive or 'better' than to work with the whole class. This assumption is clumsy and inaccurate. Sometimes it is better to work in groups; sometimes class lessons are more efficient. Until you have tried both with a variety of lessons you cannot properly judge for yourself.

The avenues chosen for possible exploration and experiment are 1) Classroom layout and 2) Ways of Working.

Classroom layout

For the first half of this century the layout in most of our classrooms remained constant. Nowadays there is an infinite variety of classroom layouts. There are some basic considerations —

- Power points: where they are (if any) and how and when you will use them. Do not cover them up or make them difficult to get at.
- Heating system: whether there are air vents to be left uncovered. Position of radiators — things like pianos, plants and of course children should not be placed too close to them.
- Windows: the position of the sun as it shines into the classrom. Arrange the desks so that as far as possible the children do not have to work while facing into direct sunlight.
- Sink: whether the children can get at it without difficulty. As far as possible position jugs, beakers, paper towels and art and craft materials nearby to reduce movement back and forth across the classroom.
- Fire/safety precautions: are they to the best of your knowledge taken care of? e.g. the classroom door or any outside fire exit must be clear, faulty electrical switches reported and mended.

Apart from these considerations, the layout of the classroom will generally be up to you. The following three layouts are described as they would be by their adherents. Use them to serve as a starting point from which to develop your own ideas based on your particular circumstances. There are of course many more possibilities and the adaptations of the three given here are as numerous as the teachers doing the adapting.

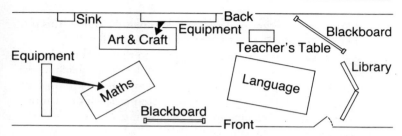

This plan is a good way to make the best use of resources in the classroom with the minimum of disturbance. Children who are working on the same subject area sit together, close to the resources/equipment which are appropriate to that subject. Group teaching is made easier in that those children who are at more or less the same stage of development in a particular subject can sit together at the same table. The teacher can, when necessary, work in close proximity with this group of children and the rest of the children can be allowed to get on in relative peace.

When a child finishes a piece of work, he can leave the table, go to the Art/Craft area to start/finish a piece of work, to the Library to read or do research for a project, and so on. In this way those children who are still working will remain undisturbed and also be less easily distracted.

Obviously this layout lends itself to the integrated curriculum, where different subject areas can be worked on simultaneously by different groups of children. This layout also makes it easy for different types of work to be carried out at the same time. For example the various aspects of a class project on say History, Geography, Environment etc., can be worked on at the same time — the reading and writing taking place at the front of the room while the drawing/painting etc. will take place at the back.

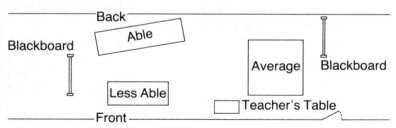

This system works well when the children are grouped according to academic ability. Working on the assumption that the most able children will need the teacher's time and attention less than the others, this plan shows the able children placed farthest from the teacher.

The less able children are placed closest to the teacher and at the front of the room. The reason for this is twofold. Some children have learning difficulties which are associated with problems of sight or hearing. To place these children at the front of the room closest to what they will be looking at and listening to can help to minimise any disability. This aspect ought to be remembered for T.V. or Radio programmes when a change of seating may be necessary. It is often the case that the less able child suffers problems of frustration and becomes easily bored. To have such children near at hand can help them and you by serving to reduce discipline problems. You can instantly spot the beginnings of restlessness or disturbance and do something about it before it develops into a problem.

An important feature of this system is that the groups are mixed up and reshuffled from time to time so that the children benefit from as wide an interaction as possible. Normally the children will have some sort of home base, i.e. when asked to go to their places they will have a specific place or table at which to sit. Nevertheless much of their time is also spent at another table. For example it would be contrary to the nature of subjects like Art and Craft to have the children sitting in groups of academic ability. Another way in which the groups remain fluid is that the ability groups will change according to subject — a child could be in Group A for Maths, Group B for Language and Group C for Handwriting. Even the ability groups within one subject will change from time to time. It would be unnaturally static to have each child in exactly the same ability group throughout the year.

The constant checking and re-checking required to ensure that each child is in the best possible group for him, at any given time will help you enormously. It will serve to keep you very well informed about each child's progress and act as a safeguard against your slipping into a state of complacency.

Although the seating plan opposite is rarely to be seen in Primary schools today, it is nevertheless worth your consideration. Obviously, for many of you the particular plan which is sketched in here will be impossible to implement since it requires each child to have an individual desk. Nevertheless something radically more formal than your usual plan could probably be devised.

One of the advantages I discovered when I tried a seating plan of this kind, was that the children *loved* it. Especially when it had the novelty of being new and different. More than once I have been asked 'Please could we have our desks in rows?' Part of its appeal lay in the fact that to be seated in a formal fashion made the children feel somehow adult and 'important'. This feeling was even reflected in the children's behaviour — for an initial period at least, until the novelty wore off.

There are many mathematical possibilities in a seating plan of this kind. The children can be seated in order of size, (height, length of foot, length of arm, etc.), they can be seated according to house number or in alphabetical order, and so on. Obviously it works well for testing purposes and it is also a useful aid in playing mental games, e.g. all the children stand, starting at one of the corners and working up and down the rows each child in turn answers a quick fire question and sits down on answering correctly.

Of course such games can be played whatever the seating arrangement but since speed is an important element the game will work better where the seating plan is based on straight lines. The children will then know exactly who comes next in the firing line of questions. In a less defined seating plan the children can become confused as to who should answer next, two children answering at the same time etc.

It may seem to you that in a seating plan of this kind there is an uneconomical use of floor space. This is true up to a point but the pushing together of two rows can be quickly and easily done to make floor space for drama, painting or whatever. The children will be eager to help here and this in itself is a worthwhile activity for them to do.

In a sense it doesn't really matter how you decide to arrange things. More important is realizing *why* things are arranged in this or that way. Equally important is that you are willing to change the arrangement to meet new circumstances if and when they arrive. Some arrangements will suit so well that you will keep them for a very long time with only slight alterations. Others will be less long lasting. Whatever happens, your classroom layout should *help* you in your daily work. It should make life easier not more difficult.

Storage

Facilities for storage vary. Here are some general hints:

a) *store similar things together* — classify according to size, shape, subject, frequency of use, etc. Naturally some equipment will fit into several categories and there is bound to be an overlap. Nevertheless *some* classification is better than none.

b) *collect similar sized containers* — the children will help collect e.g. ice cream/margarine containers. Swap flimsy/awkward sized boxes for sturdy plastic boxes which can be stored more easily. These can hold puzzles, maths and reading equipment, art and craft materials, etc.

c) *label boxes clearly* — use a broad felt pen and cover the writing with plastic film so that it will last longer and can be wiped clean.

d) *label shelves/cupboards* — this is helpful when student teachers are in the classroom and also if another teacher has to take your class.

e) *let the children share in the maintenance* — they should know where and how things are stored. That means you have to show them. Appoint a rota of children to have responsibility for a specific storage area.

f) *provide an oddments box* — so that found pieces of equipment can be put somewhere until time allows them to be replaced.

g) *have a regular check* — e.g. once a month put time aside to check over one area. To do it properly you should probably spend the whole day on it. Don't worry about 'missing work'. A day spent properly sorting through the library or the maths is as valuable to the children as 'everyday work'.

h) *throw out clutter* — at the end of the year if you find you haven't used this or that then get rid of it. Not to the dustbin. If possible store these 'could be useful' objects out of the classroom. If not then at least don't let them take up space on shelves which are used everyday.

Some possible ways to supplement existing storage:

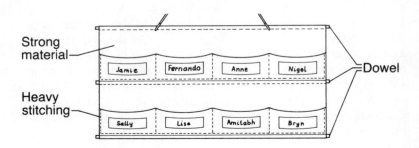

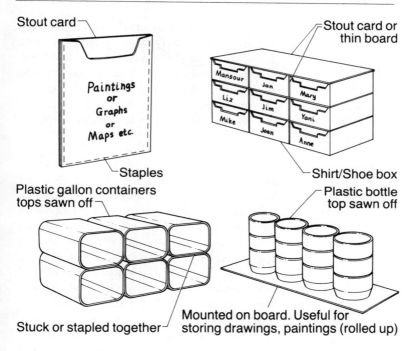

Stout card

Paintings or Graphs or Maps etc.

Staples

Stout card or thin board

Mansour · Jan · Mary
Liz · Jim · Yani
Mike · Joan · Anne

Shirt/Shoe box

Plastic gallon containers tops sawn off

Plastic bottle top sawn off

Stuck or stapled together

Mounted on board. Useful for storing drawings, paintings (rolled up)

Whatever individual storage units you have, make sure you clean them out every few weeks. Otherwise the children who are not naturally tidy (and that means most) will get into a hopeless muddle. Their desks/pigeon holes will gather an amazing conglomeration of half finished drawings, forgotten notes to and from school, rotting apple cores, mislaid rubbers, 'lost' library books etc. Set aside a specific day for this clearing (e.g. the last Friday of the month) and mark it on the calendar and ask the children to remind you. Give the day a name (Clearance Day or similar) to make something of it, and afterwards as a treat let the children have half an hour or so of free time to do what they like.

New Ways of Working

As with classroom layout, methods of working need to be scrutinised from time to time to weed out practices which have gone stale and to replace them with fresh ones. You will only find out *which* fresh ones by trying out a variety of ideas for yourself. So, the aim here is to give you *starting* points for experimentation, not a blue print for every new idea; this would clearly defeat the object of the exercise.

Sometimes you will have a clear idea about why you want to try something new. At other times you may feel that things have somehow become rather flat and that some sort of revitalisation is called for. Whatever your reasons you will probably be more successful if you approach the experiment in a spirit of curiosity, of 'let's try and see'.

Here then are some starting points. Naturally it is imagined that in each case a scenario exists which is unlike the one outlined for experimentation.

a) *Formation of new groups:* e.g. give each group a leader or leaders and approximately the same mix of ability. This would offer a contrast to say working in ability groups. Introduce practical problems (e.g. the making of a model or home made equipment) to the groups. Children who are not bright academically are often very bright on a practical level but they are seldom given enough opportunity to put this ability to good use. This system lends itself to competition between the groups but keep it on a lighthearted level (which group is ready first, etc.). If you do allow competition to stray into work then you must reward effort more than finished result. The benefits of incentive which can come from competition will only be realised when every child feels that there is a real chance of reward. Reshuffle the groups occasionally so that the children mingle with as wide a variety of personalities as possible.

b) *Give the whole class a programme of work for the day.* This can be written out on individual sheets or on the blackboard. The children work through the programme moving on from one item to the next at their own pace and as far as possible without any interference from you. You can remove groups or individuals throughout the day to give say, specific help with reading or number. This sytem means a lot of marking at the end of the day but it gives the children valuable experience. The amount of marking will of course be reduced if the children are used to marking their own work — a good practice under any system. They have responsibility for their own work and if they can choose their own activity when the programme has been completed then there is usually a high degree of industry and concentration. I have seen this system used on a permanent basis but not very successfully. The able children were under stretched and the slow children were under stimulated. I found it worked well on an occasional basis when the novelty fired the children's enthusiasm. It is also a useful system when you are suffering from laryngitis.

c) *Give one group of children a programme of work for a whole week.* Similar to the above but the rest of the class carry on as normal while the 'programmed group' work by themselves. The 'special' aura surrounding the group seems to heighten the sense of privilege and responsibility. Obviously to be fair you should see that each child has a chance to experience the programme week at least once during the session. Older children can work out their own programme for the week from the 'bare bones requirements' which they are given, (x hours Maths, y hours English etc.) Monday morning can be spent working out a programme for the week and writing out a rough time table. They can work singly or in twos and threes fitting in P.E., radio and T.V. programmes etc. into their own timetable. This system means extra work for you but the children involved get a lot out of it. It works well with a mixed ability group since there is ample scope for interchange of ideas, skills and abilities. It is equally successful with a group of similar ability (low or high) and this means you can give the rest of the class more concentrated attention because having removed one or other 'end' it is not stretched over such a wide spectrum.

d) *One or two older/abler children help the slow learners with reading/number:* the 'older children' refers to those who are in a vertically grouped class. This can be done in a number of ways e.g. in the context of daily work the abler children finish their own work then help the slower learners; or some time can be set aside each day for special Maths/English help (grouping here will depend on the spread of ability in your class e.g. one able child, one less able/one able, 4 average/one able, 2 below average etc. Provide as much concrete material as you can and let the children devise their own explanations. These can sometimes succeed where your explanations have failed because children obviously do not approach problems from an adult point of view. In this system it is important that no child is encouraged to feel superior/inferior. Also it is important that the able child does not feel 'put upon'. To work well, the activity should have the willing participation of both parties. 'Who would like to do some maths help tomorrow?' 'Who would like to have some reading help this afternoon?' etc. Think up ways to encourage willing participation, e.g. the children concerned work unsupervised somewhere outside the classroom/they are allowed to use 'special' felt pens etc. Let them see how worthwhile an activity you think this is and praise the results whenever possible.

e) *Some children work out of the classroom/home base:* to give them the experience of working without supervision. This is very easy to do and can be done with very little preparation, (check that the areas in which the children will work are available before you send them). After a preliminary discussion as an introduction to some written work simply ask who would like to/thinks they could manage to do the work unsupervised in the corridor/staffroom/library or wherever. Make it a regular feature and the children will become used to working without supervision. Often such conditions encourage the children to give more attention to the work in hand than they would do simply 'because they'd been told to'. Explain that since you will not be with them you are relying on their own good sense to produce reliable, responsible behaviour. Naturally if a child demonstrates a lack of reliability then that child is recalled to work in the classroom under supervision.

   f) *Set up a formal atmosphere and as far as possible teach class lessons:* i.e. all the children listen to the same introductory talk/watch same demonstration on say subtraction/full stops/the Stone Age or whatever, then all join in/listen to question and answers on the subject followed by written work directed by the teacher.

   This needs a formal seating plan of some kind with all the children facing in the same direction. This system is not recommended for any length of time since it really only works as long as the novelty lasts. Nevertheless it is good training for you to be able to hold the attention of a wide spectrum of ability. It is also a valid experience for the children to learn to listen and taken in that which is not pitched specifically at their exact level. On the whole though, as a continuous method, it is probably a very wasteful way to teach. So, it is at its most effective in short spells of say 1/2 days at the most.

   g) *Introduce or abandon workcards* (whichever would constitute a change for you): the introduction of workcards should be a gradual business. Probably the best ones are those you write yourself so first you have to write them. Introduce one set to begin with. You will learn as you go along how much work to put on one card and what length of time a set of questions should last. They are much more flexible than textbooks and if you write them they will be tailor-made to suit your children.

   However, the slavish devotion to workcards can be as deadening as anything else which is unleavened by variety. If you are used to dealing mainly with workcards, abandon them for a week. Dig out some text books and look through them until you have found enough material to sort out roughly a week's work for the children. You could start with all the children being given the same textbook, then go over the lesson with them and give out various suggestions for different levels of follow-up work. Or you could select some 'easy' books for a group of children i.e. books which contain work well within the children's range of ability.

That group could be left to work from the textbooks while you work with some others on a more difficult book. Even ancient books can be used in this way. As long as the information is not out of date or inaccurate the books will do no harm. Sometimes the children are fascinated by these 'old fashioned' textbooks, and I have known interesting projects come out of such work.

A by-product of this experiment is that you will see the contents of your workcards in a new light. Even if it is a case of the awfulness of some of the textbook content reminding you of the superior content of some of your workcards. On the other hand it may turn out that you are reassured (by the textbook venture) that what you are doing with your workcards is very much along the right lines. In either case the experiment will have been worthwhile.

These then are a few suggestions for starters. If you violently disagree with any of them that is not necessarily a bad thing. The question of how best to enlighten and enlarge young minds has taxed educationists and others for centuries. It will probably continue to tax them for centuries to come. Neither underestimate the particular contribution you can make to this question, nor waste your opportunity to contribute to some of the answers.

New ventures beyond the walls of the classroom

There are many and varied activities which can take place outside the actual daily work of the classroom. When you have sorted out the priority of daily work then perhaps you could think about organising an out of school club of some kind. The experience of such a club is very different to that of teaching a class of children. In one case you are working with children who have *chosen* to come along; in the classroom the children have no option but to be there. The experience of the former is highly recommended. Besides when you give something extra (i.e. over and above your contribution as a class teacher) to the school, you often gain as much as you give.

It needn't be a complicated affair, in fact the simpler the better. Nor need it take place out of school hours. Many successful school clubs operate during the lunch break. Sometimes two or more teachers share the running of a club. Parents too can be a useful source of help. The advantage here is that the club can continue even when a teacher is ill or away from school. One parent I know runs a chess club during his lunch hour at his son's school. His complaint is of a lack of back up from the school so that if he cannot attend for some reason then there is no club. This is a pity because regularity and continuity are important to the growth of a club. My own son was excited when a lunch time club was started in his school but has complained several times since it started that it was abandoned because of a staff meeting. This isn't really good enough. You cannot expect on the one hand, commitment from the children while on the other hand you display a lack of it yourself. So, if you do take on an extra curricular club, treat it as you would any other important part of your work.

There is a wide range of options, Music, Painting, Poetry, Maths, Drama, Games, Craft, Dancing, etc. Naturally you will make a much better job of something which you personally enjoy. If you have a particular hobby, an out of school club is a splendid way to spread your enthusiasm. Such clubs provide an excellent opportunity to introduce professionals from other fields into the school, artists, musicians, craftsmen, mathematicians etc. It isn't important that these people may know nothing of pedagogy. The overriding benefit to the children comes from rubbing shoulders with people who have an intimate knowledge and experience of their craft. If they are enthusiastic into the bargain, the value to the children is inestimable. Although this applies to all aspects of school life, the informal atmosphere of a club is probably more conducive to good results here than the larger and necessarily more formal set up of the classroom.

Do not be put off by the idea of organizing some sort of extra curricular activity because you feel you have no special expertise to offer. For one thing, no such expertise is required and for another everyone has something to offer.

A simple story club is very easy to organize and is usually a great favourite. All you need is a good story book, the ability to read or tell a story, and a comfortable corner in which the children can sit. If you can organize the occasional story read by a local actor, radio/T.V. personality or even local personality, so much the better.

Once you have decided to have a shot at something, try to sort out in your own mind some kind of framework around which your club can develop. e.g. is the club open to *all* the children or is it to be restricted to juniors/infants etc?; at what time will the club start/finish?; which day of the week will be most suitable?; will the children be expected to attend regularly and will they be able to come and go as they please?; will there be a charge made for materials, and if so how much?

Check with the head on points like the use and charge for materials, children staying after school, tending the road crossing etc., an explanatory letter to the parents, enlisting their help and so on. When you announce the club to the children make sure they are quite clear about the important points. For instance is it necessary to own a recorder before being eligible to join the recorder club/a camera before being eligible for the photography workshop etc. In their eagerness children often miss such important points and end up being confused and disappointed.

There are one or two things to bear in mind whilst you try to get the club off the ground:

a) After a club meeting leave things as you found them and report any damage

b) Set aside enough time at the end of each meeting to clear up any mess. Make this part of the routine of the club so that the children get used to it and learn to clear up almost automatically, (you will not endear yourself to other members of staff who have to come in next day and deal with the mess you have left).

c) If you take a piece of equipment from a central position (e.g. record player from the hall) return it before you leave school. Someone may need it first thing next day.

d) As far as possible keep all the equipment of the club in a separate place from ordinary classroom equipment. A trolley is ideal but a cardboard box will do.

e) Keep a record of attendance in a book which is kept with the equipment. This is useful when anyone takes over from you. Also the children like it and it is a useful reference generally (e.g. if a dispute arises).

Add any other points which apply to your particular school. A new venture can be at its most vulnerable in the early stages of its life so do all you can to ensure that it doesn't collapse before it even gets off the ground.

The value and importance of the extra curricular work which is done with children is enormous. Because the children have *chosen* to come and the atmosphere is relaxed the learning which takes place is likely to have a lasting quality. Moreover the criticism (to a large degree justified in my view) is often levied that school isn't like real life. The education in our classrooms has more to do with school and artificial things than it is to do with life and 'real' things. Extra curricular activity is one way to redress the balance and bring more 'life' into school. *Anything* is a possible vehicle e.g.

- *cycle maintenance* — how to mend a puncture, oil a wheel, replace a brake block, raise a saddle, etc.

- *cooking* — not only the 'one stir each' approach leading to a few cakes brought home in a paper bag, but also why not tea and toast, fried/boiled/scrambled eggs, soups, sandwiches, salads etc?

You will probably be able to think of more than one idea you'd like to experiment with in an out-of-school club. If not, the list of evening classes at the local adult education centre is as good a source of ideas as any. Most of these things are demonstrably what people like to do. There is no reason why flower arranging should be any less rewarding for a six-year old than it is for a sixty-year old. The principles are the same only the scale is different. Your predilections though are paramount. As long as you yourself have an interest in and an enthusiasm for the subject you will be able to make it work.

So having sorted out the immediate priorities and once you feel yourself to be 'in the swing', have a bash at extending your teaching beyond the walls of the classroom. You will not be disappointed.

4. Themes and variations

In this chapter we shall have a look at the use of themes as a method of working in the Primary school. First some general points, then the advantages/disadvantages and finally an example of the various ways in which a particular theme could start and then develop. Before this it might be a good idea to think about what exactly we mean by 'working through themes'. At one end of the spectrum is the teacher who brings say frog spawn into the classroom, encourages the children to observe and talk about it, and then uses this as a basis for some written work. This teacher is in a sense working through a miniature theme. At the other end is the school which 'becomes' say a community of Red Indians for a term or longer. The children experience the dress, customs, food, currency, language etc. of that community and all their written work is based on this experience. Most themes of course come somewhere between the two.

A theme can (and usually does) exist quite happily within and alongside everyday classroom Maths and English. The adherents of the thematic approach though claim that the more total the immersion in the theme, the more the children get out of it. Common sense is your best guide here. A headmaster once told me of a student teacher he'd had in school on her final teaching practice. The student had worked on a history theme around the subject of Mary Queen of Scots, and had prided herself on the fact that she's managed to organise a 'fully integrated theme'. Talking to her about it afterwards the head had asked her how she had incorporated the Maths work. She replied that the project books had been gathered in and the children had used them to work on weight! This was probably harmless enough but it does demonstrate a misguided sense of purpose. There is supposed to be some *point* in integration. In this case there was none. A definition of 'to integrate' is to combine parts into a whole. No stretch of the imagination would allow the weighing of project books to be seen as in any way part of a historical theme around Mary Queen of Scots. Either some real mathematical content should have been found within the theme (distance from France to England, measurements connected with costumes of the period) or weight should have been tackled outside the theme. There is no point in squeezing everything into a theme for the sake of some false notion of integration. When things which have no clear connection with the theme, have to be learnt, then deal with them separately.

So, first some general points:

a) There is a tendency to see the use of themes as being in opposition to a more traditional method of approach. This is a pity because done well both approaches have a lot in common and, as has been said, can co-exist alongside each other and be mutually beneficial.

b) The use of themes is in itself no guarantee of efficient learning. You should understand why you are using the method and how best to employ it. Done without due thought a thematic approach will lead to the same ends as an ill thought out traditional approach i.e. boredom, careless work, fruitless repetition, confusion and a negative attitude to books, work and school.

c) Unless you are dedicated to the thematic approach it is probably best to be mentally prepared to capitalise on those themes which present themselves naturally and which stem from such external events as a royal wedding (or indeed a staff one), national or international disasters (earthquake/famine/war/plane crash), the olympic games, a visit to the circus, etc. If nothing presents itself then leave things as they are rather than try to manufacture interest and enthusiasm.

Some of the most popular themes include: Food and Farming; The Sea; Communications; Conservation; Homes and Shelters; History — Vikings/Normans/Victorians etc.; Circuses and Fairs; Cowboys and Indians.

Naturally it cannot be deduced that these are therefore the best. Yours and the children's enthusiasm are the single most important factor in the likely success of a chosen theme. Next comes availability of resources. A theme cannot be sustained on enthusiasm alone; books, pictures, information, objects, places of interest, visiting speakers, all play an important part in keeping things going.

d) When the general enthusiasm begins to tail off, set aside a day on which to tie up loose ends and have a retrospective look at the theme. Tell the children in advance and ask for volunteers for individual readings, description of pictures, recording of information etc. Draw up a loose programme for the day; with infants you will have to mastermind the operation — 'Remember Robert painted this picture of Westminster Abbey? He's going to tell us about it now . . . and Sara wrote a poem about the baby prince, she's going to read it to you'. With older children you can leave more of the organisation of the day's programme to them.

e) A well organised system of record keeping is necessary in order to ensure that each child's progress is carefully monitored. This is especially essential in a thematic approach where there are perhaps more aspects of a child's development to be monitored (creative, social, practical, co-operative etc.), and where also there is less of a systematic progression in exercise books to use as a guide.

f) For other than 'instant' themes, preparation and forward planning are vital if the theme is to keep going. Collect as many resources as you can. There is probably a source of 'useful addresses' in the school; explain to colleagues what you are doing and enlist their help. Use your common sense. If you are doing a theme around trees then write to the Forestry Commission and ask for help or information. National bodies or large organisations (Royal National Lifeboat Institution, R.A.F. and other services, Oxfam, R.S.P.C.A., National Trust, etc.) are usually willing to give help or information or both.

g) Make some attempt to classify the material so that it is easy to use. Some of it of course may not be used. There is no need to use every scrap of material just because you have got it. The guiding principle should be that as far as possible the children are allowed to follow their own interests through the theme. They should not, therefore be diverted from a particular line of enquiry just so that an unused resource is used. If the range of materials is wide and varied enough the children can be relied upon (with some help from you) to find a reasonably fruitful path through it.

Now for some advantages of the thematic approach:

a) The themes chosen centre on known or accepted areas of interest to the children. The children themselves can choose the theme occasionally (though this sounds better in theory than it works in practice). You therefore start from the relatively strong position of having the children already interested.

b) *All* children, regardless of their intelligence or ability, can contribute to the theme, so there is a sense of community and co-operation about the work.

c) The children are given a context in which to write their own prose/poetry, e.g. imagine you are a stowaway on a Pirate ship and write about your experiences; you are an astronaut in a rocket, describe the sensation you feel in the last minute before take off. These two assignments would perhaps bear more fruitful results if the children had been involved in the situations and experiences of in the first case a theme on Pirates and in the second a theme on Space Travel.

d) The children are given a somewhat more natural chunk of the world picture to discover. One in which the various strands of learning are mixed up and interwoven. At the end of the theme they will have used their skills of reading, counting, measuring, etc., to some immediate effect. For many children this makes more sense than to practise skills as an end in itself or for the seemingly unintelligible reason that 'it's good for them'!

e) You have the opportunity to learn along with the children about topics of which you know very little. This not only gives you a chance to extend your knowledge but it also allows you to approach things in a real spirit of enquiry in which you and the children can share the enjoyment of discovery together. This is a refreshing change from the traditional approach where you seem to have most of the answers most of the time.

Now some disadvantages:

a) It is unlikely that you will get *all* the children interested in every (or any) theme. Some children will be bored at the prospect. And, to force a child to go through the motions of learning about a theme in which he or she is not interested is to defeat the object of this approach.

b) Unless the school has a policy of overall and long term planning there is a great danger of repetition. That is of the child working on the same or similar themes at different stages in his school life.

c) It is more difficult in a thematic approach to make sure that important basic skills of spelling, handwriting, the learning of mathematical facts, are given systematic practice and attention. The concern isn't so great if you are in a school which works almost entirely through themes. In this case the school has presumably evolved because enthusiastic teachers wanted to use a particular method which they believe will achieve the best for and from the children. This 'best' includes the efficient mastery of basic skills. Due consideration therefore will have been given to the problem and strategies worked out. If, on the other hand you are in the more likely position of being in a school in which there are a mixture of philosophies and methods then the fear that you are not devoting enough time to basic skills can be a real disadvantage.

d) It is probably harder (and in my experience more physically exhausting) to set up and maintain a theme as an efficient method of working than it is a more traditional set up. In the latter there are text books to help take some of the strain off your shoulders. You can if you like completely follow someone else's pattern of work for your children. With a theme *you've* got to plan the pattern of work (at least the outline) yourself, collect and collate all the material, check that the basics are not being neglected, assess the quality of the work in progress etc. Then at the end of the theme you have to start all over again. Naturally the amount of work will vary with each school. Some schools will provide a central source from which you can borrow material on a number of topics. Other schools will provide nothing in this line.

The three themes sketched out are *Harvest* (juniors), **Road Safety** (infant and juniors), *Growth* (both). They were chosen at random and the pattern of development (i.e. how one thing can lead to another) can be applied to any theme. Sometimes the theme will take a direction which you have not anticipated e.g. one of the developments in *Harvest* really strays into *Fruit*. If the children's interest dictates the direction then this is a strength of this method. It is perfectly proper to find out about say the internal structure of an apple under the general theme of *Harvest*. Indeed the link between seeds/fruit/reproductive cycle and *Harvest* is very strong. It is important though that you are able to point out such links when necessary, otherwise they could go unnoticed.

Once you have chosen the theme sort out for yourself the important aspects from the less important. Create a mental hierarchy so that you will automatically help the children while they work through the theme to give attention to the various aspects in some kind of sensible proportion. For example in the theme on *Harvest* your hierarchy could be something like the following:

a) It occurs at a specific point in the year's cycle; there is a connection with Spring planting/Summer nourishment and growth.

b) There is a strong link between the weather and the harvest.

c) There is a harvest from the sea which has a different pattern and cycle to that of the land.

d) There is an interrelationship between the various sectors of the community in the gathering, storing, treating, and distributing of the harvest.

e) Many combine harvesters are painted red.

f) Apples are harvested in Autumn.

and the children after working through the theme would be unlikely to be left with a lasting impressiong of e) and f) while missing the first four aspects.

Once you have sorted out the important aspects it is time to get down to the preparation proper:

a) Research the subject as fully as time allows by background reading and asking questions of 'likely' people.

b) Form a clear idea of how the theme could develop. Do not be too fixed about this idea rather look upon it as something to fall back on if things lose momentum.

c) Make a list of art and craft requirements and start a collection of these. Put a list of appropriate items (yoghurt pots, milk bottle tops, etc.) where the parents can see it or send a list of requirements home with the children. This will help to speed up your collection and you may be given 'extra' donations which are relevant to the theme.

d) Check on local resources. Contact the library, museum, local church, records office etc. Explain something about the work you hope to cover and ask whether there are any resources which could be made use of.

e) Talk about what you plan to do, with other members of staff. They may have useful information or material to offer.

f) Gather as wide a reading list as possible, books, prose passages, short stories, poems, notices, rules, instructions etc.

g) Prepare folders/envelopes/packets for each child — the older the child the more of this work they will do themselves.

h) Choose a starting point. It doesn't so much matter *what* starting point you choose, so long as it is interesting/eye catching/ enjoyable.

Here then are some starting points and possible lines of development for a theme on —

Harvest *An apple or apples brought in by you or the children*

Buy a few pounds of apples (cheap at this time of year). Give one to each child to look at, feel, smell, cut in half, then eat or as a dramatic starting point, simply dish them out to be eaten. This will instantly focus attention more effectively than a verbal introduction — 'today we are going to think about the *Harvest.*'

This starting point can lead to —

a) different varieties of apple; varieties of other common fruits; work on world map, tracing fruit and vegetables to country of origin; pictorial representation of fruits linked to country of origin; graph work on most popular fruits; costing of fruit in local shops (this information used for work on money sums).

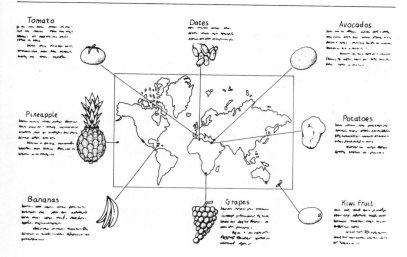

b) dissection, internal structure, classification of various types of fruits; difference between fruits and seeds relationship to one another, and fruit and seed dispersal; collection of examples of different methods of dispersal: sycamore seeds, thistledown, coconut with outer shell, nuts, berries etc., and display of same; requirements for germination and growth; parable of the sower; planting of bulbs; sowing of mustard and cress; germination of broad bean.

c) food value — classification of different sorts of foods according to nutritional content; collage work on 'health-giving foods'; diet, exercise and rest; comparison of a baby's food intake with that of children in the class; individual diet charts of food consumed in say one week, class graphs — to show number of potatoes, slices of bread, apples etc. consumed in one month — comparison with Third World — daily intake of food amongst people living on the borderline of starvation.

• *Picture of a Combine Harvester*

a) various stages in harvesting grain; the various designs and functions of farm machinery — development of same over last 100 years; visit to an Agricultural Museum; visit to a farm; designs of various tyre treads of tractor tyres; drawing of life-size tractor and car tyre — comparison of same, drawing of both to scale; comparison of different methods of harvesting, pictures of hand picking, scythe etc; foods harvested in different countries — rice, tea, coffee, etc.; animals which are involved in harvest work; harvest mouse — poem *To a Mouse* (Burns).

b) making of a model combine harvester, cardboard boxes to represent various sections to cut, thresh, winnow etc.; written descriptions to accompany children's own diagrams of a combine harvester (real or imaginary view).

● *Sheaf of Corn*
a) separation of grain from stalks; grain as starting point in bread making chain; each stage researched, written about, illustrated etc.; large wall display *The story of Bread*; collection of different sorts of bread — white, brown, wholemeal, soda, unleavened, etc. bread tasting session! — most/least popular breads — baking of bread; writing recipes.

b) various aspects of straw: display of Corn Dollies, research into customs and folklore of the past — link with pagan festivals — harvest festivals of the present day; methods of preparing and storing hay/grain — associated words — hay stack, hay cock, hay rick, hay maker, etc.; various uses of straw — hat making, thatching, bedding for animals and

Thick lid — Cover — Boiling water — Bowl

Cardboard box — Potatoes — Straw — Cardboard box

people, hay-box — making of same to demonstrate that hay is a poor conductor of heat, experiment to show how heat is retained inside box — fill a bowl with boiling water, add salt, porridge oats, or potatoes; place in hay-box and leave several hours or overnight, after which time the contents may be eaten.

● *Visit to a Farm, Garden, Orchard or Allotment*
Children actually *do* some harvesting: interview of farm worker, gardener etc., (from list of questions compiled before visit if necessary) recording of event and experiences — class book results of interviews — e.g. how weather can affect the harvest, how extra help is needed at *Harvest* time, the worst/best *Harvest* in memory of person interviewed, illustrated account (communal or individual) of Day in the Life of a Farm Worker during *Harvest* season.
Invited speaker — *baker, greengrocer, fisherman, farmer, lorry driver, etc.*

This to be used as a starting point in the gradual build up of chain of events which transforms say corn in the fields to bread on your table; map showing route of local (or nearest) produce to different parts of the country and abroad — visit to supermarket or local shop; choosing of one item (children to choose their own) to be used as focal point in chain of events to bring food from source to supermarket e.g. baked beans — harvesting, drying, sorting, cooking, canning, packing, loading, journeying, unloading, storing, displaying, etc. done in booklet form or mounted as a wall display; collection of labels, wrappers, packets from foods used in children's homes — collage work, graph work or linking of wrappers on world map to country of origin.

Road Safety

There are two aspects of road safety in the Primary school: road safety education, and road safety training. Both are valuable in themselves and should ideally complement each other. Nevertheless they are quite distinct from each other and the doing of one cannot be taken as substitute for the doing of another. Therefore when you embark upon a theme of road safety do not assume that by the end of it the children's actual behaviour on the roads will necessarily be affected.

Before we go on to the actual theme let us quickly look at the training aspect of road safety. This involves repetition, routine and actual physical practice. Take the children to the actual kerb side (another adult will be needed to help if you take a large group). 'Play' at crossing the road properly with and without the aid of a road crossing patrol. Repeat the process in the classroom or hall simulating the kerbside with ropes or tapes. Obviously the younger the children the greater the need for this kind of training. Also, the training will have more effect when the children are young enough not to have developed good or bad road safety practices of their own. Nevertheless it is true to say that children at all stages in the Primary school ought to have regular practice sessions in road safety. The frequency of the practice sessions will vary with the age of the children and locality of the school. Once or twice a term may be sufficient for top juniors. For reception children once a week would probably be more suitable with (just before home time) a *daily* verbal reminder of the main points of road safety.

● *Visiting speaker*
Most primary schools are visited at some point during the session

by a road safety officer. The visit may prove to be spontaneous starting point for a theme of road safety or you can plan for the visit to be a starting point. Usually the contents of the talk, film or whatever are of a general nature. You can choose to explore particular aspects best suited to your children. Infants will need to learn words like pavement, road, kerb, zebra crossing, traffic, vehicle etc.; large 'street scenes' painted, labelled — frequently referred to — used as a basis for simple written work; flannel graph or cellograph boards used with all the necessary parts for a busy road: vehicles, people, traffic-lights etc. — children can make parts themselves where appropriate, three dimensional models — own toy vehicles brought in and used on model; road games invented — rules written for future use, e.g.

  a) Throw the dice to choose your part:
    i)   person
    ii) bicycle
    iii) three-wheeled vehicle
    iv) car or van
    v)   traffic warden or policeman
    vi) lorry or bus
  b) Throw dice again to choose your leader
  c) Leader puts people in place

With Infants it is a good idea to leave the 'rules' as open ended as possible so that they are open to interpretation. Once set on the track the children will have no trouble in inventing the 'game' as they go along (main features here are the development of language associated with the theme, the role playing involved and the clarification of ideas NOT the playing of the game itself). A school crossing patrol sign can be brought in to the classroom — examined, words read aloud, copied, displayed on wall etc. A child's size version of the sign (or 'lollipop') can be made to be put in dressing-up or props box. The children can choose to be vehicles of various kinds — arm shields drawn in the shape of a vehicle

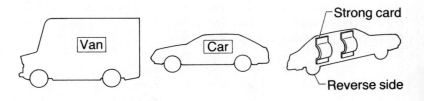

to be slipped over forearm — children 'drive' along road till road crossing patrol makes them stop — a group of 'pedestrians' cross in safety — patrol walks back to pavement — 'traffic' continues.

• *Story:*

Story told to children of 'Polly's road accident' — details tailored to suit individual locality — story acted by children — different kinds of accident discussed — plays to show different situations (crossing road from behind parked car, playing with a ball in the street etc.), lists and pictures of possible injuries — broken or fractured limbs, cuts and bruises, damaged eyesight etc. Sorting game — board or card showing road, pavement, park, playground, zebra crossing, traffic lights etc., box of pictures to be placed on board in suitable positions e.g. child walking to school, child playing, dog on lead, bus, bicycle, parked car etc. — the making of the parts for the game is a worthwhile activity in itself *provided* that there is adequate provision made for language development associated with the activity e.g. 'this boy is playing with a ball, he will have to go in the park', 'where do you think your van should go John?' etc.

• *Life sized version of nearest road sign:*

Children shown the sign and try to guess where it could be found outside school — short outing to the actual sign, photograph taken, meaning of sign explained and discussed, pictures of road signs collected which can be seen in close vicinity of school, simple matching cards made for games like — road sign families snap etc. Basic signs STOP, SLOW and GIVE WAY used in the classroom, furniture arranged to form roads (to include crossroads, T-junctions etc.), some children are vehicles driving along till they have to react to others who are road signs. Traffic lights introduced — included in game, these can also be used as signals with children's every day activities e.g. red 'light' (traffic lights drawn on cards with red light coloured) — children stop working, amber light — children stand behind their chairs, green light — children go out to play etc.

Juniors will be able to take Road Safety education much further. You could use similar starting points or especially contrived ones:

• *Tape recording of traffic flow on road outside school:*

This could lead to counts on various categories of vehicles; the discovery that there is more traffic at one time of day than another, (why?) or more on one day of the week than on others — market days, rush hours, bank holidays etc.; accumulated data leading to graph work, averages, percentages and so on. Speed and distance work to encompass such things as — stopping time — correlation between m.p.h. and stopping time, speed limits — variation in these according to environment also comparison with other countries, different penalties for speeding offences — link with maximum speed limit and number of serious or fatal accidents, other factors leading to serious or fatal accidents — fatigue, drink/drugs, mechanical failure, faulty tyres — car maintenance — basic requirements needed to pass M.O.T. — talk from local garage mechanic.

- *Bicycle display in hall or playground:*
Children to bring in their own bicycles — short written description to be displayed alongside bike — name, age, any special features etc. — large diagram of bicycle on wall — various parts named and function explained — as many real parts as possible displayed and labelled (chain, brake cable, tyre, inner tube, pedal, saddle, wheel spoke etc.) — many of the items can be borrowed from a second-hand bicycle shop. Care and maintenance of the bicycle — puncture mending — an 'expert' from the children could demonstrate along the lines of a cookery or gardening programme on television — cleaning, oiling, replacing of chain, lowering or raising the saddle etc. Cycling proficiency — blank road maps drawn by children, route and position of cycle from point A to point B drawn in — some to have deliberate mistakes e.g. cyclist wrongly positioned for a right hand turn — these to be included in a 'Spot the Mistakes' folder — each sheet in folder to be given a title and three or four deliberate mistakes. When folder is functioning the child will choose a sheet, copy the title into his or her own book and describe the mistakes presented. The child will then copy the sheet into its book with the mistakes corrected. Advanced cycle tests devised by the children — entrants judged by the children — questions made up and printed out on card for — cycle, driving, pedestrian proficiency test.

- *Highway Code*
Different groups of children to take responsibility for learning one section of the code — one representative from each group to go on to a panel to form a kind of 'Brains Trust' — members of panel answer or discuss questions raised by rest of class — panel to be changed frequently so as to give every child the opportunity to be in the 'firing line'. 'Mastermind' — one questioner interviews 4 contestants who try to gain the title of Mastermind of Highway Code. Road signs from surrounding area found in Highway Code — painted/drawn to actual size — other

signs from different localities painted/drawn — display on classroom wall
or corridor — suitable picture of type of environment (painted or cut

out of magazine) made to correspond to sign — alternative road signs
devised — road signs devised for different countries e.g. Africa, Switzerland,
Australia, different planets, etc. Motorway signs — special features —
differences between motorways and minor roads — photocopied pages
from roadmaps used to trace routes from home to named town or city,
calculating the distance between given points on a map — plotting the
most direct route between two points. Diagram of own town centre —
arrows used to show traffic flow of one way system — devising a one
way traffic system for a real or imaginary town/city centre — parking
regulations investigated — penalties for parking offences — new parking
regulations devised — new penalties. Dialogues between parking offender
and traffic warden written and narrated by children.

Suggested additions to Highway Code to reduce number of road
accidents — alterations in existing traffic laws to suit local needs. Dramatic
interpretation of road accidents, written account by the children of —
'If only I had looked/listened/stopped/checked etc'.

Growth

• *A Bulb*

Each child to plant a bulb, or, different groups given a different
variety of spring bulb (daffodil, hyacinth, snowdrop etc.) to plant — what
will happen to the tiny plant inside the bulb over the next few months?
— it will start to grow — what is growing? — children offer suggestions
— collection of growing and non-growing things — table of objects can
be placed in front of wall display or relevant pictures/poems/prose, take

one aspect of growth e.g. increase in size to be looked at more closely — observation of some quick growing plants — broad bean, mustard and cress — simple illustrated description of connected experiments, — expedition to local shop to buy bread and butter for mustard and cress sandwich feast — written invitations to another class or adult members of school to come to share in the feast — different elements of the feast traced back to source — e.g. — butter — milk — cow — grass, bread — dough — flour — wheat, — pictures by children to illustrate these chains, experiments to discover the basic requirements for growth to occur (placing of one plant in darkness, starving another of moisture, placing another in an extreme condition of cold, — another in dark position with light coming from one side only etc.) — written description or series of pictures of experiments and ideal conditions for the encouragement of germination and growth, series of illustrated accounts of the various stages in the growth of a bulb — different time scale of different bulbs — duration of bloom after it has appeared etc. — story *The Life History of a Crocus* — movement, drama or mime to depict the various stages in the growth of the bulb.

- *An Animal* (child's or teacher's pet brought in)

Short study of the animal itself then comparison with others — leading to simple groupings — e.g. large, medium size, small,/vegetarian, flesh eating,/land dwellers, sea dwellers,/egg-laying, non egg-laying etc. Children given random lists of animals and categorise the animals according to given headings; pictures, diagrams and photographs to show three stages of development — infant, young and mature in various animals (kitten, puppy, bird, caterpillar, frog, human being etc) — comparison

of different rates of growth and consequent variation in age of maturity
— use of reference books to answer specific questions on habitat, diet,
life span of various animals — one or two animals selected to be studied
in some detail — booklets made — *Life History of the Honey Bee* to be
read aloud, to be displayed, to be used as reference books for further
research by different groups of children.

Some live animals to be studied at close quarters — butterflies (from
caterpillars), hamsters, earthworms, etc. Care needed here to ensure that
the animals do not suffer any kind of discomfort or distress because of
the children's enthusiasm. Diagrams drawn of one of these animals —
main body parts labelled — comparison with human body parts — e.g.
claws/human finger nails, fur/human hair — nails and hair continue to
grow after maturation — experiments to show rate of growth of nails
and hair — how much increase in length is shown in one week/two weeks
etc. Graph plotted or estimation made on length nails would be in 6
months were they to be left uncut and the rate of growth to remain constant — pictures drawn (to scale where appropriate) to illustrate relative
length of nails after one month, two months etc — model cardboard or
plastic nails made to stick on to existing nails, poems — 'We are the Long
Nails', story 'The Plight of the Long Nails'. Similar work on the growing of hair — measurement of the longest hair in school — stories from
literature — Rapunzel, Samson, Rip Van Winkle.

● *Collection of photographs of children as babies*

Photographs displayed and numbered — matching game — on a
list of names the child puts the appropriate photograph number beside
the name — photos of siblings as babies — can children spot whose brother
or sister this is etc. — some very alike others less so — (find a suitable
alternative for those children who cannot produce a photo and take care
that no child feels left out or uncomfortably 'different').

Children gather all possible information about themselves as babies
— time and place of birth, weight etc. — similarities and differences between them and now — colour of hair, eyes, length of hair, weight etc.
Display of some of children's baby clothes alongside clothes of present
size — similar display of toys of babyhood alongside current toys —
newspaper(s) from year of children's birth (it is often possible to obtain
back numbers by writing to the local or national office) comparison of
news of that year with that of this year.

Stages of development — first smile, tooth, words, steps etc. —
note individual variations yet see the similarity of the overall pattern —
one or more mothers invited in with their babies to demonstrate bathing,
feeding, weighing, changing etc. — visits recorded by children in their
books — communal or individual interviews held to ask specific questions — extra safety precautions needed in the home where there is a
baby or toddler — list of possible dangers — catalogue of accidents which
have happened to members of the class — *An accident which need not have
happened* as a title for written work perhaps leading to drama — *'Spot
the hazard'* — pictures showing obvious safety hazards for young children
(unguarded fire, loose wire, open door, hot drink left within baby's reach)
redrawn with hazards corrected or removed — recording of accidents
which have occured within children's own homes or in homes of relatives.

● *Storm*

Taking another aspect of growth — that of gradual development
— the storm used as a starting point for the question 'How did it start?'
— movement, mime, pictures, written descriptions of wind growing
stronger, sky growing darker, thunder growing louder etc. — frieze along
the wall of the gradual development of a storm, Children help to compile a list of ways in which things can grow without necessarily increasing in size — growing richer/poorer, growing more beautiful, growing
old, growing cold, etc. Another list can be compiled by a different group
of children showing how growth can constitute visible change — village
can grow into a town, disagreement can grow into a feud, minor mishap
can grow into a major catastrophe (poem *For the want of a nail*), stream
can grow into a river. Simple fun with numbers — repeated addition
of a number to show the regulatiry of this sort of growth.

$$3 \longrightarrow 3$$
$$3 \ 3 \longrightarrow 6$$
$$3 \ 3 \ 3 \longrightarrow 9$$
$$3 \ 3 \ 3 \ 3 \longrightarrow 12$$
$$3 \ 3 \ 3 \ 3 \ 3 \longrightarrow 15$$

Maths work — sorting various labels into sets — necessity to place some labels in more than one set etc. — discovery that various arrangements are possible.

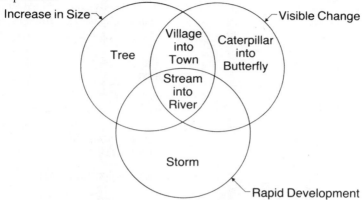

Selection by children of a story/poem which they have heard/read to illustrate an aspect of growth (collect as many as you can put in the book corner for the duration of the theme), e.g. *Jack and the Beanstalk, Henny Penny, Hans and the Hole in the Dyke, The Ugly Duckling, My Shadow, The Enormous Turnip, Little Drops of Water (hymn), Pinnochio,* and so on. Children go on to write their own stories to illustrate one or more aspects of growth.

- *Trees*

Expedition to various local trees — height measured (or approximate height estimated) — approximate age ascertained — old records possible source of information on when trees were planted — old prints/pictures — interviewing older members of the community. Collecting of seeds from trees and planting of same — display of various fruits and seeds linked to parent tree — each child to plant an acorn — estimate height of sapling by say end of term — plot graph of sapling's growth — check on accuracy of estimation at the appropriate time — placing of tiny sapling beside parent tree — photograph taken — diagram drawn to scale or representative picture (according to age of the children). Importance of trees — literature from Forestry Commission or talk from same — work of Forestry Commission — work of different kinds associated with growing plants and animals — farmer, shepherd, midwife, cowboy, florist etc. Each child or group to choose one job to research, and compile a detailed account of the work of a . . . . . ., — illustrations and samples where appropriate (sheep's wool, grains of wheat, piece of fishing net etc.). Different aspect of growth from trees — the growth of coal seams — leaf fossils to be found in coal from thousands of years ago — other growing solids which are mined — diamonds — experiments to demonstrate the growth of a crystal — blue copper sulphate (nearest

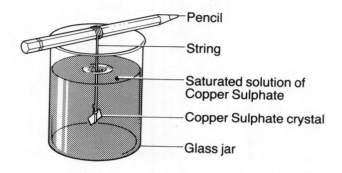

friendly secondary school can help out here) or simple salt crystals — suspend a length of string in a very strong solution of salt and water — wait several days — observe growth on string — wait a few more days, remove some of the crystals — study them through a strong magnifying glass. Children record the experiments in simple diagrams with a few sentences of written description (to be done by teacher in the case of younger children) — growth of an icicle, pictures drawn to illustrate the same icicle in one day, three days, ten days etc. — stalactites and stalagmites — making of same in plasticine, plaster or clay. Drama to encompass written work — *The Stalactites and Stalagmites in Conservation, Diary of a Stalagmite* etc. Music — starting with the children's voices — one group count in a 'growing' voice from 1-10 — another group crouch down into a small shape then start to grow as the voices grow — leading to

1 2 3 4 5 6 7 8 9 10

the use of percussion instruments as signals to suggest growing and diminishing shapes. Children split into groups — each group to work out a movement sequence around the theme of growth — one group performs the sequence to the rest of the children — rest of children say what the sequence suggested to them — performers explain their intentions and interpretations.

The outlines here are by no means comprehensive. There are many directions which perhaps you would like to follow and which have not been mentioned. Similarly there will be directions given here which you will choose not to follow. Some directions may even seem to you to be incomprehensible. This is to some extent understandable and even unavoidable unless a detailed step by step guide is given. Since this could defeat the whole purpose of thematic work, such a detailed framework has been purposely omitted. You must pick and choose your own path through the labyrinth of possible options. Discard ideas which do not seem to you to have much potential for development and add ideas of your own. The more confident you feel about the theme yourself the better able you will be to guide and encourage the children.

Two tales to end this chapter. One shows how much can be gained by a willingness to exploit educational opportunities as they present themselves. The other shows what may be lost by an unwillingness to do this. A willingness and ability to spot, seize and exploit such opportunities is of course an important ingredient in the classroom whether or not you work through themes (as the first tale demonstrates). Nevertheless this educational opportunism lends itself particularly well to the thematic approach and so the tales are included in this chapter.

On entering the school gates one morning, I picked up two cardboard rectangles each punched with 6 holes (the sort which are used to keep cream and yoghurt pots in place).

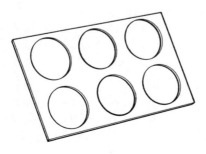

They had presumably fallen from the milk lorry when the school milk been delivered earlier that morning. I put them on my table intending to mention them to the children after assembly, making some point about litter and how we could all help — then throw the cards in the bin. However, after my little chat, one of the children (six to seven-year-olds) pointed out that there were the same number of holes on each card. Someone else offered that this made 12 holes altogether. We looked at the cards, counted the holes, in ones then twos, one child even managed to count the holes in threes and fours. We then cut the cards into 6 smaller cards each bearing two holes. We made 'sums' together using our experience with the cards —

'Polly cut two holes off a big card, who can write a sum about this?'

$6 - 2 = 4$

'We counted six twos to make twelve'

$6 \times 2 = 12$

The children recorded these sums in their number books. The more able children went on to make up more difficult sums by themselves while I worked with a less able group and helped to draw 12 holes, write a number line to 12 etc. The cards were used as templates to make identical shapes which were made into masks — litter masks put on for a litter search of the playground.

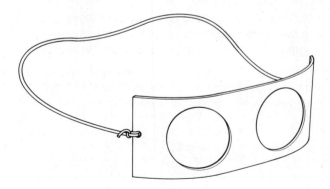

We also used the cards as stencils to paint over, to make all sorts of patterns. Two of the patterns were chosen to make the covers of a big story book entitled '*The Cardboard Litter.*' We made up the story together:

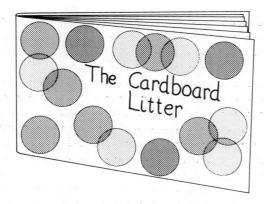

Mrs Soper found some litter on Thursday.
Here is a picture of it.
She put it on her table.
Polly cut off two holes.
We made up sums about it.
Here are four sums . . .

Different children illustrated each page. When the book was finished we put it on the book corner where it became a much loved favourite. Since I had contrived to include as many words from the reading scheme as possible, it became a useful consolidation exercise too.

There is nothing special about the above story and it is typical of the sort of thing which happens every day in lively classrooms up and down the country. It does serve to show though how things can develop almost of their own volition IF you will allow them to.

The second tale comes from a nursery school where the children were mostly four to five year-olds, and came to school either in the morning or afternoon. Ten or so children stayed all day and had lunch in school. I was helping out as a supply teacher for the day and happened to be on lunch duty. For pudding there was ice cream with thick red jelly. Rather a lot of the jelly was left over and the cook asked the teacher in charge if she would like to give some of it to the afternoon children. 'Oh no we don't have time for that just throw it out' replied the teacher. The afternoon children began to arrive and drifted to one activity or another. Some of them seemed to drift rather aimlessly through the whole afternoon. I thought how the red jelly could have provided a focal point for the children to be brought together, how they would have enjoyed such an unusual treat, how we could have talked about red things, drawn and painted red pictures, started a collection of red objects to make a display, dissolved a lump of red jelly with hot water, perhaps made a different coloured jelly the next day etc. The time which the teacher had said we hadn't got seemed to be in plentiful supply. It could have been better filled by giving the children something to enjoy which could then have become a basis for no end of related work. Instead they did the usual (I had been to the school before and knew the pattern), a variety of disparate activities, seemingly unrelated to each other or to anything in the children's lives.

Now, it goes without saying that most of the children probably got a lot out of the afternoon. And, of course not every single opportunity can be seized and developed. As an aim this would not only be unrealistic but also just plain silly. Nevertheless there are occasions when with a little effort you can set off a line of development which will provide the children with interest, enjoyment and a proper climate for learning.

5. The Curriculum

Some of you may not be entirely clear in your own mind about what is actually meant by 'The Curriculum'. The trappings of technical jargon, often tacked on to any study about the curriculum, can confuse rather than clarify things. In this chapter we shall attempt to:
- look briefly at what is meant by the word 'curriculum'
- make suggestions about the aims of a Primary school curriculum
- talk about the dangers of an overcrowded curriculum
- offer some suggestions about content.

So, what do we mean then by the word curriculum?

Really, nothing much more than 'a course of study'. That doesn't sound too problematical. But it is the content of that course of study and how it is organised which can cause such heated debate. Questions about what to include or omit, how much emphasis to place on each subject, what are the most efficient means of giving and receiving information etc., not only show how deeply people feel about these things but also that there is a constant striving by some to improve the curriculum.

These debates can be interesting and sometimes even illuminating but as a new teacher you will be more concerned about a curriculum which actually works for you in the classroom. A young teacher once complained to me that at college the 'integrated day' had been put forward as an excellent idea and also reasonably easy to organize. The whole thing fell apart when she'd tried to put her ideas into practice with a class of seven to eight year-olds. There are many ideas which sound good in theory but which will simply not stand up in practice. Not at any rate until you have some experience behind you. So, at this stage practical considerations are of the utmost importance. If you have an idea, think it through in practical terms before you start. Say for example that you would like painting facilities to be permanently available to the children. First ask yourself things like where is the best position in the classroom for the activity, who will look after the paints, where will the paper be stored, what will the children do with their finished paintings etc. This will save you needless heartache later on.

There are of course many things which 'work' well enough, but this does not make them automatically desirable in the curriculum. This really brings us to the next section.

The aims of a Primary school curriculum

First some *questions* and *answers*. The answers are mine and are not of course the only ones.

Q: Why should we bother to work out the aims of a curriculum?

A: Without aims your work could lose purpose and become wasteful and irrelevant. Not that aims in themselves are any guarantee against such things but you are probably less likely to go astray with aims than without. Besides, the working out of aims is in itself a worthwhile activity and provides a focal discussion point for staff.

Q: Should the elements of a curriculum reflect its overall aims?

A: Yes and this may sound obvious but there are many examples to be found of schools which have fine sounding aims which are not borne out in the work of the children. There are other schools in which the connection between the aims of the curriculum and the work of the children has not even been thought about.

Q: Should the various elements complement each other or be seen as separate entities?

A: The more a curriculum can be seen as a sensible whole which has something to do with life and living the more valuable it will be. An attempt should be made therefore to merge the various elements whenever possible so that these are seen not as 'subjects' but as really useful and enjoyable parts of the children's lives.

Q: Are some subjects more important to a Primary school curriculum than others?

A: Generally speaking yes, though there can be no hard and fast list of subjects. In order to do their best, teachers must be allowed (within reason) to draw up their own lists placing their own particular emphasis.

Q: Will all teachers have the same hierarchy of subjects?

A: Yes and no. The answer to this question is really contained in the answer to the previous question.

Q: Should the curriculum of a class be linked to the curriculum of the school?

A: Yes, in order to save time and to reinforce the idea of a sensible whole curriculum, the aims of a class curriculum should be in tune with those of the whole school, for example, if the aim was to teach a fluent, legible handwriting style. This would not be achieved if each class teacher taught his or her own choice of handwriting style without recourse to an overall school policy.

Q: Should the curriculum of a school change from time to time?

A: Yes, if it is a living curriculum which meets the shifting needs of the pupil, then it must change from time to time, (e.g. the needs of most who had to undergo an 11 plus exam 20 years ago are not the same as those of most pupils now who have to go on and find their various places in a comprehensive school). And, in these circumstances, any school which had the same curriculum now as it had 20 years ago would be open to criticism.

These questions and answers are not supposed to bog you down, but only to remind you that there is more to your work than meets the eye. They will also help you to think a little about the curriculum in your own classroom and in the school at large.

What then, should a Primary school curriculum aim to do? The following tentative suggestions are offered as a basis for thought and discussion and not as a prescription. The more you can chop and change and refine them to your own way of thinking the better.

A Primary school curriculum should:

• welcome and entice the children into a process of growth through learning

• stimulate and foster a curiosity about themselves and the world they live in

• foster first an awareness, then a caring consideration for others who share their world and the wider world beyond

• teach basic skills of listening, talking, reading, writing and counting.

Of course these aims cannot be achieved by the curriculum alone but in this chapter it is the curriculum aspects upon which we shall concentrate. As you work out the content and method of your curriculum ask youself, 'Will this work in practical terms, is it in tune with my aims for the curriculum, could it be improved upon?' But before we go on to the actual content, a word about overcrowding.

Some dangers of an overcrowded curriculum

In recent years one fault has become common to many Primary school curriculums — that of overcrowding. This has come about because of a lack of understanding and communication between theorists, specialists and general teachers in the classroom. Advocates and devotees of one discipline or another have argued for its inclusion and importance in the curriculum without bearing in mind the balance of the curriculum as a whole. Theorists have lectured on the breaking down of subject barriers and the need to include as many areas of experience as possible without really taking practical considerations into account. The result has been that many teachers have felt that they must cram everything in somehow. In some cases quantity has assumed greater importance than quality. Naturally this happens at great cost to the teachers and the children.

For example, in an overcrowded curriculum there is a greater likelihood of:

i) lack of thoroughness

ii) dilettante attitude to work

iii) the elements of a curriculum merging into a jumbled mass of bits and pieces instead of complementing each other to make more sense of the whole

iv) long term development of some subjects (Maths, French, Science) being hindered or even harmed, and unqualified teachers (that is teachers with little or no expertise in a given field) being given responsibility for important areas of the curriculum (remedial education, science, music)

v) the task of Secondary school teachers being made more difficult — children may be unnecessarily 'put off' a subject by their Primary school, they may have to 'unlearn' some things when they reach Secondary school — a sufficient grounding in basic skills may not have been given to help the children to make the most of what the Secondary school has to offer

vi) overall pace of classroom life being too rushed for the child to absorb and assimilate information

vii) same rushed pace preventing teacher from research and experiment in areas of particular interest in the classroom — children picking up half truths and piecing these together to form an overall hazy and inaccurate impression.

An overcrowded curriculum is of course not the only cause of such faults, but I believe it is certainly one cause.

As much can be gained by attempting to tackle fewer subjects thoroughly and in greater depth. Also fewer risks of the sort outlined above will be run.

This is not to argue for a dull narrow curriculum. Certainly in the primary school there is a sense in which the world is the classroom and the classroom is the world, so that there is nothing which is barred from observation or enquiry if the need arises. But, there has to be room in the curriculum for the enquiry to take place, and time also for the teacher to do some relevant background reading. One of the glories of primary school education is its spontaneity. Too many fixed points on a curriculum will have a constricting effect on this spontaneity.

The number and variety of subjects in a curriculum will be (or ought to be) largely determined by the enthusiasm and expertise available on the staff. It can happen that long after a subject has ceased to be a worthwhile part of the curriculum it continues to be included. For example, if the enthusiastic member of staff who introduced and sustained a subject leaves the school, it can then be 'given' to a much less enthusiastic member of staff to deal with somehow. The temptation to keep something in the curriculum is greater if expensive equipment has been bought as a teaching aid. And so the curriculum becomes cluttered and overcrowded.

Certainly we want the children to have a rich and varied educational diet, but too rich and too varied all at once can lead to mental indigestion and our object will be defeated.

The wisest plan for you initially will be to tackle as much as you feel you happily can. Do not feel pressured into biting off more than you can chew. You will make a much better job of things if you feel you are in control. The feelings of panic or of not being able to cope can be started off simply by trying to do too many things at once.

Curriculum Content

It is not the business of this book to argue for this or that hierarchy of subjects but of course some subjects are more central than others to the Primary school curriculum. There can be no doubt for example about the need to include the '3Rs'. It is how to include them which causes debate. It is hoped that they will be seen in the light of the 1980's/90's so that reading and writing are seen as creative and recreative as well as functional. Also that arithmetic is extended to embrace an all round mathematical approach which seeks to increase the child's understanding as well as to give practice in those things which must be learnt by heart. Apart from the 3Rs the subjects here are to be found in the curriculum of most primary schools but of course there will be exceptions, and there will be some schools which cater for subjects not mentioned here.

Since it would not be possible nor indeed desirable to exhaust the possibilities of any one subject, the suggestions here are only starters. The aim is to help you to formulate ideas about how you would like to organize your own curriculum. It is important therefore that this section is not seen to be prescriptive. Indeed the more debate and disagreement it engenders the more use it will be.

1. *Reading*

We start with reading since its mastery can, unlike any other single subject, help (or hinder) a child's progress in a very wide variety of subjects. The actual teaching of reading is of course outside the scope of this book. The two aspects of reading which are looked at are Reading for Information and Reading for Pleasure (though strictly speaking of course the two are really inseparable). First a glance at oral practice which is common to both aspects.

a) Oral practice

Two basic skills which I believe are not given enough attention are those of speaking (clearly) and listening (attentively). They are so basic that they are often overlooked. Children are assumed to be able to listen attentively and speak clearly. Some of course can, but by no means all. Those who cannot are often blamed rather than helped. It seems to be me that one of the first jobs of our nursery schools and classes is to give adequate attention to these skills. You cannot assume however that just because a child has been to nursery school he or she will therefore have had any help in learning how to listen. So, it may fall to you to take responsibility for these skills to give them the attention and practice which they need.

Since they are unquantifiable you may receive little recognition for your efforts but do not let this put you off. By helping the children towards the acquisition of a clear speaking voice and an attentive ear you will be doing them a valuable service. You will also encounter less problems with written work. Time and time again mistakes and misunderstanding in a child's written work can be traced directly back to a lack of oral practice. Of course, conversation is as valuable as anything and it has the added advantage of being natural. But it would be difficult to find time to have enough ordinary conversation with each child and so here are some suggestions for games to practise and improve the skills of listening and speaking.

i) Obeying of softly spoken or whispered commands (pick up your pencil, close your book, touch your head, look at the roof, point to the window). These can become more complex for older children (put your feet together, then put your left hand on your right shoulder, then look at the door). Vary the response i.e. sometimes the whole class, sometimes a particular group and sometimes individual children to respond.

ii) Writing down/drawing of softly spoken words, sentences, names, numbers etc.

iii) Listening to well known rhymes to pick out certain words e.g. 'There are two two-syllabled words in this verse listen out for them and see if you can tell me at the end what they are.' Then read the rhyme aloud or let a child read it.

Jack Sprat could eat no fat
His wife could eat no lean
And so between them both you see
They licked the platter clean.

iv) A variation of the above is the listening to a piece of prose or poetry (use the children's own writing when you can). The children signal e.g. put a hand up or write down each time they hear a word in a given category (words starting with 'p', ending in 'll' etc.) Word categories are chosen to suit the passage and the age of the children.

v) Reading aloud by child of a passage from the blackboard (or similar). The others give a signal if things are not sounded, or if they are mispronounced. Speech defects or irregularities are of course taken into account here. Naturally these are not penalized.

vi) Giving and receiving of instructions — one child describes a picture/pattern to his partner who tries to reproduce a similar picture/pattern on the blackboard.

vii) The old ring game. The children sit in a circle, one child starts the game by whispering a message (word, song title, phrase, command etc.) to her neighbour, who in turn whispers it to the next child and so on until the message travels all the way round the circle. The last child announces what she heard then the original message is read from a card then held up for all to read.

Make up games of your own to suit the children (e.g. by using local street names). A large part of the value of such activity is the fun the children get out of it so they should never be laboured. Naturally the games in themselves will not make the children better listeners but they do help a little to teach them what listening is and how to do it.

When the child starts to learn to read, he or she should read aloud daily, not necessarily to you, it could be to an older child, a parent helper, a student etc. At the early stages it is important to keep a daily rhythm going, so 2 minutes each day is better than 10 every few days.

Once the child is reading fluently there is still a need to read aloud. Older children should read aloud at least once a week, younger children every other day. Keep up the habit of reading aloud all the way through the Primary school, to improve pronunciation, spelling, sentence construction and to increase confidence. Once the child has learned to read, use a wide variety of reading material, poetry, jokes, cereal packets, Radio Times etc. Make 'read aloud' cards — extracts printed or written clearly on stout card. Covered in plastic the cards will be more durable and can also serve as tracing cards. These cards are useful in that the children become accustomed to hearing them being read aloud and the poorer readers have the advantage of semi memorization when they come to read the cards. If they are written in the school's agreed handwriting style the cards can also double as handwriting copy cards. The children can read aloud to a group, the whole class or you alone (older children still benefit from your praise and individual attention). Throughout the year they will experience all three.

I once used a successful device with infants for helping the children to lose their self-consciousness and to speak out. This was an imaginary radio programme which we called '*Listen In*'. The readers would stand behind the blackboard holding whatever material was to be read. The imaginary radio (sometimes drawn, sometimes made from a box) was placed in front of the board and the 'audience' would gather round in readiness for the 'programme'. Someone would switch on and the announcer would describe what the content of the programme was to be then the readers would begin. Surprisingly often on these occasions children who normally found reading aloud rather difficult, would manage to produce a much smoother flow of words than usual. The fact that they wouldn't see their audience seemed to help them to project their voices without thinking about it.

A variation on this with juniors would be the reading of news snippets (national and local) on an imaginary T.V. news bulletin. The children could take it in turns to gather the news during the week and the bulletin could go out once a week.

Read aloud to the children when you can (infants every day, juniors 2 to 3 times a week at least). Let them hear records or cassettes of children's stories, there are some excellent ones around but there are some dreadful ones too so have a listen yourself before you play anything to the children. Cassette recorders can aid reading in many ways. With infants you can record well loved tales from the reading corner. The tales can then be 'read' along with the taped story. Many recorders have a set of individual earphones which enables one child to listen without disturbing the others. Older children can read a page each of a short story or an extract from a book then listen to it being played back.

Another successful device to encourage fluency in reading is the reading aloud of short plays. The children enjoy the dialogue and such plays provide a lot of reading practice for the comparitively small number of words which an individual child has to read aloud. There are a number of books available on the market but try to write your own as well. It isn't difficult to invent simple lines from well known tales (or even unknown tales), and there is no harm in inventing a few extra characters so that you can include more children. Older children should be encouraged and helped to write their own lines. Give help with expression and voice production to help make the reading more interesting.

Reading aloud is a most important aspect of reading. It heightens awareness of words, increases the child's self-confidence and helps to improve self-expression. Generally speaking it is neglected. Try to make adequate provision for it when you plan your own curriculum.

b) Reading for Information

In other words the ability to understand instructions, notices, timetables, T.V. and radio guides, recipes, directions, signs etc.

The material can be divided into three categories
i) Information which gives warning e.g. DANGER
ii) Information which instructs e.g. PULL
iii) Information which tells (you something) e.g. EXIT

Information which gives warning

It is as well to start with the first category since the sooner the children learn to recognise words of warning the better. Start with the school — take the children for a walk round noting any danger signs e.g. fire instructions. Go on to collect dangers signs from the home, supermarket, public transport, countryside etc. Read them together and discuss meaning; are the colours used for the sign significant, is the position of the sign important? Warning signs ought to be obeyed — make a wall display of real signs or facsimiles of same alongside list of words from the signs — danger, keep out, private, do not enter, do not touch, keep off the grass, beware of the dog etc. Collect pictures cut out of magazines, or drawn — pictures then held up — group of children decide which sign or group of words is appropriate to the picture.

Stories written *If only he had read the sign, Not to be ignored, The day the sign fell down* and so on. Home assignment — children asked to locate and copy a notice or sign from a public place — bus, theatre, super-market (or village shop), park, farm etc. These are then brought back to the classroom, coloured or painted, and a short description written about each one; a wall display may be mounted. Children then choose one to copy and describe in their books — plays made up by children — these to be based on a warning sign in the vicinity of the school (plays can also be developed from the childrens' stories).

Information which instructs

Again a walk round the school may provide some ready made examples here or you could take the children on an expedition round the town or village to look for specific examples: 'shut the gate', 'lower your head please', 'please take a basket', 'keep to the left' etc. The same sort of use could be made of this information as was made in section (a).

Collect instructions from games — Snakes and Ladders, Scrabble etc, also electrical appliances — washing machines, food mixers etc. (you may have to simplify some of these) — stick on to card alongside ques-tions which you have made up to test the children's understanding of the instructions of a particular device e.g. 'what is the maximum number of players allowed to play this game?', or 'is the on/off switch for this gadget (television, food mixer, washing machine, electric drill) on the right or the left?' Children may then invent imaginary gadgets of their own and write instructions to go with them e.g.

Instructions for use of the Sockbox:
- Sort socks to be stored into light colours and dark colours.
- Remove lid.
- Place light colours in section marked L.

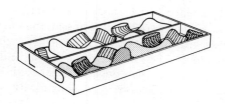

- Place dark colours in section marked D.
- Replace lid.

You will find that the children can be very inventive here but remember the main object of the work is to help to sort out their naturally rambling written style into precise, step by step instructions. Do not allow the object to become obscured in the devising of the inventions themselves. This sort of work is of course very good practice for later précis work.

Collect directions from the packets of 'easy made' foods — jellies, instant pudding, potato, rice, cake mixes etc. If you can actually make some of these things in the classroom the pitfalls of carelessly read instructions can be well illustrated when a jelly fails to set or a cake rise etc. The directions from these packets can be mimed — each onlooker has a copy of the directions — checks to see that each one is carried out properly by the child doing the mime. There are many possible variations of this — each onlooker is given two similar sets of directions — object is to guess which card is being mimed — the child doing the mime deliberately misses out one of the directions — others spot the missing stage at the right time and interrupt the mime.

Children given simple written assignments — Write out directions to someone from another planet (who understands our language) for the

- preparation of a bowl of breakfast cereal
- making of buttered toast
- sharpening of a pencil, etc.

Assignment cards for simple making and modelling projects can be useful here. The projects must be short and simple e.g.

HOW TO MAKE A SHIELD

- Cut an oval shape from thin card (approx. 400cm by 250cm).
- Draw a pattern on the front.

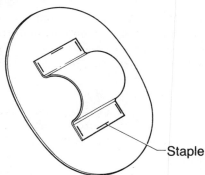

Staple

- Cut a strip of card measuring 20cm by 10cm.
- Stick or staple this strip to the back of your shield so that it fits over your arm.
- Write your name on your shield.

Information which tells you something
Collect local bus/train timetables. Simplify these if necessary. Make timetable cards to use in question and answer games — group of children each with a copy of a timetable — the teacher or a child asks:
'When is the first bus into town after midday?'
'At what time will the 8 o'clock train reach Hull/Crewe/Dover/Cardiff?' etc. Questions eventually written on cards for future written work. Same sort of activities can be applied to T.V. and radio guides. In the oral games introduce an element of speed to add an extra dimension e.g.
'At what time did *Jackanory* start last Thursday?'
'On which day can you see *Pinnochio*?'
'Which programme follows *The Archers* on Friday afternoon?' . . . etc.
The children start with the guide closed in front of them — as soon as the question has been asked they open the guide to find the required information. Again the questions are eventually written on cards for written work later. Collect pamphlets and leaflets of various kinds (dental care, health education, school notices etc.), to be used in oral and written comprehension.
Before we leave reading for information let us quickly mention filling out forms. It falls roughly under the general umbrella of this section, though of course it involves writing as well as reading. Simple forms can be made to be filled in by the children — these can range from name, age and picture of themselves to a more detailed profile including headings like date of birth, country of origin, schools attended etc. Forms can be devised to cover many aspects of the child's experience–applications to go to school camp, to join a cycle club, to join the recorder class, etc. They will have questions such as —

- Have you ever camped before? . . . . . . yes/no/don't know.
- Do you own a sleeping bag? . . . . . . yes/no/
- Have you ever mended or helped to mend a puncture?
- For how long have you owned a bicycle?
- At what age did you learn to ride a bicycle? . . . . . .
- Do you play a muscial instrument other than the recorder? . . . . . .

• Do you own a recorder . . . . . .

These applications can be purely imaginary. The purpose of them is to give the children the experience of form filling in a variety of ways. Vary the form of answer from the yes/no to the writing of a simple sentence to the ringing of the appropriate answer.

It should not be outside the scope of the infant room to give the children some practice in reading for information. Certainly infants can and should learn to recognise and understand words like DANGER KEEP OUT etc. Also they should learn to recognise instructional words like DRAW, COLOUR, WRITE. Even the following of a recipe can be of great value with pre-reading children — recipe is written out in large letters on blackboard —

ONE PINT OF WATER
ONE PACKET OF JELLY

a) Put jelly into bowl.
b) Add boiling water.
c) Mix well.
d) Leave to cool.

— The teacher points to words as everyone reads them together. Much is made of each stage in the recipe e.g. MIX WELL — can you mix well? Lets all mix well (exaggerated arm movements going round and round). When jelly has been made each stage in the recipe is read again, then children are asked to repeat the stages in the correct order — 'Who can tell me what we did first?' Good, and what came next?' etc. At the end of the jelly making session several of the children — even the non-readers — will be able to 'read' the recipe from the blackboard as you point to the words. They will not necessarily retain the recognition of the words — but no matter. The point is not so much to teach the words themselves as to accustom the children to the process of making sense of symbols. Work of this kind is not only a good foundation for later work on reading for information, but it is also a valuable part of the children's general reading programme.

In reading for information we are trying to help the children to extract as quickly as possible the essential points from a written message. Bear this aim in mind when you start to devise exercises of your own for the children. Then you will be likely to give the right sort of practice to help them to develop the skill of reading for information.

c)   Reading for Pleasure

Even before the children have mastered the mechanics of reading you will encourage them to read for pleasure — by reading to them yourself, by providing a wide variety of books which they can 'read' without having to know the words: books like picture books, nursery rhyme books, books to feel, even books to smell (these have a picture page of an orange/banana/strawberry/cup of coffee, which when gently scratched release the appropriate scent), books to investigate physically with ribbons to tie, tabs to pull, flaps to lift etc. — all have a part to play. Anything which will encourage the children to want to read is to be sought after.

Once the children have taken the first steps along the path of reading they sometimes need an extra boost to keep them going. A useful enticement can be to allow them to take their books home, (when they can read 10 words/pages/half the book/the whole book or whatever suits). Much can be made of this big event — 'well done Carol, you have tried hard. Now you can read to page 15 I think you can take your book *HOME*, and read it to mummy and daddy.' It will not always be a good idea, but DO allow those who want to take their books home to do so. Insist on a protective covering being provided and make it quite clear to the parents that the books must be well cared for. There will of course be the odd accident, especially in those homes with babies and toddlers. In some cases you will be able to ask the parents to pay for the damage or loss, in others you will not. In any event the total loss throughout the year should never amount to anything serious. Certainly never serious enough to excuse a school policy which forbids the taking of reading books home by all children at all times. You may think that such a policy would never exist. I myself would hardly have believed it possible until my eldest son went to school. The school had recently purchased a brand new reading scheme. One of the good points of this scheme was the beautiful illustrations in the early books. My son told us about one of the characters in his reader and I asked if he could bring the book home so that we could all have a look. I was told that this wasn't allowed. Later I brought the matter up at a meeting of the P.T.A. It became clear that the fear of the books becoming dirty, torn and lost lay behind the decision to forbid reading books home. It seemed that the fact that children's general reading development was not being encouraged on *EVERY POSSIBLE* level was less important than keeping the books clean and new.

I tried to point out that the advantages to some children of being allowed to take a book home were considerable. It was then suggested that any child who wanted to take his reading book home could take a book at an equivalent level from the old reading scheme. This scheme had been in use for over twenty years and was filthy, battered and torn. It ought to have been replaced years ago and was certainly fit for the dustbin now. To suggest it as a viable alternative for a child's brand new reading book was a downright insult to the children. Reading is so important it must be encouraged on *every* front. Problems of dirty/torn/lost books are relatively easy (given the will) to overcome. Problems of the non-reader are not.

If possible create an area in the classroom or just outside where the children can go to select and browse through a book when they have a spare moment. This area ought to be attractive and comfortable to sit in. Insist that it is a quiet area, but allow two or three to enjoy a book together so long as they do not become too noisy. Those of you in open plan schools will have the reading areas already set up. In these cases co-operation between members of staff is necessary in order to ensure that the best use is made of these areas.

Once the children have mastered the mechanics of reading you will have to sustain their interest and encourage them to go on reading for pleasure. Provide a *wide* range of reading material in both level and interest. Read passages from various books in the class selection to tempt the children. It is surprising how a book can be ignored for months and then suddenly become very popular after a reading of one or two pages by you. The pages can be chosen at random and you can read on until you reach a suitably suspense-laden page, at which point you shut the book saying it can be found in the library/book corner for those who would like to know what happened next.

Set yourself to read at least 3 children's books a term. Keep a personal review of each book you read — this need only take minutes on finishing the book. If you wait 6 months you will probably have forgotten most of it. Compare your own reviews with those you read in the press and journals. Soon you will learn how to interpret press reviews in order to ascertain whether or not the book appeals to you — despite what the reviewer actually says. Keep a list of books which you would like to read aloud to the children and read to them at *least* once a week. Encourage the children to suggest books which **they** would like to hear you read aloud.

Also — encourage the children to write reviews of books they have read to include in a communal class review. This can be simply a loose leaf folder with the pages indexed in alphabetical order. It is interesting to see what different children say about the same book, and the review can be a help to those children who find difficulty in choosing a suitable book for themselves. Do not make the writing of a review a compulsory task. For some children this would ruin the experience of reading the book. Sometimes it is enough to read the book, enjoy the experience and leave it at that.

Introduce/encourage the children to whatever library services are available. Children's librarians are usually extremely helpful. They welcome parties of children to visit the library and will often, if invited, come to give a talk to the children in school. Some libraries run book review talks which are useful for whetting the children's appetite.

There may be a paperback book club or shop operating in your school. If not you could find out about the possibility of starting one. Literature is usually sent to the Head by the publisher or bookshop. Ask the head if you may have a look at the literature. Alternatively write to your nearest bookshop or the publisher direct and explain that you would like to start a book club in your school.

Do all you can to make reading an enjoyable activity. Make sure the reading books are stored tidily and displayed attractively. Appoint children to give the bookshelves a daily check so as to keep the books in reasonable order. Probably the simplest method of storing fiction in a Primary classroom is by alphabetical order of the author's surname.

Never force a child to finish a book but insist on his reading a minimum number of pages (not less than 20 not more than 50), before the book is rejected.

Have at least one weekly slot on the timetable for silent reading together. Insist on a minimum of noise during this period, and try to create an atmosphere of serenity, (i.e. *don't* use the time to re-vamp a wall display).

Comics have a part to play in encouraging children to read for pleasure. Have a wide selection in the classroom and make sure they are stored in some sort of order and are kept reasonably clean. Appoint children to check them regularly, and throw out any comics which have become too torn or dirty. Old comics can be used to make work cards of various kinds — this can be a useful activity for the children to do themselves. Cut out the appropriate pieces from the old comic — puzzle pages, joke strips, etc., arrange them in place on the card before sticking them onto the card, then add any necessary questions or instructions.

Not all children come to discover the pleasure of reading by the same route. Provide as wide a variety of reading material as you can so that you help as many of them as possible to discover the delights of reading for pleasure. To help children learn to read, to want to read and to continue to enjoy reading is a very important part of your job. Give it the attention it deserves.

2. Writing

a) Handwriting

With infants, a daily handwriting practice is ideal — much of what they do at this stage will be incidental handwriting practice, painting, drawing, colouring and so on. Besides this incidental practice there ought to be provision made for specific practice which is directed towards helping the child to form letters correctly. It is easier and quicker to write an 'n' as a downward stoke with an arch attached   than the many amazing variations which the children will invent for themselves. Handwriting, like tying shoelaces, will gain very little from the discovery method of learning. It is best handled in a formal way — you show the children how to form the letters, and they copy.

It is important that the school has a consistent handwriting policy. Time is wasted and anxiety created where a child is told to do one thing in one class and a different thing in another. Find out as sensitively as you can what scheme of handwriting exists in the school. If none exists perhaps you could suggest (equally sensitively) that some scheme should be adopted. The actual scheme itself is relatively unimportant so long as you have some guidelines about how to teach children to write which are compatible with what the children will be taught in the rest of the school. If the children are taught nothing they can pick up cumbersome handwriting techniques which will hinder their development.

Reception children ought not to be rushed into writing letters. Great fun and excellent handwriting practice can be had from a 'drawing game'.

The children are seated comfortably so as to have a good view of the board — much is made of starting at THIS side and going all the way along to THIS side (pointing from left to right with exaggerated arm movements) now we are going to draw a whole line of straight soldiers — |||||||||||||| next a whole line of lovely fat sausages 0000000000 now some tall men and small men ||;ı||ıı||ıı|| . .. . . etc. All the while the children are writing you go round and correct pencil holding and position of paper etc., giving encouragement and praise. Later these patterns can be put on cards for the children to copy by themselves. Use thick felt pens and bright colours to make the activity more attractive. Learning to form letters is an extremely difficult thing for small children. Do not become so concerned with actual letter formation that you fail to appreciate real effort, even when the end result is a mess. The main point of this work is to help the children towards the mastery of an easy flowing handwriting style. Gentle persistence and daily practice will be more effective than ranting and raving when a child starts at the wrong side of a page or forms a letter wrongly. In time, letters linked to the above patterns are introduced. The letters are not introduced alphabetically but in stroke related groups i.e. all the letters which need more or less the same movement are taught together so that the child consolidates the practice of that movement and fluency is encouraged. A possible grouping could be

coadgqe

rnmbhpk

iltj

uy

wxzv

fs

The groupings vary slightly according to the particular style to be adopted. The actual grouping is relatively unimportant. The important thing is that the letters *are* grouped in accordance with a sensible writing policy. This way the children gain the maximum benefit from the writing lesson. To introduce letters alphabetically for handwriting purposes is a waste of time e.g. the child is introduced to the shape a and practises a line of the letter. Just as the shape and rhythm of the stroke become familiar the child has to learn a new shape that of the letter b . By the end of a line of these the experience of the first shape has practically been wiped out. So, until the children are confident about forming all their letters, keep the practice sessions in stroke related groups.

Once the children have learned to write they still need a regular practice session, to encourage good handwriting habits. As with infants, this can only be done as a formal lesson. You remind them how to form the letters and they copy. The exercises to practise specific letters will be followed by a piece of prose or poetry especially chosen to include the letters to be practised. The children will enjoy inventing suitable rhymes themselves. Praise must be given for effort here NOT end result. For some children the creation of a beautiful page of handwriting is effortless, for others the creation of a barely legible page is enormously difficult. Only you can be the judge here of praiseworthy effort. Make it clear to the children that it is effort which is being praised. On other occasions of course you will want to show and praise the best end results so as to show the children the kind of standard at which to aim. This sort of praise is fine so long as it is not given to the exclusion of praise for effort etc.

Now and then it is a good idea to let the children be their own judges. Here is an activity which helps the child to focus attention on handwriting and to encourage a critical approach to it. When you have ten minutes or so in hand, ask everyone to collect a piece of scrap paper (which should always be freely available) and write down a sentence about anything they like. At first some of them may not be able to think of anything, so say that if anyone is absolutely stuck they can copy something from the walls. In time they will be able to make up a sentence quite easily. When everyone has finished ask them to look at their words and then circle the one which shows the best handwriting. Now they write the words again trying to improve the general handwriting standard of the first sentence. Ask the children to write their names on the papers before you collect them in. Clip them together in a paper clip so that you can quickly flick through the sentences when you have time. Read a few good examples back to the children (on the same day if you can manage) and point out the details which impressed you (the even spacing of words, a particular letter, the balance of the capitals with the small letters etc.). Do not make too much of the content of the sentences otherwise children who do not have a flair for this will be put off trying altogether. Concentrate on the handwriting and eventually the children will do the same. It is a good quick easy way to top up the proper handwriting practice which you may not always have time for.

Some of your children will want to (especially if there is an enthusiastic member of staff) develop their handwriting skills as a creative outlet for their self-expression. This is excellent and of course ought to be encouraged. It should not be forced on all the children. Nor should there be undue stress placed on 'a beautiful hand'. A pleasant easy to read handwriting style is perfectly adequate. There is a difference between formal lettering and functional handwriting. Speed is not an element of the former. It is an essential part of the latter and the children will need it increasingly as they progress through Primary school and on to Secondary.

Allow individual variations in style as long as these do not spoil the clarity and legibility of the handwriting. A lasting memory I have of handwriting in my Primary school is of a lesson in which we had to copy a line of the capital H. The teacher Miss K. walked round to inspect the books. She asked six of us to bring our books out to the front of the class. I was particularly proud of my efforts that day and felt sure we were about to receive some high praise. When I saw Miss K. take her belt from her drawer I felt less sure. We were asked to look at our books and then look at the board and say why we had been asked to come to the front. Eventually one of the six came up with the reason — we had all copied the letters as ᚻ (a relic from a previous teacher) instead of H . We were all given a stroke of the belt and sent back ignominiously to our seats. At the time I felt it to be a most unjust punishment. In retrospect it seems to have been pointless as well. The least of its effects would seem to be to improve the handwriting of any of the six offenders. The tale also reminds us of the importance of having a consistent handwriting policy throughout the school.

Provide handwriting practice cards for use in spare moments or for those children who would benefit from extra practice. You could increase the appeal of this activity by allowing the children to use thin fibre-tipped pens. Provide a variety of colours and allow the children to use them for only this purpose so that the pens remain in good condition. It is surprising how much practice the children will get through when they feel that there is an element of a 'treat' about the work. Do not allow these cards to take the place of a weekly lesson. There can be no substitute for that. Also the cards should be written in the school's agreed style. There is widespread belief (borne out in practice), that a child can practise and improve handwriting by copying ANYTHING, even printed pages from books. This is absolutely not true. A child who has never been taught the correct formation of letters cannot 'divine' this formation from a page of print. Copying from print therefore, in the absence of proper handwriting lessons, can hinder rather than help progress. When handwriting practice is sought the children should copy the actual style. Anything else will not be as efficient. Finally, don't nag on about handwriting *all* the time or you will undermine the effectiveness of what you say and do during the handwriting lesson. For example, curb the urge to make comments like 'good but the handwriting could be better.' They are a waste of time, and the last thing they do is to improve the handwriting one jot. So, first make sure that your children know how to form each letter of the alphabet by an efficient economical method and one which is in keeping with the policy of the school, (better still if this policy fits in with the local secondary schools). Then see that they have regular pleasurable practice sessions so that you help them towards a clear fluent handwriting style which will be an asset to them throughout their lives.

b)   Written Language

Terminology is a problem here. For, of course, handwriting is written language, creative writing is too. The specific meaning of the title here is functional rather than creative writing, (which we come to in the next section). Obviously it is artificial to divide things like this, and there are overlaps at every turn, and one is, in a sense part of the other. Nevertheless there is a broad difference, and to begin with we will look at the functional side. The first question to consider is — 'Why do we practise written language in the Primary school?' Mainly so that the children will be able to communicate with their fellows. Communicate their needs, wants, responses, reactions, thoughts and feelings. An important (and often overlooked) point to remember is that for most of your children this will *not* be a major feature of their adult lives. Generally speaking the amount of written practice in school is out of step with the needs of a child's adult life.

Another important point to remember is that spoken communication comes before written. It is more important in the Primary school to give the child sufficient practice in communicating orally before you ask for written work. Before a child can communicate orally of course he or she has to have something to say. So often in written work the problem is that *the child can think of nothing to say*.

Your first job then is to stimulate and feed the children with a wide variety of impressions and experiences.

For example:

a)   visit the fire station, take a bus trip into town, make cakes, plant bulbs, go to the theatre, etc., and talk to them about what you do. Listen too to what they have to say, exchange words, ideas, opinions, feelings so that they feel what they have to say matters to you. A rich and varied diet of experience will help your children's writing as much as anything.

b)   take the children outside the classroom, talk with them and listen to them about what you see, the colour of the sky, the shape of the clouds, the bare or budding branches, the shape of the school buildings, the telegraph pole, the post box, the pattern of bricks, roof tiles, paving stones and so on. Again exchange and encourage comments and ideas, passing on information and enlarging knowledge when you can.

Although the point of the above is to indirectly improve written work, do not follow up every single outing, walk, conversation with a written account of it. How would you like it if every time you saw a film, heard a concert, received a gift etc., you had to 'write about it'? You wouldn't. Nor do the children, and if they don't like it they don't learn much. Trust them occasionally to take in what they enjoy so that they gradually build up an inner store of experience from which to draw when they need it.

More specific preparation for written work will vary, but the more you can help the children at this stage the better. Let's imagine you want the children to practise descriptive writing. A good preparation would be to produce a box of unseen objects, blindfold a few children in turn as they choose an object from the box to hold up to the rest of you, and describe in detail before they guess what the object is. Vary the objects: apple, fir cone, silk handkerchief, leather glove, lavender bag, sea shell, piece of chocolate, whistle etc., so that the child can utilise all his or her senses to explore and describe the object. Let someone choose an object for you to describe — the children love to see you perform and besides it is good practice for you to see the exercise from their point of view. This is an example of giving the children reasonable preparation for written work. An example of little or no preparation would be to simply tell the children to choose an object and use as many adjectives as possible to describe it. The more you can give the children at this stage, the more you will get back. What does it matter if they give you all your own words back? At least they will be using (I hope) suitable words in a proper context. As soon and whenever they can the children will be creative and original but you cannot force them into this. In the meantime give them as much help as they need. Expect effort of course, and show them your genuine disappointment when you don't get it. Still, you will be more likely to have effort from them when they feel that it isn't all one way, when they do all the trying and you do all the judging.

Often too they are trying in the dark, so try always to ensure that they know what they are about before they start. They don't always ask if they are unsure.

I once had a 'slow learner', John, who was drawing a picture of a ship on the blackboard and labelling as best he could. During the labelling he came to me to ask how to spell 'sea to sail on'. As I was some distance from the blackboard and working closely with some slow readers I asked an able child nearby to write out the phrase for John to copy on the blackboard. Some time later I glanced at the blackboard and saw boldly written under the ship 'sea to Ceylon.' A minor misunderstanding which fortunately for John I was able to put right. Major misunderstandings, however, abound. The onus is on us and not the children to prevent these.

Perhaps a surprising hindrance to fluency in writing is the use of reference books. When fluency is the main aim, go easy on the reference books at least until the children are confident about handling them. If you make them look up every single spelling or reference point you will not only hinder fluency but you could put them off altogether. So when a child wants a spelling or some background information, simply give it rather than directing her or him to the reference books. If you cannot give the required information then help to look it up. It will be quicker and you can teach some incidental reference skills as you go along. Eventually the children should be helped towards the comfortable and confident use of reference material, but too much too soon hinders the writing and does nothing to develop the skills of using reference material either. Specific lessons should be carefully planned to develop these. The children should be directed to a named reference book then asked specific questions relating to chapter *x* page *y* etc., so that they are encouraged into the world of reference material. The ubiquitous and clumsy 'Look up and find out all you can about . . .' is so vague and unhelpful that it is no wonder many children are put off before they even start.

Finally when you have succeeded in encouraging the children to *want* to write, don't undo all your hard work by covering their work with your corrections. Take note of the mistakes of course and use them as the basis of practice exercises. Point the mistakes out to the children *after* you have praised what is praiseworthy. Explain that you will give some practice exercises to help to strengthen these weak spots. Naturally if there is nothing praiseworthy then you cannot praise, and of course if a child presents sloppy careless work he or she should know that you think it *is* sloppy and careless (you will only know what is and isn't sloppy by 'knowing' each child). Nothing will be gained by pretence. Nevertheless you will probably help the children more by being interested, supportive and encouraging than by being unnecessarily censorious.

With infants you will at the beginning have to do the actual writing yourself. At this stage the children will be very eager to communicate information about themselves and their families. Encourage this flow of information, selecting when necessary a suitable piece to be written in their book. Gradually they will learn to copy what you have written and then go on to compose their own simple sentences. Naturally some children will be able to discard your help before others. Only by knowing your children will you be able to judge which of them need to continue to copy the whole sentence, which of them need to copy part of the sentence and which of them can be encouraged to compose their own sentence. Never force a child into composition before he is ready. He will learn nothing and his confidence in his ability to write could take a severe knock. Much more will be gained by allowing him to remain at the copying stage for a few extra weeks/months.

There are, of course those children who need to be pushed rather than coaxed over hurdles. For such children, firm insistence on their ability will probably do their confidence as much good as anything — 'come along Simon I know you can write this story yourself, let's do it together on the blackboard first.' When the sentence has been written more or less by the child himself, say how you *knew* he could do it and how well he has done etc., — 'now you can copy it into your book.' On such occasions the child is usually so amazed by his achievement that he is motivated to 'write his own stories' again and again.

Having made every effort to encourage the children to *want* to write, take note of what they say in their writing. Read out the interesting pieces or let the children read them out themselves. Draw attention to the good points, 'Jill has written such an interesting description of her cat that I thought we all ought to hear it.' Jill reads the piece. 'Did you notice how she told us three things about her cat's coat? That it was black soft and shiny' etc. If the children feel that you can be relied upon to give their writing your full attention and appreciation then they will be more inclined to apply themselves to the content of what they write.

When you have reduced the problem for the children of 'not being able to think of anything to write', there comes the task of passing on the accepted conventions of formal writing so that communication can be effective. However good fluent and original a piece of writing may be, it will lose most of its value if it is not readily understood. This brings us to the next consideration . . .

c)   The Arduousness of Writing Correct Language

When you come to teach grammar give some thought to why you are doing what you are doing. The main aim of teaching grammar in the primary school is to help the children to understand something about the structure and rules of our written language SO AS TO IMPROVE THEIR WRITTEN WORK. It often happens that too heavy an emphasis on grammar has completely the opposite effect. As a young teacher I often heard a colleague lamenting 'we did hours of sentence analysis last week and now their writing is worse than EVER' — as if it were the children's fault. The possibility that the work had seemed perhaps pointless to the children, and had muddled rather than helped them did not seem to arise. These days of course the children are looked at in a kinder light and the suitability of the work in a more critical one. Nevertheless in the cry for back to basics you must be on your guard to ask what basics and why, (that is, what are they going to do and how do we know they will do it?).

Part of the problem is that many grammatical exercises are so divorced from what the children say and write. They become exercises for their own sake and not for the sake of the children's writing. As a child I did my fair share of 'filling in sentences' with such phrases as 'a gaggle of geese' or 'a pride of lions'. I don't think I have ever once used such a phrase since leaving Primary school, though I've seen plenty of geese and lions since then. Large chunks of the grammar to be found in textbooks do nothing to improve the children's writing. This is demonstrable. And yet far too many of the wrong kind of exercises are still dished out in our schools. Unless, and this is crucial, the exercises are linked to the children's own writing and experience, they are a waste of time.

Timing is an important factor in the effective teaching of grammar. Introduce something too early or too late and you will waste valuable time and energy. Find the optimum moment and your job will be made that much easier. Finding the optimum moment will not be as difficult as it may sound. Firstly it can usually span several weeks or even months. Secondly there are recognisable signs that the children are ready for this or that aspect of grammar, (they ask about a certain aspect, or their writing suddenly becomes full of apostrophes or bereft of full stops or whatever). At first you will have to work on a trial and error basis and of course you will make some mistakes but eventually you will be able to 'feel' when it is the right time to introduce this or that aspect, and to be able to judge from the children's writing as to who is ready for what.

A friend of mine once commented to me that she always had trouble with quotation marks. 'The children are fine until I start to 'do' quotation marks, then everything goes haywire — they put quotation marks round proper names, at the beginning of sentences, round whole sentences, in fact anywhere and everywhere but where they ought to be.'

It sounds as if the work was introduced before the children were ready for it. Grammar should be the servant of language not its master. Look at the children's writing for what is needed. Then having given the children a suitable exercise for a specific purpose put it to work as soon as possible. Refer to it in the daily work of the classroom, incorporate it into imaginative writing, functional writing, and oral work. Look for examples in stories, poems, reading books, prose passages etc. Gradually and naturally the children should get the message. Use your knowledge of the children and their writing to:

a) get the timing right i.e. to introduce a grammatical point when it is needed and not before;

b) keep the exercises within the children's comprehension and experience;

c) provide as much oral practice as written practice, and you will help them towards clear thinking which is a sure basis for good writing. Grammar then, will not be a stumbling block for the children but a tool to refine and improve their written style.

d) Spelling

It became unfashionable for a time to 'teach' spelling in the formal sense. Unfortunately this meant that for many children spelling was almost ignored — they picked up what they could and muddled along somehow. Now it has been realised that spelling is very necessary on a Primary school curriculum. It is fraught with difficulties since there are so many existing myths about spelling, and a real lack of understanding about how children learn to spell. The process starts of course before children come to school. It is continued in the Infant room with all the exercises which are designed to aid and develop visual perception. At this stage the children are learning to sort and order all sorts of objects into sets of shape and size and colour. When the time comes to teach letter formation it is a good idea to leave the letter names till later. The children will find it much easier to talk about and draw, a tunnel for **n** or a snake for **s** (or whatever) and it focuses attention on the actual shape of the letter. Part of the spelling process is to do with mental recall of a series of shapes. Gradually the single letter names are learnt, then blending of two letters is introduced so that eventually the children can not only recognise *cat* as a whole shape in the 'look and say' method but can sound it out as *c-a-t* as well. Many teachers favour the building of groups of words with the same sound — *oo-* look, book, took/*ee-* feet, keep, meet/*ing-* ring, sing, king . . . and so on. It is useful at this stage to show the children that one word can belong to several categories. The use of sets helps here — use big plastic hoops on the floor or draw big circles on the blackboard — scatter a variety of more or less 'known' words on the floor — make sets of words starting with *t*, rhyming with *gate*, ending in *ing* etc. — a child offers a word as being suitable for a par-ticular category, if right, he then finds the word on the floor and puts it in the appropriate hoop, or you write it in the appropriate circle on the blackboard. The handling of wooden or plastic letters helps those children who find it difficult to distinguish one letter from another and many of the games/apparatus to be found in the Infant room are incidental aids to spelling though they may be used for other reasons.

Older children are very often denied this kind of practice in visual perception, though quite clearly many of them still need it. Often it is assumed that the more they read the better they will spell. This is not necessarily true. The skill of reading is a very different one from that of spelling. Good spellers are usually good readers but very often a good reader is a poor speller. You cannot therefore rely on reading as a significant aid to spelling. Devise games which encourage the children to look closely at the structure of words. Even older children can benefit by describing letters according to the visual forms they suggest and not just by letter names. By doing this the child really has to think about the form and order of the letters e.g. 'Spell the word *nest* by describing the letter shapes in their proper order' — a tunnel (n), an egg (e), a snake (s) and then a signal (t). Together with the children, make up your own descriptions of the letter shapes, 'e' could be a loop, 't' could be a hook, etc. This may sound painstaking but it does encourage close scrutiny which is an important element in spelling.

A useful, though not widely used, aid to spelling is the typewriter. The removal of the effort of handwriting seems to allow the child to concentrate more on the spelling. Also, thought is needed about each single letter to be depressed. There is too the added thrill of 'having a go' on the typewriter (which will only apply as long as you keep the machine in good working order). Limit its use to specific times or for specific purposes, otherwise it will soon be disregarded or even damaged and broken.

Make up communal spelling lists from the children's writing (to include those words which cause most frequent trouble to your class). These can be displayed *THEN CONSTANTLY REFERRED TO* (otherwise they will be ignored as part of the wallpaper). Encourage the children to compile individual spelling dictionaries — when a child asks for and is given the spelling of a new word, he writes it down in his own spelling dictionary. Gradually he will build up a list of words to which he will constantly refer. The words will then become so familiar that they can be written *automatically*. This is an important aspect of good spelling. A communal class dictionary offers the children a wider selection of words to refer to before coming to you for the spelling of a new word. This can be a strip of cardboard on the wall or a large loose leaf folder if you are short of wall space. As with the displayed spelling lists, make sure you refer to the dictionary from time to time. A regular weekly spelling session (apart from all the incidental spelling which goes on during the week), will help to concentrate the children's minds. Vary the form of this so that it does not become stale. It could be a — straightforward spelling test, a guessing game (write down the name of a musical instrument which rhymes with middle), list building — write a list of all the words you can think of which start with *c* and end in *e* (you would do this with those children who needed your help), spelling of simple commands — children can do this to each other — s-i-t d-o-w-n, s-c-r-a-t-c-h y-o-u-r h-e-a-d etc. If you decide to employ rote learning of lists of words, then select words which the children will be able to use in their everyday writing and give them plenty of opportunity to write. Writing has much more of a direct effect on spelling than reading does.

The complexities of the spelling process are not thoroughly understood and certainly not widely recognised. There is no ONE way to teach it — and you'll probably do a better job if you use a variety of methods.

e)   Creative Language

This area of language work can be —

- one of freedom and experiment
- one which can greatly enhance a child's appreciation of language
- one in which success/failure are not necessarily linked to academic ability
- one which can bring almost immediate satisfaction to the child.

In order to achieve these ends you must understand what creative writing is about. It is not a matter of taking away all the rules and throwing words onto a page in any old order. The words have a function to fulfill. They will: convey feeling, mood, atmosphere, make sounds, paint pictures and so on. There are standards to be sought, not those of precision and correct spelling but those concerned with self expression, word flow, the choice of words for a particular purpose etc. In creative writing the children will wallow in words, enjoy the sounds the words make when put together in a certain way, paint pictures with words, etc.

Of course not all of us can be creative with words. For those children who find this work difficult do not turn it into a chore for them. Good creative writing is as hard to achieve as 'good' anything else. The idea that it is effortless or that it comes naturally to children is nonsense. Nevertheless it is unquestionably a valid part of language. And, as a source of enrichment and enjoyment your children deserve access to it.

Some Ideas: Word Shapes

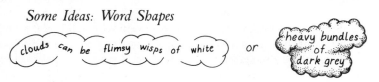

Children choose an object about which to make a wordshape. Provide a list of ideas (but encourage them to make up their own ideas when they can) — a rocket, ship, raindrop, cloud, candy-floss, mud, wellington boot, kitten, bottle of milk, mirror etc. the outline shape of the object is drawn simply as an outline or use the letters themselves

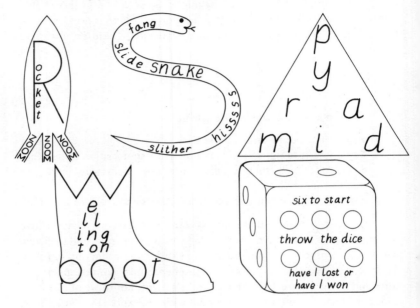

the shape is then filled with words which can be connected in any way with the original idea. Do some collectively to begin with to give the children the idea — those children who need to could use one of the collective efforts as a basis for their own.

Mood Words

A compilation of words of a certain mood — fear, terror, cold sweat, beating heart, horror, monster, vile, ghastly, ghost, black, death, slime, dark cloud, sickness, clammy hands.

Smile, sunshine, bubbles, singing, sweetness, bright, gay, joyful, glowing, twinkling eyes, golden, happiness, buttercups, shining — children use the list as background material for a poem or description. e.g. *Twinkling Eyes*

She was a girl with twinkling eyes
With laughing lips and a sunshine smile
Her voice was bright, her hair was glowing
Where she went there was no knowing.

The compilation of these lists is a useful way to show how the same words can create a different impression when set in a different context e.g. the words 'beating heart' could be included in both of the above lists.

Haiku

The children usually respond very well to this form of Japanese poetry which uses the very minimum of words to convey a picture, story or message, e.g.

Wind lifts suddenly —
Balloon lurches from small hand,
Clutching nothing now.

Evening sun — old man
Pushing barrow to a fire —
Smell of burning leaves

Spring is in the air
Buds on the plum tree to day
To morrow blossoms

There are reasonably strict rules which govern Haiku e.g. the syllables or points of stress in the three lines should follow the pattern 5/7/5.
If Haiku proper imposes too much restriction for your children, there are many poems which are not strictly Haiku but which employ the miniature form and economy of words. For example:

Chalk box	Hidden well
Cupboard rocks	Ned fell
Chalk falls	Loud yell
White walls	From well

This as an activity where, very often two minds are better than one. The children can experiment in pairs keeping a record of lines they liked even if they couldn't make a complete poem. Place all the unfinished lines in a box and shuffle them around. The children can select new slips of paper and try to complete a poem which has been started by someone else.

Children's Names

Children use the letters of their first name to describe themselves:

```
                      s        s   s
   h              s    l t      m   h
 S A R A H      P E T E R    K A T Y         I n t e r e s t i n g
 e p i c e      o a a f o    e l a             M a l e
 n p g t l      r s l t n    e l n           s t R o n g
 s y h i p      t y l   g    n   n             t A l l
 i   t v f      y     h          e             N o i s y
 b   e e u      g     a          d
 l   h   l      o     n
 e   a          i     d
     n          n     e
     d          g     d
     e
     d
```

Riddles

These are single verses which describe something in an imaginative way but do not name it.

> e.g.
> I am white
> And I fall from a hedge
> I cover the ground
> And don't make a sound.   (Snow)

> You cannot see me
> Only the mischief I do
> Leaves from trees, hats from heads
> Lids from dustbins, roofs from sheds.   (Wind)

> I am round and not round
> Soft and hard
> I could become a chicken
> Or some other kind of bird.   (Egg)

Words to make sounds

There may or may not be a meaning to these. It is the sound that is the prime factor:

'Twas brillig, and the slithy toves
Did gyre and gimble in the wabe
All mimsy were the borogoves,
And the mome raths outgrabe.

'Beware the Jabberwock, my son!
The jaws that bite, the claws that catch
Beware the Jubjub bird, and shun
The frumious Bandersnatch

Lewis Carroll.

The Computer's First Christmas Card

jollymerry	Mollymerry
hollyberry	Jerryjolly
jollyberry	bellyboppy
merryholly	jorryhoppy
happyjolly	hollymoppy
jollyjelly	Barrymerry
jellybelly	Jarrryhappy
bellymerry	happyboppy
hollyheppy	boppyjolly
jollyMolly	jollymerry
marryJerry	merrymerry
merryHarry	merrymerry
hoppyBarry	merryChris
heppyJarry	asmerryasa
boppyheppy	Chrismerry
berryjorry	asMERRYCHR
jorryjelly	YSANTHEMUM
moppyjelly	*Edwin Morgan.*

These are two examples — look for more to read to the children. In poems like the two above it is the sheer sound of the words takes precedence over their meaning. In others the sound of the 'meaningless' words will ADD to the meaning —

> e.g.
> It goes fwunkety,
>   then shlunkety
> as the washing goes around.
>
> The water splunchesses
>   and it slunchesses
> as the water goes around.
>
> (from The Washing Machine by *J Davies*)

Make lists of words which can conjure up a sound — bang, crash boom, warble, knock, clap, stamp, clippety clop, hammer, thump, roar, shout, hiss, whisper, hum, splish splash, whistle, screech, whine . . . etc. These can be used in the same way as the 'mood words' to aid the children's compositions.

Ask the children to close their eyes and think of a word whose sound they particularly like (not necessarily 'sound words') — that is, a word which they actually enjoy saying aloud. The children usually respond to this quite well and the lists are usually varied and interesting — liquorice, mechanical, plunder, chrysanthemum, rubbish, plop, tesselate . . . are some of the words which I have seen crop up on such lists. Apart from the enjoyment which can be derived from simply reading these lists the children will also enjoy selecting some of the words to make 'verses':

> liquorice and lollipop
> mechanical and plop
> shilly shally shilly shally
> tesselate the lot.

Work like this, while being enjoyed for its own sake also has a valuable contribution to make to the study of more formal poetry and prose. It can help the children to pay closer attention to what the words say, how they sound and what they mean.

Treat it seriously and give it its proper place alongside the other areas of language work, and creative writing will be a valuable addition to your curriculum. If you overestimate its importance or misunderstand the contribution it can make, you could do more harm than good. So, be clear about your aims, and tailor the work accordingly.

In a sense, it is unnatural to divide language into separate areas. Each of the three areas outlined here is present in the others, and all three can be present in one.

To be most effective, you must be quite clear about the essential elements of each area. More important, the children should be clear. Whereas careful copying and excellence of presentation rank high in handwriting work, they rank lower in creative work (unless for display).

A worthwhile exercise to illustrate that the three areas are part of a whole is as follows. Allow a child a free rein on a piece of creative writing. Make another lesson to correct the spelling and grammar. Let the child spend a final session on copying out the piece in his or her best handwriting.

It would not be desirable to do this too often otherwise the value of the work of each individual area would be lost. Mostly you will concentrate on each area for its own sake. The children will have many opportunities to observe that language is a rich and complex fabric made up from many strands. These opportunities crop up *naturally* without you having to contrive situations.

The more the children can talk, read and write using 'real language', the more they will find out about how it works and therefore how to use it effectively.

3. Mathematics

At least half of your Maths syllabus will be taken up with Arithmetic. Although it is a very small part of Mathematics proper it is neverthless a very vital part. It is important, not only as a foundation to all future mathematical study, but also as a tool which the children will need to use throughout their lives.

So for our purpose here let us think in terms of —

Arithmetic
- as a tool
- as an offshoot of Mathematics,

and

Mathematics   as an environmental factor.

Arithmetic as a tool

It is not the purpose of this book to say what should and should not be included in a Primary Maths syllabus. I would remind you though of the dangers already mentioned of an overcrowded curriculum. Certainly in Mathematics 'first things first' is a helpful directive. That is to say that basic number work ought to have precedence over other areas of Maths. It is *NOT* to say that very young children are to be denied the pleasure and experience of Mathematical discovery. *NOR* is it to say that we make the children do page upon page of mechanical computation. It is simply to recognise that an important part of our job in teaching Maths in the Primary school is to give the children a firm grounding in basic number. Something has gone wrong if a child spends more than a minimum of time in the secondary school on basic computation practice. Secondary teachers understandably wonder what on earth we do in the Primary school when they receive children whose manipulation of the four rules is clumsy, halting and innacurate.

An overcrowded curriculum which denies the children sufficient experience in the manipulation of the four rules may be one reason why they fail to reach a reasonable standard of numeracy by the time they leave the Primary school. Another major reason is, too much computation too early — that is before the children *understand* what they are supposed to be doing. Computation should be the *LAST* stage in the learning of a new concept. It should come *AFTER* practical experience and oral discussion. Very often the first two vital stages are missed out, and the children have to grapple with a new concept *AND* its computation at the same time. Many teachers, anxious to give the children 'a good basic grounding in number,' force-feed the children too early with pages of written computation.

A six year old acquaintance of mine was struggling with subtraction using tens and units

$$
\begin{array}{cc}
T & U \\
2 & 6 \\
- \ 1 & 7 \\
\hline
\end{array}
$$

. Allowing for exceptions this is generally speaking too early. On being questioned by her mother about the sums it became clear that the child had not the least understanding of what she was supposed to be doing. When you come to introduce a new concept, err on the side of being too late rather than too early. If the child is not ready to understand a concept then *NO AMOUNT* of written computation will help him to understand, *NOR* will it serve to make him ready. At best it is a waste of time. At worst it can have long lasting harmful effects (lack of confidence, half understood concepts which affect the forming of other concepts etc.). Besides this, you will cause yourself needless anxiety and distress. There is nothing more likely to increase your blood pressure and anxiety in the child than forcing him to do formal written work before he is ready.

You may need to do some oral and written tests to find out what the children's various stages of development are. This information coupled with general guidelines (ask the head about these if you are not sure), will help you to select material from textbooks to add to that which you will make yourself so as to give the children a reasonably well balanced, relevant and interesting scheme of work.

Once you have sketched out a rough plan for the year or term you can then devise practical activities to precede and accompany the written work. For this, above all, is essential to good mathematics practice in the Primary school. It must be active. Not for all the children all of the time, but for most of the children most of the time. There is no shortage of possibilities here, besides the wealth of experience embedded in model making and craft work there are also the various role playing games — shopping (vary the shop to suit the need — baker/counting; greengrocer/addition or subtraction in weight; fabric shop/linear measurement, etc.). These role playing games are very often not encouraged beyond the infant room. This is a pity because although the need for such games diminishes as the children grow older, it very rarely disappears altogether, and so many children are forced to abandon concrete objects and situations *long* before they are ready to think and operate in purely abstract terms.

The result is a dislike of Maths, a lack of confidence about numbers, their use and application. This lasts all the way through Secondary school and beyond, producing the results discovered by the Cockcroft Committee in 1982. It is crucial therefore that we make a proper start in the Primary school.

The children ought to have concrete experience of all things mathematical: half a litre, a quarter of the children in class, more than/less than, three times as many, four times less, the circumference of a tyre/paddling pool, the area of the playground, the height of a tree/the school, the length of the pavement outside etc. When they come to apply their arithmetic to practical problems they will then have some sense of what they are doing as opposed to merely manipulating numbers on a page. So, before you ask a child to do page 56 or a blue sum card, ask yourself what, if anything, the content will mean to the child.

Proper active Maths in the Primary school demands conversation. Conversation between child and child, between child and teacher and between teacher and groups of children. It is through conversation about activity that ideas and concepts are awoken, shaped and developed. Also unless you converse with the children you will not know what their understanding is. Pages of written work do not necessarily tell you anything about a child's understanding. For example $48 - 22 = 62$ written in a child's book could easily lead you to believe that that child had little understanding of the subtraction process. In fact it could be that this child understands quite well that $48 - 22 = 26$, but is still reversing letters and numbers. When he says 26 in his head, he writes 62. Now, unless you know the child well you will not discover his mental reasoning unless you ask how the answer was arrived at. You can learn so much from the children's errors, as indeed can they. But you must allow time and space to talk about them. Certainly a cross beside the (in this case) 62 does nothing to help anyone.

Conversely a page of 'correct' sums could lead you to believe that a child had a sound understanding of subtraction until that child is stumped by a simple problem involving subtraction. I can hear myself as a young teacher exclaiming to such a child 'but we spent a whole *week* on subtraction last week' and see the child assume a suitably shameful expression. He was probably also thinking 'what on earth has that got to do with it.'

As far as possible and of course it isn't possible all the time, the children should have a stake as it were in the task they are being asked to perform. Trudging round the playground with a semi-efficient trundle wheel discussing last night's T.V. is hardly active participatory Maths. Sitting at a desk working on computation for an understandable and desirable end comes nearer to it. The point is that it isn't the actual activity itself which matters, as much as the attitude which you and the children bring to bear on it.

The emphasis on understanding and purpose in Primary Mathematics doesn't mean that there is no place for memorization. There is a very definite and deserved place for it. And ability to recall the basic

(+ − × ÷) facts INSTANTLY takes away an enormous amount of drudgery for the children, so that you owe it to them to see that these facts are learned as quickly and as painlessly as possible. Teach that for every single number fact there are 3 others e.g. $8 + 4 = 12$ ($4 + 8 = 12$ and $12 - 8 = 4$ and $12 - 4 = 8$); $3 \times 4 = 12$ ($4 \times 3 = 12$ and $12 \div 3 = 4$ and $12 \div 4 = 3$)   and you will reduce the burden of learning hundreds of individual and separate facts.

Daily oral practice is essential. It needn't be much longer than ten minutes but it should be regular to be effective. Vary the pattern — quick fire questions to the whole class; children working in pairs timing each other with a stop clock or digital watch; one group working outside the classroom with an elected 'question master' to practise the blue cards; 8 times table, story of ten or whatever. The children can keep a personal record of their scores. Occasionally you can given them ten minutes or so to learn a table etc., then let them try to beat their own record for speed and accuracy with a multiplication table/addition + subtraction to 20/subtraction within 14 and so on.

Systematic written practice is also essential but not necessarily every day. Two or three weekly sessions of half an hour or so is probably enough, but you will be the best judge here. Remember though, a major fault in our Maths teaching is that we bore the children by expecting too many worked examples (written sums) from them. Most Maths text books ask for 20 examples when 10 would do, and 10 when 5 would be enough. The purpose of these examples is to show you that the child has mastered a particular point. Either she has mastered it and becomes bored by showing you over and over again, or she hasn't, in which case she shouldn't be doing the examples anyway.

If you aren't already equipped (either from the school or yourself) there are plenty of books and cards on the market which offer systematic practice. You should thoroughly understand whatever system of graded examples you use however, so study them before you organise and distribute them around the classroom.

There isn't a blueprint for *THE BEST* way to organise such material, but keep the organization simple. Such material is only a means to an end and should never get in the way of the end itself (to help the children to memorize the number facts as quickly and painlessly as possible). Nevertheless despite all your efforts the cards/sheets will inevitably become muddled from time to time so check them over occasionally, and of course let the children help.

Each of your children will be at a certain stage of mathematical development: learning to count on in ones, learning number bonds, grappling with place value, subtraction, division etc., or doing preparatory work leading up to one of these stages. Part of your job will be to find out in various ways what the level of understanding and ability is, then to provide work at an appropriate level, to consolidate what has been learnt or to stretch the child a little to lead on to the next stage.

The problem of providing work at the right level is perennial. It is also crucial, but don't despair. If you are aware that it is a problem you have already gone half way towards solving it.

Besides if you ensure that at least half the child's mathematical activity is to do with real problem solving, i.e. concerned with problems which the child is actually interested in solving, then you have a sound guide towards meaningful and purposeful maths.

To sum up then, under the heading '*Arithmetic as a TOOL*' we would aim to help the children to —

a) Have an understanding of the four rules of number ($+ - \times \div$).

b) Discern something of the relationship between these rules.

c) Be able to manipulate up to four figure number (including decimals and fractions) using these rules. This involves having an understanding of place value.

d) Be able to apply these rules to Measurement and Quantity of all kinds — Time, Money, Length, Capacity, Weight etc.

e) Be able to apply the number system to a variety of problems including Averages/Percentages, Ratio/Proportion, etc.

This in itself is quite a list. There is no need to feel that you must cover absolutely everything. Sort out your priorities according to the school, the children and the environment. Far better that you take time enough over what you DO cover so that you and the children understand it for its own sake, and also how it fits into your scheme of number/maths work as a whole. The more the children understand about the work they HAVE done, the easier it will be for them to understand and absorb new work. Many children struggle along and never really understand anything properly. These children have the problem further compounded each time a new piece of work is introduced. Take stock from time to time. Ask yourself if the children are spending too long/short a time at a particular stage. Devise tests to show what they have absorbed on recent work. Above all TALK with them about their work and LISTEN to what they say, and this more than anything else will teach you how to improve your work.

Arithmetic as an offshoot of Maths

Concepts such as regularity, order and pattern are at the very heart of Mathematics. In your number work in the Primary school you can encourage the development of these concepts from a very early age. The process will have started of course even before the children come to school. Most young children have experience of one to one correspondence in everyday activities like — putting one toothbrush into one slot, one button into one buttonhole, one cup into one saucer etc. Also a sense of order can be learnt from stories like 'The Three Bears' and 'The Three Billy goats Gruff.' The reception teacher will continue to provide incidental mathematical experience. She must also lead the children along a more structured path to the discovery of numbers, the recognition of their names and shapes, the cardinal/ordinal numbers, counting on and counting back etc.

Use everyday objects when you can, to extend the children's ideas of number. You can — count, add, subtract, multiply and divide using — buttons, pencils, fingers, books, pages, tables, chairs, dinner money, water etc.

The inclination to order, classify and quantify our environment is a NATURAL one. It is present in the children AND it is at the heart of Mathematics. USE this natural inclination. So often it is blunted or even stifled altogether by the work of our schools. Time and again the cart is put before the horse and children are asked to manipulate figures on a page before they have any real experience of what these figures represent in the real world. No wonder they get it wrong, become confused and end up 'no good at Maths.'

Let the children see and enjoy then, the inherent regularity and pattern of numbers. As well as being worthwhile activity in its own right it also helps them to learn the basic facts talked about in the previous section.

Much of the equipment (not necessarily Maths.) to be found in an infant room like mosaic tiles, unifix cubes, cuisenaire rods, marbles, etc., lends itself to number, pattern and discovery. You of course have to be aware of the mathematical ideas which are important to learn so that you can help the children to make the most of these activities.

If you are hazy about these ideas then do something about it. Attend an in service course, speak to colleagues, ask questions, do some reading, do some thinking. You have to be convinced that what you dish out to children is worth the effort (yours and theirs). Otherwise, what is the point of you being in the classroom at all?

Juniors should have access to such equipment too. The fear that they will waste time 'playing with baby toys' is unfounded. In general children do not play with toys which are below their level of interest and ability. The same equipment can be played with over and over again at different stages in a child's development. And at each stage the child brings and takes something different to and from the activity.

Juniors who have access to a wide range of apparatus most commonly found in the Infant room, will gain experience from it commensurate with their age and ability.

Alongside the use of concrete material, the use of number lines of various lengths and the 100 square helps the children to formalise and further develop their ideas about the underlying pattern of number. e.g. Using the (0–10) number line:

- start at 0 and 'visit' every second number

0	1	2	3	4	5	6	7	8	9	10

- start at 1 and visit every second number

0	1	2	3	4	5	6	7	8	9	10

- start at 1 and colour in half the number line, the even numbers, the odd numbers, etc.

1	2	3	4	5	6	7	8	9	10

- using the single line to 20; colour the two squares in which you can see the figure 3 — red; the figure 4 — blue; the figure 5 — yellow etc.

0	1	2	3	4	5	6	7	8	9	10	11	12	13	14	15	16	17	18	19	20

- using the double number line to 20 — give the instruction 'make this into a number line to 20 by adding 'ten' to each number in the bottom row'

1	2	3	4	5	6	7	8	9	10
1	2	3	4	5	6	7	8	9	10

- using the number line to 30 — start at 0 and jump up in threes till you reach 30

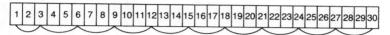

- using the number line to 100

start at 0 and jump up in fives, sevens, tens etc.

Gradually the children will see the pattern emerging.

Make large number lines with bold figures — cover these with clear plastic and put them on the floor. This is useful where wallspace is limited. More important it gives the children the opportunity to HANDLE the number lines.

A child can pick up a number line to 5 and PLACE it on top of a line to 10 and SEE that half the line is left uncovered, or pick up a number line to 10 THREE TIMES and place it on top of a number line to 30 in order to cover it, and so on. If you have room make a number line to stretch right across the floor from wall to wall. The children can then actually walk along this line and invent games based on the line — a number line to 100 is probably the most useful here. One child can walk along the line while the rest of the group count aloud. Various patterns can be invented — stop at every 4th, 6th number, hop over every 10th number, stamp at the ¼ ½ ¾ mark etc.

Similar kinds of exercises can be done in the children's books and probably ought to be done to consolidate the above experiences. The two are NOT the same however and the doing of one should not be substituted for the doing of the other. For most children, the actual handling of the material is a great help towards understanding.

100 squares can be used in the same way. Make one for the wall (they can be bought commercially), and make sure that the children who are using it can see it clearly. Use it to count aloud (communally and individually) to 100, to count in tens — 7, 17, 27, 37, (point as you do this or let a child point), to count to 100 and CLAP at the end of each line — reverse the process and count back from 100 to 1 still clapping at 90, 80, 70, etc. Let the children HEAR the rhythm as you stress every 2nd, 3rd, 4th number (use a variety of sounds clapping, tapping, piano, recorder, percussion instruments).

Besides being fun this sort of activity does help the children to develop their ideas of number. It is also a good foundation for later work leading to place value. If a child can visualize the position of the number 34 on the 100 square he will be better able to think of it in terms of

3 tens and 4 units (though of course he will have several aids to help him to understand place value).

When you come to use the hundred square for written patterns much of the same ground will be covered.

For example — put an empty 100 square on the blackboard and let 10 children each complete a line. When the square has been completed use coloured chalks to pick out various patterns —

- all the even numbers
- all the odd numbers
- start at one and circle every 3rd number
- choose a number from 1-10, circle it add ten, circle that etc.
- choose a number from 91-100, circle it, subtract ten, circle that etc.

Eventually the children can discover that all the multiplication tables form regular patterns on the 100 square.

Extend the children's experience of the link between number and pattern. Let the children use bricks, crosses, gummed shapes, to make patterns based on

a) a sequence of number

2,1,2,1,2,1...   ⊗ × ⊗ × ⊗ × ⊗ ×

3,2,3,2...   🞆🞆🞆🞆🞆🞆🞆🞆

3,2,1...   ⊗ ⊗ × ⊗ ⊗ × ⊗ ⊗ ×

b) a single number

4

5

6

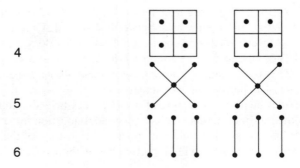

Help them to perceive, and direct their attention to number patterns in the environment — in wheels, walls, gates, window panes, paving stones, door panels, floor tiles, fabric patterns, fish scales, a honeycomb, a snow crystal etc.

Many children find the fascination of actual numbers very appealing. There are books on the market to give you ideas for number games and activities, magic squares, lotto, dominoes etc. Some suggestions are fine, others are more suitable for long car journeys or wet playtimes, i.e. the educational value is pretty limited. This is fine so long as the activity is recognised for what it is — a harmless bit of time filling. When it's active participatory Maths you're after look closely at such activities. Some of them are dressed up to look educationally responsible and exciting. Close inspection shows them to be something else. Ask yourself what the activity does, and how does it do it. And don't be misled by attractive book covers or grand sounding aims.

The really fascinating behaviour of numbers can engage the child's mind for long periods of profitable activity. e.g. ask the children to write out the 9 times table then add the digits of the answers

$$1 \times 9 = 9 \qquad 9 + 0 = 9$$
$$2 \times 9 = 18 \qquad 1 + 8 = 9$$
$$3 \times 9 = 27 \qquad 2 + 7 = 9 \qquad \text{etc.}$$

Better still, aim to provide the kind of environment in which the children will make such discoveries for themselves. This of course is easier said than done and most of us fail more often than we succeed. Nevertheless it is an aim worth striving for. One way foward is to keep up your own interest and enjoyment!

There are numerous books easily obtainable (from libraries, colleges of education, teachers' centres, colleagues) in which you can learn more about the fascination of numbers. Take the trouble to visit the library or a bookshop and have a browse. You could be replenished with ideas for further work with the children, and the ideas in the books may spark off some ideas of your own. Take advantage also of any in-service courses which may be available. These can be an excellent source of stimulation. They are often dismissed as being a waste of time and containing 'nothing new'. A lot depends on *your* attitude when you attend these courses. If you keep an open mind and look for material which could be adapted for your use, there is often plenty to be found.

Before concluding this section I would like to mention one very important yet often neglected skill. That is the child's ability to ESTIMATE reasonably accurately. Estimation is something the children ought to be familiar with from the very beginning of their primary school days. It is valuable in that it:

a) Concentrates the mind.

b) Increases the children's confidence in their ability and readiness to 'have a go' at answer.

c) Helps to 'fix' facts — an estimation (how many ½ litre mugs will fill this litre jug) followed by the children's discovery of the correct answer, will give that answer greater meaning.

d) Helps to develop concepts — the more the children estimate (how many metres long is the corridor, how many people were in assembly, how many minutes it will take to do a given task), the nearer they will come to a clear and precise notion of measurement and quantity.

e) If they are accustomed to making a rough estimate first then they will be less likely to accept a glaring error in an answer. They will for example know that $640 - 320$ cannot be nine hundred and something.

Very often the children are denied a sufficient amount of practice here in order for them to become proficient. When you come to think about the content of the Arithmetic in your curriculum remember to make room for estimation. It is not time consuming and can be slotted into your existing scheme of work without and effort apart from that of remembering how important it is.

So, under the head *'Arithmetic as an offshoot of Maths'* we would aim to help the children to —

i) Appreciate the regularity of number

ii) Discern something of the underlying pattern of number

iii) See some of the patterns of number in the surrounding environment

iv) Know some of the fascinating properties of number

v) Be willing and able to estimate approximate answers

Mathematics as an environmental factor (being evident everywhere in our physical world)

For many of you the beauty and satisfaction of Maths, will not be immediately obvious. You may feel unsure of your ground because of an unhappy experience in your own education, or you may simply dismiss yourself as being 'no good at maths'. Take heart. You need not be a mathematician in order to make an excellent job of exciting young minds in the discovery and joy of mathematical exploration.

Firstly, if you concentrate on what you *do* know you will be surprised at what this amounts to —
— that a triangle has three sides
— that a rectangle has four
— that these shapes are to be found in and around the immediate environment
— that there is a relationship between parts and the whole (sides to perimeter, diameter to circumference)
— that these relationships are CONSTANT and can be written in 'shorthand' or as formula e.g. area, length, breadth a = l × b . . . and so on.

Secondly, you can extend your knowledge fairly easily. Most primary schools will have an adequate source of reference books for your needs. If not, use the library, local college or teacher's centre. Discuss your problems with colleagues. Ask other members of staff to clarify difficulties. No one will think ill of you and most will feel flattered to be asked and delighted to help out if they can. You may even spark off a lively staff discussion in which everyone will learn something.

Whatever you do, do NOT be discouraged from attempting Mathematical discovery with the children. Choose those areas of Maths which seem to YOU to be relevant and worthwhile (most of the prescriptive lists of Maths to be covered in the Primary school are far too full). Having chosen an area, find out as much as you can about it — play the game, do the puzzles, make the shapes before you introduce the work to the children. If you prepare yourself like this then you will have the confidence to learn *with* the children and be able to tackle the problems which crop up. If you are unprepared and/or unsure of your ground you may well feel inclined to abandon things at the first hurdle, thereby passing on the belief that Maths is a mystery which only a very few can understand. This may be true at a higher level but at the Primary stage the fun, satisfaction and enjoyment of Maths should be available to all of your children. Moreover it is well within your capabilities to make it so.

Naturally not every child will take what you make available. It is as unrealistic to expect everyone to be moved by the beauty and satisfaction of Mathematics, as it would be to expect everyone to be moved by Gray's Elegy, or a Beethoven Quartet. People are different, and children are people. Your job is to see that the Maths you offer is sound. Then at least the child's assessment of her ability in, and aptitude for the subject will be an accurate one, not one made false by false Maths (boring or incomprehensible or both).

The following are some ideas for you to think about as starting points in terms of Maths as an environmental factor. The extent of exploration and development will depend on your particular circumstances — the age and stage of the children, the attitude towards Maths in the school, your own interest in and knowledge of the subject, etc.

Basic Shapes

The children ought to have ample experience of HANDLING the basic geometric shapes. These should be presented in a variety of materials — wood, plastic, paper, card etc. The children should build with them, make patterns, cut them out, colour them, paste them together and so on. In this way they will become familiar with the properties of the various shapes. The handling itself of course is not enough. Conversation is absolutely vital here in order to give the children the appropriate vocabulary (angle, circumference, diameter, diagonal, etc.), and also to help them to sort out and clarify their ideas. Again, bring in the environment.

Draw the children's attention to — circles in wheels, clocks, bottle tops, triangles in leaf shapes, roofs of buildings, squares and rectangles in boxes, windows, doors, pavement slabs etc. Devise work which will help them to seek out and recognise these basic shapes in and around their immediate environment.

Three Dimensional Shapes

It is important that the children have an opportunity to work with three dimensional shapes as well as two dimensional ones. Provide activities which will encourage them to spot the relationship between a circle and a cylinder, a square and a cube, a triangle and a cone or pyramid etc. Again talk is essential during these activities otherwise much of the mathematical potential will be lost.

Food packages are an excellent source of 3D models. Use them to let the children discover and cut out the circle from a cylinder, the squares from a cube, the rectangles from a cuboid etc. Show the children how to 'explode' the various 3D solids into their two dimensional faces. Attractive wall displays can be made from 'exploded' 3D models. Reverse this process and let the children build 3D models from two dimensional shapes.

Again, draw the children's attention to the presence of these forms in the world around them, noting that often the properties of the shapes are connected to their function, e.g.

ball bearings, castors (spheres)
hinges, bottles   (cylinders)
boxes, bricks   (cubes, cuboids)

Great enjoyment can be had in making up 'crazy inventions' i.e. objects made from shapes which are not suitable for their function (bicycles with square wheels, chairs with conical seats, spherical dice etc.).

Symmetry

This is a very important mathematical concept with far reaching implications. At the Primary stage though it is enough for most children to stick to concrete examples. Symmetrical examples from the natural world (plants, flowers, crystals) can be studied then spotted in man made designs of all shapes and sizes. The pleasure of symmetry can be seen on the face of a 5 year old involved in the simple yet satisfying act of folding a painting to make a symmetrical shape with one axis of symmetry. This is an excellent starting point (but it IS only a starting point).

From this starting point you can go on to discover symmetries of more than one axis, symmetries of three dimensional shapes, symmetry by reflection, rotation, translation. Wallpaper and fabric designs will provide plenty of examples of these last three devices. The children can cut out the patterns, move them around to make new patterns: *actually* reflect (using a mirror), *actually* rotate (fixing the centre of the shape with a drawing pin) and *actually* translate (using tracing paper).

Take the children around the school, into the playground and outside to look for examples of the various types of symmetry on which they have been working in the classroom.

This is an area which usually fires the children's imagination. There are dozens of examples readily to hand and they will inundate you with suggestions, ideas and questions. Make sure you know enough about the subject so as to be able to capitalize on this enthusiasm, to be able to lead the children on towards seeing the Mathematical implications of what they are doing.

So far we have started from a particular aspect of Maths then gone to find examples in the environment. Turn the process round occasionally — start from the environment e.g. find all the patterns made by roof tiles, wall tiles, floor tiles, house bricks, window panes etc. and use them to lead the children to discover tessellation — which shapes will tessellate and which will not. Another example of starting from the environment is to ask the children to bring in empty cardboard containers from home (matchboxes, cereal packets etc.). Make a collection of similar shaped food containers in varying sizes. Use these to show the children the difference between everyday similarity and the more exact Mathematical similarity. This will involve the use of ratio and proportion. Let the children use their knowledge of these to make scale models of their toys. Even quite young children have an innate sense of ratio and proportion. This is demonstrated in their drawings and models. Try to provide activities which will develop this innate sense so that the children have something to rely on i.e. a memory bank of experience, when they come to work out more abstract problems later.

A word of warning for those of you who have studied Mathematics at a higher level. You may be inclined to ASSUME that the children will see the Mathematical implications of what they are doing. For the most part — they will not. It is better that you spell things out so that there is as little chance as possible of confusion arising in the children's minds because you have assumed that they would understand what you have left unsaid.

Graph Work

There are several aspects to graph work in the primary school. It can be seen as

a) A creative activity
b) A means of displaying information or data
c) A means of finding out information quickly
d) An aid to prediction
e) A means of showing relationships.

The spectrum is very wide. It ranges from the very simplest pictorial representation of children's heights to the more sophisticated straight and curved line graphs showing algebraic relationships. Take the children only as far as they can comfortably understand. An important point to remember is that children need a WIDE VARIETY of experience of graphical representation before they are able to understand the Mathematical implications. Therefore allow them *plenty of time* at one stage before moving them on to the next. Better that a top junior is still working at the block graph stage with a sound understanding of what he is doing than to have him working on single line graphs with only the haziest notion of what they are all about. A short discussion about a completed graph will tell you how much a child has understood and whether he is ready or not to move on.

These discussions are a very necessary part of graph work. They will help a child to learn to 'read' the graph. Being able to read the graph (and perhaps even make some simple predictions) is more important than being able to make the graph. After all graphs are a form of communication. They are made *in order* to be read. This fact is sometimes overlooked and the children are given practice in the making of graphs with insufficient practice in the reading of them. This is like teaching the children to spell without giving them the opportunity to write.

Usually the children respond very well to work on graphs. Increase the appeal by allowing them a free rein with colours and materials. Here is a random selection of graph work in the primary school, but your own ideas will be better suited to your particular school and children. Eventually the need for precision and clarity of presentation will become evident but do not place too much stress on this at the beginning unless there is a real need for it.

3D Block Graphs

These can be appropriate at all levels. They are 'instant' and can be quickly cleared away when the point has been made.

Red and blue bricks piled in two columns on the floor (each child placing an appropriate coloured brick on one of the piles) will provide an 'instant block graph of 'Numbers of Boys and Girls in our Class'.

Yellow and brown bricks for 'Children with Light Hair/Dark Hair.' Blue brown green bricks for 'Colour of Children's eyes in Class 2'.

Where time and space allow ACTUAL cereal packets stuck to the wall in a column graph will provide a dramatic and obvious display of 'Favourite Cereals'. Things do have to be dramatic and obvious especially with young children or when you are just beinning to introduce graphs in order to help the children to get the point e.g. halved conkers stuck on to thin card to show 'Number of Conkers won in a Week/Found each Day', or toy cars/lorries arranged to represent the results of a traffic count done outside the school.

2D Block graphs

Use coloured sticky shapes/outline drawings/labels etc. Each child sticks one in the appropriate column on blank paper or card. (Large squared paper can also be used. Here the children colour in the appropriate squares to make a column for the graph.)

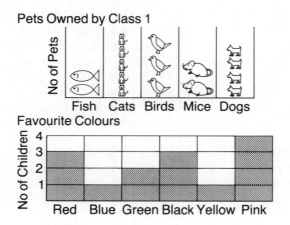

Single Line Block Graphs

These are still essentially block graphs in that there is no real relationship between the data on one axis and that on the other. Points are plotted on the graph and these can be joined by a line (e.g. in a temperature chart). This line can show trends but because the graph is a block graph, it is the points themselves which are the only accurate measures.

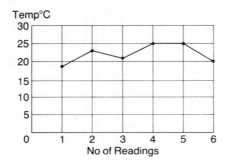

Graphs which show a relationship

These come about when the data on one axis *has a bearing upon* that on the other. Usually the data on the vertical axis is dependant upon that on the horizontal axis:

a) Straight line

e.g. to show the relationship between multiplier and multiplicand

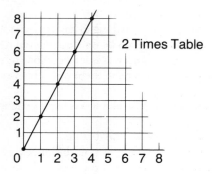

b) Curved line

e.g. to show the relationship between the area of a rectangle and its width — the perimeter being constant.

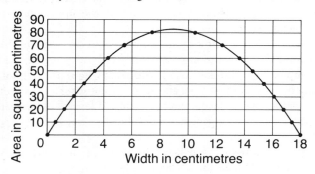

Most children are surprised to find here that the area can change though the perimeter remains the same and eagerly go on to find out the smallest/largest area to be had from a given perimeter.

Curved stitching

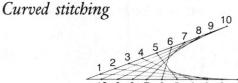

This is an enjoyable way for children to explore mathematical relationships. It is not difficult and there are plenty of books around to show you how to start. Read and experiment yourself a bit before you start work with the children. And, let them experiment with rules and straight lines before you introduce needles and thread.

There is ample satisfaction in curved stitching as an activity in itself. Once the children get the hand of it there can be no stopping them. For many though, the mathematical implications will not be obvious or even interesting. It will be up to you to help to tease them out. Questioning is as good a way as any, e.g.

- I wonder what the curve would be like if we halved the angle between the axes?
- Where have you seen a curve like this before?
- Do you think this line would go on forever in this direction? etc.

Some children may overtake you and lead the way to fresh questions and experiments but this is no cause for worry. Indeed it is the very nature of successful teaching.

These then are a few suggestions from the hundreds of possibilities. It is a very good thing to be able to 'make a picture' to describe and convey information which would otherwise have to be communicated by a method so wordy and laborious that the information became incomprehensible.

Graphs, like so many things become clear and easy to do when there seems to be a real need to use them. My husband admits to having been completely in the dark about the graphs he did in school. Now he wades happily through page after page of statistical analysis, drawing and comparing graphs at quite a sophisticated level. His mathematical ability cannot have changed that much but he does see some point in what he is doing.

As far as possible then keep the point of the work within the childrens' sights. Where some aspect is clearly proving too difficult for a child to see the point of what she or he is doing, leave it alone for the time being. Not only will you benefit her long term mathematical development you will have valuable classroom time as well.

Finally, do keep reminding the children that their graphs are representations of real things in the physical world. This awareness will help them to notice when a result on the graph makes no sense. It is when they lose sight of what the graph is supposed to be representing that they can go badly wrong.

There may be occasions when you want to separate one aspect of Maths and deal with it in isolation. For the most part however you will be dealing with all aspects at the same time

e.g. Taking a traffic count/Measuring the length of the school hall involves —

Arithmetic — as a tool
— as an offshoot of Maths.
and Mathematics — as an environmental factor.

It is important that you try to help the children to see that all the various strands of Maths that they do are not separate entities. That is that they are linked to each other in various ways as well as being linked to our physical world. For this is the point which so often gets lost in our schools, namely that Mathematics is in and of this world. It has to do with real life problem-solving and the pleasure and satisfaction this can bring. It makes sense and it should help us to make sense of our surroundings. It was not invented in order to fill up school text books and the children should not be practising maths exercises in order to be able to do maths exercises. There is a point behind the exercises and this point should be brought in at every opportunity. As far as possible the children should follow each practice session with some practical application, so that practice exercises are never seen in isolation from what they represent. They are therefore seen to be useful and worth doing.

So, make your mathematics as 'real' as you can, talk with (not to) the children about their work (especially their mistakes), and finally give them time. Time to soak in new ideas, time to develop time to mature. I think it was John Locke who said 'never trouble yourself about those faults in them (the children) which you know age will cure'.

The single biggest cause of failure in Mathematics is that we expect too much of the children, too soon. Time and again we force them to grapple with abstract notions without first giving them enough concrete or 'real life' examples.

Children need time to develop and development is a process which can be helped and encouraged certainly but never hurried.

4. Music

The first aim of teaching music in the Primary school is to foster a love of music in the children. It is part of our primitive inheritance and it has a power of communication over and above words. A much needed unifying balm in a world where we seem to be splitting into ever smaller and separate 'specialisms'. All children deserve access to the joy and enrichment which music can bring to their lives. Unfortunately not all children are given this access. There is a vast variation in the quality of musical education in our primary schools depending on the talents and enthusiasm of the staff involved. What can you do to ensure that your children gain maximum exposure to the resources which are available?

Use other members of staff

Is there a member of staff whose musical talents with young children are obvious? If so — approach that person. Work out an exchange of classes which would be of mutual benefit. If there is a visiting specialist music teacher you can benefit enormously. Ask about her work with your children and how you could help. Sit in on her class from time to time and try to give some back up lessons in your own time. You needn't go to every lesson. Most of these visiting specialists will realize how precious the free time is to you. Do show some interest though. It will be a poor reflection on your general attitude if you take no interest whatsoever in what others do with your children.

Radio and T.V. Programmes

There are some excellent programmes available. You will gain more from these if you USE them to suit your purposes as opposed to passively listening to them week by week. Read the accompanying notes for the teacher in order to be well prepared for the actual broadcast. Make sure the children are comfortably seated and in a suitably receptive mood BEFORE the broadcast actually starts. Half the value will be lost if you have to spend the first few minutes issuing instructions and generally settling the children. Ideally broadcasts should be taped and played at your convenience but this is not always possible. If you must hear the broadcast 'live' then do all you can to make conditions as favourable as possible.

Refer to the broadcast during the week if you can 'that's the same rhythm as we heard in Music Time' etc. Practice if necessary so that the children can join in when invited to do so. A quick re-cap may be needed on last week's programme before the new one begins so that the children can key in immediately. Follow-up work is sometimes suggested in some of the pamphlets. This is fine up to a point but bear in mind the actual broadcast should be the 'high spot' or focal point. Beware of any work which would diminish this fact and reduce the important of the broadcast. The broadcast should be looked forward to and enjoyed. Part of the point of these broadcasts is to offer the children a direct and immediate experience. They work best when the medium is exploited e.g. when they produce audio and visual effects which you could not do. They are at their worst when they are simply switched on to be used as a replacement teacher.

Daily Experience

Since music is in and around us all the time it should be part of the children's DAILY lives in school. It can come in a variety of settings —

Assembly — songs, hymns, musical accompaniments
Listening to records
Participation in Radio or T.V. broadcasts
Performance of one or more children to rest of class
Movement to pitched and unpitched percussion
Learning a new song
Singing some old favourites together
Formal music lesson.

Obviously you cannot be expected to tease out the musical essence of every single opportunity. Because of the many pressures on you there will be times when the children will have to make what they can of the music presented to them. Sometimes this will be nothing. This is fine as long as it is not the general pattern. The degrees to which some of the above are seen as 'music' by the children will largely depend on your attitude. There are many simple things which you can do to heighten or lessen the musical experience. e.g. — the assembly hymn — make sure the children know the words and tune well enough to be able to join in with confidence, and enjoyment. There is nothing enjoyable about trying to sing half-known words to a half-known tune. It is a rare child who does not enjoy a really good sing-song. This means singing well known words to well known tunes. One only has to listen to any coach load of children coming home from a day's outing or to a camp fire sing-song. So when it comes to teaching a new song, aim to have the words and tune learnt as QUICKLY as possible so that the children are able to sing with confidence. Without the confidence there will be no enjoyment and without the enjoyment what's the point?

Use a variety of methods to lighten the chore of teaching a new song. Read the words, together, singly, in groups, in question and answer form (with the class divided into two); whisper the words, shout the words, whisper one verse, shout the next, speak the next etc. (end in a soft voice rather than a shout in order to keep things in control); use a tape recorder to tape the children's efforts and play it back to them; mime the words or part of them; write out any difficult words or 'sticky spots' in large letters on card which can be held up at the appropriate point in the verse. Use some of these and invent more of your own so that in the learning of the words the enjoyment is retained.

Similarly with the tune — a variety of methods will help you to teach it in an enjoyable yet efficient way: tap, clap, stamp and rhythm, beat the rhythm using percussion instruments; play the tune on the piano (even non-players can copy a simple tune — ask someone to play it for you then you can copy) at the normal pitch then at the highest and lowest possible pitch — this always goes down well with the children and it does help to 'fix' the tune in their heads; play the tune or have it played on any other available pitched instrument. As with the words use the tape recorder to let the children hear their own efforts.

Finally, before you embark upon the actual teaching of the song, the children ought to hear it played in its entirety so that they have an idea of what it is they are aiming at.

Live Music

Give the children the experience of live music as often as possible. Sources may be as varied as —

instrument players within the school — pupils AND staff
instrument playing parents
secondary school pupils/orchestra
local band silver/brass/pipe etc.

local pop group/operatic society
professional musicians . . . and so on.

Make contact with possible sources. Invite them to come to school
to play, sing, talk about an instrument or whatever. There is a great deal
of untapped wealth in the area of muscial education in the primary school.
With comparatively little effort you can stand to gain a great deal yourself,
as well as perhaps greatly enriching your children's musical experience.

Having made every effort to tap all available resources is there any
more you can do to improve your own approach to music with the
children? There are two main aspects to be considered — Musical Appreciation and Musical Performance. Obviously the two are closely linked. Much
of the work you do will directly or indirectly affect both aspects. For
our purposes here however it may be helpful to look at each aspect
separately.

Musical Appreciation

The aim of your work here will be to help children to develop
a discriminating ear, to enable them to appreciate music in all its many
forms, so that, eventually, each one will be able to choose, understand
and enjoy the various kinds of music which most appeal to him, or her.

In order to do this you must provide as wide a variety of music
as possible, pop, classical, church, film, T.V., music from other countries, etc. Encourage the children to suggest music which they would like
to hear so as to gain some idea of their tastes. You can then provide
music from other categories to give a balanced cross section.

At appropriates times (not every time) after listening to a record,
tape or live performance, you can discuss with the children such things
as clarity of words/instruments, feelings aroused if any, speed too
fast/slow?, images suggested (if any), attitude of performer — did she
show pleasure, nervousness, boredom etc. When you come to listen to
a complex orchestral symphony it can be helpful to tease out one or two
strands of the music and let the children hear one line played on the piano,
recorder, xylophone etc., then let them hear it embedded in the symphony. Story lines help here too — Peter and the Wolf, The Nutcracker,
The Sorcerer's Apprentice, Peer Gynt, The Firebird etc.

Some stories from Opera are very suitable for the primary school.
Indeed since Opera is a form to which children naturally respond it is

a pity that it is so neglected. There are plenty of operatic highlights around on records and there is no shortage of reference books in which you can find the story lines. After listening to some of these records you will probably find that you like some arias better than others and you may be tempted to find out more about the operas from which they came. You will then be in a position to tempt the children with tit-bits like Papageno's arias from the Magic Flute perhaps, and other favourites of your own. There is no need to go into details of the whole story. Roughly sketch in the plot then set the scene for the particular aria which you intend to play to the children.

Even seemingly unsuitable operas can work well. I once took a group of about twelve 10 and 11 year olds to a performance by the touring Welsh National Opera Company of 'La Traviata' (the story of a courtesan who loves and is loved by a nobleman, she sacrifices her love to safeguard his family honour and eventually dies of consumption). I had the help of an American student Mrs King at the time. She and her husband were very interested in and knowledgable about Opera. Several weeks before the performance we had lunch time meetings where we took the children through the story and played several different recordings (from records borrowed from the record library) to them. The evening of the performance was an unqualified success. The children sat with rapt attention for almost the whole of the three hour long performance and their animated conversation during the interval also clearly delighted members of the audience who were nearby.

Next day the children shared their experience with the rest of the class (some of whom had been to the lunch time sessions but had elected not to go to the performance). They told the story in their own words — 'here's where Alfredo's dad asks Violetta to give Alfredo up' etc., and played pieces from a record to illustrate the story. They painted pictures and made a model theatre. Finally they did an assembly to share their experience with the whole shool.

Because of the enthusiasm of Mr and Mrs King the children received support and encouragement which was out of the ordinary. Apart from this their's was no special case. The school was in a working class area and none of the children involved had parents who would be likely to play or listen to opera in their homes.

There are so many possible ways to enjoy opera that its appeal can be to a much wider spectrum of people than other muscial forms. It is a great shame that so many children leave the primary school with no experience of it whatsoever. Even if opera has never appealed to you personally you could do no harm by giving it a try. Sample some 'popular pieces' yourself first. It is certainly worth thinking about in terms of how it could enrich the children's musical education.

Musical Performance

Remember that here too an important ultimate aim is enjoyment. When choosing a song to be performed by infant children remember that small muscial steps are easier for them to cope with than large jumps. Tunes therefore which are made up of reasonably small intervals (gaps between the notes) will be easier to teach than those which are made up of larger intervals. Similarly, simple rather than complicated rhythms are a better choice for infant children. You may want to extend the experience of singing together by introducing percussion and perhaps some pitched instruments. After some 'free play' when the children can experiment with the instruments at will they can listen to, then copy a musical pattern to refine their sense of rhythm. Much use can be made of their own names to make up rhythm patterns —

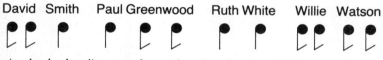

David Smith   Paul Greenwood   Ruth White   Willie Watson

simple rhythm lines can be made using the actual children as models

Kevin and Katy and Richard and me

— children stand in a row and another child claps the appropriate rhythm in front of each child saying the name in time with the rhythm.

You can best decide whether or not and when to introduce the French rhythm names ta, ta te etc., but do not be in a rush to introduce them. It is more important that the children spend time in developing a sense of rhythm than in learning the rhythm names, (the two are not the same thing). The teaching of the names should come after the children have had a good grounding in basic rhythm work, i.e. when they can copy a simple rhythm, make one up for others to copy, beat and keep time to a simple tune. The same applied to musical notation, DO NOT BE IN A RUSH TO INTRODUCE IT. Probably the best muscial experience occurs in the Primary school when concentration upon musical notation is kept to a minimum. In my own muscial education in Primary school the cart was put before the horse as it were. I was never so lost as when we had to make muscial sense of what to most of us was a meaningless pattern of dots and lines. The same applied to singing from the tonic solfa sight reading books. The task or indeed the point of the task was beyond most of us and the musical input was absolutely minimal. We struggled along as best we could trying to act as if we knew was going on. But the whole exercise was largely a waste of time.

When the need arises introduce musical notation which is linked and CAN BE SEEN TO BE LINKED to real music. To begin with, introduce the musical notation of songs THAT THE CHILDREN ALREADY KNOW

e.g.
London's Burning
Jingle Bells

Obviously there comes a time when, in order to be able to give a more sophisticated performance the children will have to learn something of music's discipline and the hard work which is required in preparation for a polished performance. This 'time' has more to do with aptitude and experience than chronological age.

The two aspects of musical notation which will concern you are Rhythm and Pitch. Up to a point you can deal with them separately but the sooner the children come to the stage when the two aspects are seen as part of the same thing the nearer they will be to real music.

Make larger than life cards to show the rhythms which fit your needs

use these to make up a rhythm. Individual children can hold the cards — other children or groups clap the rhythm (with simple rhythms this is usually enough to give the children a clue to a tune of the same rhythm).

e.g. Baa baa black sheep have you any wool

Baa baa black sheep have you any wool

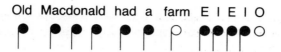

The next stage is to introduce the stave. This can be made from thick card (corrugated card works well), and made to measure to 'fit' the rhythm cards. when the children can clap the rhythm the cards can be slotted on to the stave.

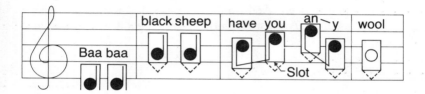

Now the tune can be sung to 'la'. Finally the words of the tune can be matched to the notes and the song can be sung following the notes as you go. One would not wish to reduce every song to this sort of treatment but it is a useful way to introduce musical notation in a way which makes sense to the children.

A vitally important and yet greatly neglected part of a child's musical education is the ear. The widespread belief that a child either has or has not a musical ear and that little can be done to improve things is just not true. There are of course 'natural musicians' but most of the rest CAN improve their musical ability in one way or another with some effort and a little help.

One way to help to train the ear is to sing a note or play one on the piano and ask a child to repeat it, play another and ask the child whether this is higher or lower. Gradually refine the process e.g. play a note on the piano, ask the child to sing the note above, two notes above, two notes below, etc. Play the correct note immediately after the child's effort and let him correct himself. This need not and indeed should not, be a painstaking business. A few minutes is long enough for any one session. Those of your children who need this training will experience a sense of achievement even after a very small step forward.

A great many people admit to a wish that they were 'more muscial'. They feel that the ability to understand and appreciate music is a real lack in their lives. Help your children to be able to make as much as they can of the musical opportunities presented to them. Top up your own musical knowledge if you need to. Learn to sing the tonic solfa, learn to play it. Its notes are those of a major scale. If you don't know what a major scale is then find out. It isn't difficult and some members of staff are bound to be able to help you.

Start with enjoyment, sing play and listen together. Making musical dialogue besides being good training for the ear is marvellous fun. For example in the scale of C Major one partner (or group) picks out a 'tune' on the piano, xylophone, chime bars or sings it from the sol-fa. The other invents a musical reply. Add words then gradually increase the number of notes used etc. A question and answer is a good way to start e.g.

```
        doh  me                    soh  doh
         c    e                     g    c
        he    llo                  he    llo


     doh  me  soh               soh  me  doh
      c    e   g                 g    e   c
     are  you there?            yes  I'm here


 doh  me  soh  doh            doh  soh  me  doh
  c    e   g    c              c    g    e   c
  do  you  like me?           yes   I   like you


      doh ray  me  fah soh        fah soh  la  te  doh
       c   d    e   f   g          f   g    a   b   c
      will you sing this song?    if  its not too long
```

Don't start work like this until you are equipped with a few 'basics' (knowledge of some major scales and how the minor scale is made from the major) but don't be put off by not having them. They are very easy to acquire. If you are prepared for the children to be more musically responsive than you are then you can learn along with them. You can begin to share with them in the endless pleasure of the amazing world of sounds and their relationships.

Finally, those of you who at the beginning cannot bring yourselves to sing even a note in front of the children would do well to learn how to pick out simple tunes on the piano or recorder. Ask a member of staff to teach you or teach yourself. It is not as difficult as it may seem and could even lead to a deepening interest for you personally.

Those of you who are gifted musically will be in a position to spot talented pupils. These ought to be encouraged to develop their musical potential as far as possible. It may be up to you to point out the potential of a pupil to the head, the parents, the music specialist or whoever can take the child further. On a more general level though, you may be at a slight disadvantage in that you cannot understand how the (less musical) children approach something which to you is almost second nature.

Good instrumentalists (usually pianists in Primary school), should not be assumed to be best equipped to give the children the best musical experience. A most unmusical experience is to listen to a group of children scambling in the wake of a polished pianist dashing off a song on the piano with such flourish that the children are almost unheard and all but forgotten.

The finest singing I ever heard in a Primary classroom was from a class of 11 year olds whose teacher was a monk called Brother Martin. I never saw a piano in the room but before the children started to sing Brother Martin would close his eyes then 'hum around a bit' until he hit the starting note. The children would then glide right into the middle of that note sounding like angels.

You don't always have to be 'an expert' in order to be expert at something.

Art and Craft

Art and Craft (like Drama and Science) in the Primary school is more a method than a subject. That is, it matters more how things are done than what things are done. Unfortunately for many children its a rather hit or miss affair. If you are lucky you learn some useful and worthwhile techniques. If not, you leave the school with little or no idea of the attitudes skills and techniques necessary for an enjoyable participation in Art and Craft.

How can you ensure that your children can make the most of the various activities which will make up their Art and Craft?

And, what is this 'most'? Sometimes it will be the sheer pleasure and discovery which can come from 'messing about' with new materials (or old ones used in a new way). Sometimes it will be to make a specific object to as high a standard as possible. Always it should be associated with enjoyment and enthusiasm. First, then, a quick glance at some of the activities themselves.

Drawing/Painting:

with — fingers, crayons, chalks, charcoal, pens, pencils, paint brushes of all sizes (ask for old paint brushes from home to swell your collection) and a variety of paint.

Printing:

with — a variety of shapes and textures e.g. cotton reels, yoghurt pots, pieces of sponge/string/cloth stuck on wood, potato cuts, rubber letters/numbers, hands and feet;

on — paper of different textures (e.g.sandpaper, blotting paper) wood, fabric, glass.

Weaving:

with — paper, wool, string, straw, cane, plastic strips, old tights etc.

on — the materials itself e.g. tights can be woven or platted together to make a rag mat (the tights can be died first to increase the interest of the activity and add to the fun), a flat loom (easily made on stout card) or one made from a tomato box, matchbox or similar.

Modelling/Sculpture:

in — clay, plasticine, papier mâché, soft/stone, soap, polystyrene, stiff paper (for paper sculpture),

to make — animals, plants, abstract shapes, masks, 'useful objects' to take home as presents etc.

Woodwork:

with — a variety of shapes and textures of suitable wood, nails, hammer, hand drill, saw, sandpaper, glue, hooks, hinges and handles etc. (This is widely considered to be an appropriate and valuable activity for the Primary school but there seems to be little expertise around about what and how the children gain from it. If you haven't got it youself you should 'borrow' such expertise from a parent or member of staff so that the children get the most out of the activity.)

Sewing/Knitting/Crotcheting

with — thread, wool, cotton of various colours, and needles of various sizes on a variety of cloth.

These are some of the possibilities open to you for Art and Craft. Naturally you cannot do everything, but you can make sure that what you do do, you do properly.

There are two aspects to be considered as far as the children's work is concerned: experimentation and achievement.

Experimentation

This is where the object is to allow the children to experiment with a material in order to acquaint them with some of that material's properties and possibilities. Obviously the end result here doesn't matter. Allow the children simply to enjoy the handling of the materials. Some children will impose their own end result and will want to produce 'something'. This is fine, but those who feel no need to 'produce' anything at this stage mustn't be forced to. Sometimes these sessions can be usefully slotted in before a more formal session e.g.

Clay — each child in a group is given a lump to play with for 5-10 minutes. Let them know when the playing time is coming to an end, then tell them to roll their clay into balls. Explain that you are now going to show them how to make something (say a thumb pot or coil pot). While you show them the technique stage by stage, you can also show some of the properties — 'see how it breaks if you press too hard', 'we can mend this crack by rubbing a little water over it' etc. You can let them copy you as you go along, then give each child a second piece to mould without your help.

Free experimentation doesn't *have* to be followed by a more formal session, but if it is experimentation for its own sake then make something of it. Work alongside the children as they try out this or that and talk with them about what they are doing. Keep an eye open for any discovery or piece of work by a child which is worth sharing with others. Do not go on too long, or much of the point will be lost. Stop before the children lose interest so that they are eager to continue next time. Certainly give them some time to themselves when they can do and discover whatever they like but this must be in conjunction with a planned approach of your own. You cannot give clay to children then leave them to 'discover' its properties by themselves. They won't, and what is more their interest in the material will quickly dwindle into boredom. Clay especially seems to suffer from misuse in nursery/infant schools. It is not as accessible to young children as a bowl of soap suds for example, or a lump of dough. It is more formal than these and children have to be helped to become acquainted with it. To dump lumps of it on the children's table in the hope that by themselves they will discover its properties, is to misunderstand the material. The point about clay is that it can be baked. The child can see its properties change and also enjoy the pleasure of making something which is almost permanent (vase, pot, etc). When the end result is not to be a baked or dried object, some other modelling material (plasticine, dough, etc) would be more appropriate.

Experimentation is the place for model making where various boxes and food containers are stuck together and left at that. The children need to handle the various shapes and relate and compare one to another and of course TALK about what they are doing. Similarly with woodwork or collage work, the end result is not vital here. The important thing is that they experience a wide variety of materials shaps and textures, that they sort, arrange and classify these in different ways so that they can learn about the varied forms and textures which go to make up the physical world.

There are of course times when the end result DOES matter, i.e. when the point of doing something is not only to enjoy the doing but also to arrive at a satisfactory end result. This brings us to the second aspect — that of achievement.

Achievement

The aim here is to help the children to experience the satisfaction of having produced something worthwhile. Here the cereal boxes will *not* be left unpainted nor will the paint be so thin that the words CORN FLAKES can be seen showing through. This is where the children will learn the care, concentration and hard work of craftsmanship. Many children lack the application required to produce a satisfactory end result and yet they can surprise themselves at what they do produce when a little help is given and a bit of pressure is applied. This was brought home to me by my own son when he was aged 4.

He had done several 'abstract' paintings when I suggested to him that he might try to paint a person. 'I can't *do* persons' came the slightly disgruntled reply. Without thinking I said 'Oh come along now a person has a head and body and arms and legs you could do one quite well, have a try'. He applied himself, became totally engrossed for the next few minutes and the result was a charming picture of a little friend 'Joanna'. He was delighted with his efforts and the praise he was given further increased his sense of achievement. It probably also increased his estimation of his own ability. The satisfaction to the child on these occasions is worth the restriction of freedom.

There are those who think that any form of adult intervention is a restriction of the child's freedom and a curbing of self-expression. Time and again I have seen this to be demonstrably not true. On the whole children suffer more from too little input than too much. This applies to your work in Arts and Crafts as much as anywhere else. The secret lies in knowing when to intervene and when to leave a child alone. There is no magic formula for this secret. The best way to learn it is 'by doing' i.e. by working alongside the children giving as much help as you think is needed, noting the outcome and adapting your approach as you become more experienced.

When it comes to making things (usually as a gift for someone) like woolly balls, hand stitched mats, pots for pins, pan holders, soft toys etc., the end result should not have the stamp of 'adult' all over it. Nor should it be unrecognisable and not worth giving. I once helped a junior teacher by doing a weekly stint of sewing with her class of 8-9 year olds. I came half way through the term and the children had already started to sew felt rabbits. Half of them didn't know how to thread a needle, tie a knot, cut a length of thread from the skein etc. Consequently they were forever standing in a queue waiting for one of the above tasks to be done for them and their progress was infinitessimal. Most of them could have learned how to do these things for themselves but no one had taught them. At the end of the year there was a mad rush to finish the rabbits and the result was a few presentable stuffed rabbits and twenty odd candidates for the nearest dustbin. The thing is the children *knew* the standard was poor. It seemed to me that this activity didn't teach the children anything except how to do a thing badly.

There is of course the occasion when the child is genuinely pleased with an end result which you think is frightful. In such cases you ought to respect the child's judgement and, it is only by knowing your children well that you will be able to tell whether or not a finished result is praiseworthy.

Often in your Art and Craft there will be both experiment and achievement going on at the same time. Nevertheless it is a good idea to sort out your aims before you start — do you want the children to explore the possibilities of painting on glass say, or do you want them to express their feelings about a thunderstorm through pictures or do you want them to make a reasonable and recognisable five pointed start? . . . and so on.

Having sorted out your aims, make your instructions and explanations as clear as you can. Be precise and fill out your explanations with examples. So often, our instructions — so clear to us — simply bewilder the children. An incident occurred whilst I was at college which illustrates the gulf which can exist between teacher and taught. We had been asked to invent a texture using everyday materials — foodstuffs and things generally found around the house. I was not entirely clear about what was expected and in retrospect I realize that I was confused about the differences between texture and design. Anyway I made an attempt. I stuck halved polo mints at half inch intervals on a rectangle of card (A). In the spaces between the mints I stuck on some sprinkled tea leaves. 'Textures' were duly collected for marking. Really we ought to have been given a mixed bag of textured surfaces (fur, silk, brick, sandpaper, wallpaper, velvet etc.) to handle discuss, describe classify, take rubbings of etc., before we made our own. It was clear by the results some of us produced that we were not at all sure what we were supposed to be doing. Nor were we enlightened when the work was given out again a week later. It could have been explained to me that what I had done was not really a texture at all but that the textural possibilities of polo mints are, in fact quite interesting (B) (C).

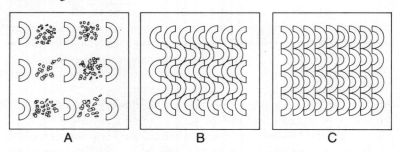

A   B   C

Instead I was given the mysterious assessment of 6 out of 10 and left almost unenlightened apart from what I learned from seeing the interesting textures which others had produced.

Though this incident took place with adult pupils it is relevant to any stage. It is easy to assume that just because you know what you mean the children will too. There's no harm in making extra sure by giving a few examples of what you mean and then asking some questions at the end of your explanation. Certainly this would have helped to avoid the above misunderstanding.

Clear instructions and full explanations are especially important when you intend the work for display.

Display

Where appropriate, discuss the display in advance with the children. Discuss how it could be arranged, talk about size and colour etc. If you have definite ideas about how you want the finished display to look you must be very specific with the children in order to avoid frustration and dissappointment. This is especially true with younger children who are more likely to interpret what you say in their own idiosyncratic way. There may be a case to be made for saying 'No Tom, we won't have your snowman on our picture, we said we would have all the snowmen white. If you'd like to go and do a white one he could go on the picture', but not for 'This isn't a snowman Tom. Snowmen aren't green. Go and do a white one'. While display is an important part of life in the Primary school it must be said that there are many excellent teachers whose rooms are visually disastrous. Nevertheless a good display can serve to reinforce and consolidate weeks of work, stimulate further interest, and help to create a caring environment. All children love to have a piece of work on display. In order that they can take a pride in their efforts the display should be attractive and effective. A crayon drawing may look fine on a desk, but it can fade into insignificance up on a wall alongside commercially produced visual aids. Children are very ready to take a pride in their work if you help them to, and there's not much scope for pride in a dog-eared drawing attached to a dull pin board by a single drawing pin.

There are some who feel that too much interference in the children's work is an insult to the child. This is to imagine all children as prima donnas which they are not. On the whole they are sane and reasonable people who welcome interference which is going to help their efforts to look better. I encountered a head in a nursery school who admitted to me that she had a 'thing' about adult interference in children's work, 'and since its my school I insist for example that *only* rectangular mounts are to be used for the children's work.' Asked why rectangles were fine and any other shape wasn't, the reply was that there was a convention of framing pictures in rectangles, which meant that it was therefore less of an interference in the children's work. It seemed a most odd way of preserving the children's creative freedom while at the same time firmly stamping on the creative freedom of the staff (some of whom may well have wanted to mount the children's work on circles, triangles, irregular shapes or whatever). Moreover the visual result was a dull, monotonous and uninspirational in the extreme. Is it not by rubbing our ideas together and by copying, swapping and adapting them that we are educated at all? This extreme stance was probably a reaction against those schools at the other end of the spectrum where the display is so perfect in its unvarying 'high standard' that it is almost unnerving. One asks oneself where are the 'good trys', the 'not bads' the 'quite goods' the 'could be betters' — or how many attempts have been made to get to this standard and at what cost? Good display is admirable but it shouldn't become an obsession. Motives are important. If the adult intervention is more for the child's sake than the sake of the display — that's fine. If it is the other way round, the balance is wrong.

So, experiment with some 'effects' in order to mount a decent display which doesn't take hours and hours. Keep a stock of various sizes of backing paper cut in a variety of shapes — eventually the children can choose and mount their own pictures. Infants can manage this quite well with a little help and efficient tools (staplers, glue sticks). Old wallpaper books are a good source of attractive mounting paper.

I learnt whilst on my second teaching practice that a thick marking pen can enliven a communal picture enormously. The children had made a long winter frieze composed mainly of robins and bare tress. They had worked hard but somehow the result was rather dull and lifeless. I said so to the teacher who then quickly added outlines to some of the birds, legs to others, the mark of a wing to others so that   became
, then an outline to some of the trees. Within minutes the frieze was transformed. This sort of help would have been so welcome from the college art department.

An efficient stapler is invaluable for mounting a quick display. The sophisticated gun type is not necessary. Open up an ordinary one and it will do the job of fixing flat craft work to the wall quite well. Take care when using sellotape, it can ruin a freshly painted classroom in the space of a term. The 'Blue Tack' type of adhesive is useful within limits but it must be used properly — keep it clean and warm and knead it

thoroughly before use. Use a small amount — many people think that
the bigger the lump the stronger the hold. This is not the case. Also a
good deal of pressure is required. Trial and error will quickly teach you
how much to use for what weight and what pressure to apply.

Words can improve a display by setting it in a recognisable context. For example, imagine a display of a set of coloured paper circles
of varying sizes. It looks pleasing enough but it could be made more
interesting by the addition of say

    a) a title — 'Bubbles on a Windy Day'
    b) the clearly printed name of its creator upon each circle
    c) a question — 'Can you find the largest/smallest circle?

To see children take note of and discuss a display makes it more
than just a pretty backdrop. It then earns its keep as it were, as a valid
educational aid as well.

Some members of staff may show a special talent for display. Ask
for help if you feel unsure. You will learn a lot by mounting one or two
displays with 'an expert'. Look at attractive displays in your own and
other schools, in large stores and shop windows, and copy or adapt them
to your own situation.

Beware of always choosing 'the best' for display. It must be most
disheartening for a child never to have work displayed. Besides this there
is the effect on the child's idea of 'my ability' to be considered. In my
primary school I was firmly in the group of children whose work was
rarely if ever displayed. My one crayon design to be displayed in 7 years
has stuck in my mind. The fact that I can, 25 years later reproduce it
accurately perhaps indicates how important such an apparently small thing
can be to a child. Make sure therefore that each child's work is displayed
at least once in the year.

Now lets look at two aspects of Art and Craft in the light of the
following question, *How can you improve standards and increase individual
satisfaction for the children?*

Preparation and Organisation

These are of course vital in order to get the most out of your work
in Art and Craft. Much of the section on general classroom organisation
and storage applies here.

Not only should the children know where and how things are stored
but they should be able to take things out and put them away with as

little disruption as possible. As an Infant teacher I was caused constant annoyance and irritation by the children's painting aprons. A child would lift one down only to pull several others in its wake. No matter how often I sorted them out they seemed to be in a permanent muddle. Some years later I noted in a local nursery school the simple yet efficient use of two hooks to store the painting aprons

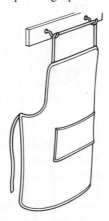

It was almost impossible for the children to get them in a muddle, (they did of course but only occasionally).

Children have to be helped to be organised simply telling them is not enough. So, your organisation should make it *easy* for the children to do art and craft work.

For example there should be a supply of cut up materials sorted into colours for collage work (the children can make this themselves, an old shirt box filled with margarine tubs works quite well);

- ready mixed wallpaper paste, (it keeps for ages in a screw-top jar);
- some paint and brushes where they can be got at easily; a communal roll of sellotape which the children know how to use (e.g. they fold over the end after cutting a piece so that it is easy for the next person to take some);
- a supply of drawing paper and mounting paper;
- a specific 'home' for useful items like the stapler, hole puncher, drawing pins, paper clips etc.;
- a supply of wool and string, and so on.

Label boxes and jars clearly so that visiting helpers (parents/students) find it easy to keep things in reasonable order. You will probably change and improve your storage as you go along. It is a good idea to wait until you have new children before making any radical changes otherwise a lot of time can be wasted. Keep you eyes open for ideas and storage devices which work for others and seem to be adaptable to your needs.

The children should know what to do when they have finished or when time runs out, how to clear up, wash a paint brush, replace the lid of a glue pot, etc. Some schools keep paint brushes permanently standing on their heads in paint. While there may be valid reasons for this like time saving it should not be the child's whole experience. The washing of a paint brush and care of materials generally ought to be an integral part of Art and Craft education. It is hard work to train children in the dull business of clearing up but its part of your job and if you make the effort at the beginning it will pay dividends later on.

Part of your preparation and organisation will include the provision of not only a variety of materials but also a *variety of the same material* e.g. paint, string, glue. To be able to choose the right tool for the job will help the children not only in Art and Craft but in many other areas too. In order to develop this ability the children will need more than one variety of say glue from which to choose. It is frustrating and off-putting for a child to try to stick something with glue which is not strong enough for the job. The same applies to wood/nails, needles/thread, modelling materials, paintbrushes, etc. There is no need for huge choice. The message to be got across is that some tools are more suitable for a given task than others. By choosing the most suitable tool available the task in hand is made that much easier and the finished result is likely to be more satisfactory. This message can be got across by as little as two varieties of glue, sticky tape, string, etc.

I once asked a head to order some poster paint blocks for me. He seemed surprised saying that solid blocks were rather restrictive and did not give the children the experience of mixing colours as powder paint did. This is true up to a point but it is not the whole story. I argued that the children should have the experience of both and that in some cases blocks had advantages over powder. Not the least of these is the fact that it does not need to be mixed — a great boon where time is short. (For example a child may want to paint a car yellow, the point here is not to mix blue and green until the 'right' yellow emerges but simply to get the car painted. In such a case poster blocks would be the right choice for the job. Moreover the having of poster blocks in the classroom could mean the difference between the child being able to paint the car at all or not.) Finally we agreed that in most cases powder paint gave the children a better experience of colour and texture etc., but that there was no harm in them having the occasional experience of solid blocks as well — and he ordered the blocks.

Stimulate interest before you start

In the light of the question at the beginning of this section this is well worth doing when at all possible. Talk round the subject first. Find out what the children already know or think about it e.g.

Picture of a Cockerel — you want the children to make a picture of a cockerel in paint, crayon, collage, etc. Firstly you could ask if anyone had ever seen a cockerel and get them to say where and in what circumstances etc. Ask them to describe what they saw in detail. Then you could show several different representations of a cockerel — discuss each one — the similarities and differences between them and so on.

You could look at some of the details of the actual bird either on a nearby farm or on a filmstrip. Observe such things as scales on legs and feet, claws, arrangement of toes, sheen on feathers, colours of various feathers, shape and colour of cockscomb, size and colour of eye, size and shape of break etc., also observe the strutting walk — children can imitate the jerky movements. Think and talk about some of the characteristics of a cockerel — is he proud, gentle, fierce, timid, etc.

Teach some useful techniques — the addition of white to represent the sheen on a feather; printing with mesh or net and sticking on sequins to represent scales; gradual mixing of two or more colours to achieve the desired shade, etc.

Make a collection of pictures from colour magazines which show all or any part of a cockerel.

Once your start investigating in such detail things will often begin to develop by themselves. The children will offer ideas of their own and bring in materials which can spark off further work.

Naturally you will not always have time for such detailed preparation nor would you wish to. Spontaneity is one of the glories of Art and Craft in the Primary school. Nevertheless a detailed investigation of a subject is always a responsible educational activity and the standard of Art and Craft output after such preparation usually bears witness to this.

Finally, don't forget the value of close observation. It is fundamental to high standard in Art and Craft yet so often it is sadly neglected or even completely ignored. Again the children have to be helped to 'open their eyes' simply telling them isn't enough. Try an experiment — ask a group of children to draw an orange making it as life-like as possible. A week (or so) later give each of the same group of children an orange to look at for say a minute to handle, smell, discuss, see how many descriptive facts they can compile together etc., then ask each child to draw an orange. The comparison between the two sets of drawings should give you food for thought.

Inspiration

Much of your art and craft will be linked to work going on in other areas of the curriculum. Here you won't have to think of 'what to do'. When it comes to Art and Craft for its own sake there will be times when you lack inspiration. Where can you go for help?

Magazines/Children's comics — flick through these from time to time. If it happens that you find something in a magazine in a doctor's waiting room ask if you can have the magazine and explain why. Tear out the relevant pages and stick them in a loose leaf folder. Even if you never use some of the ideas it will be a comfort to be able to browse through the folder when you are stuck for ideas.

Children's work — start now to keep examples of children's work (with their consent), and notes of ideas which prove successful. Date and name the children's work and jot down the ages of the children. This will help to jog your memory when you come to thumb through the collection at a future date.

Art Galleries/Museums — these may or may not operate an education service but at any rate organise a visit. Do some preparation yourself first. Before you take the children check on what they will see. Read any available literature on the exhibits so that you can help the children (and yourself) to make the most of the visit. (This is not the same as a regular 'pleasure' visit. Generally speaking our children do not have enough access/exposure to original art. There is a strong case to be made for taking them reularly to a gallery, just for pleasure. To be most effective the children should be taken in small groups of about six, and as far as possible it should be a voluntary activity.)

Novelty — naturally you cannot use this often or the point is lost but it's worth bearing in mind for when an opportunity presents itself. A colleague and I once took the top junior class to the annual school camp. On our return to school we were expected to set up a display for the rest of the school showing different aspects of the week's camp. Towards the end of the week I became slightly alarmed at the marked lack of drawings, paintings, writings and exhibits of any kind. On Thursday afternoon two of the children returned to our base carrying an old desk lid asking if they could paint a picture of the campsite on it, (the camp was also the county dump for unwanted classroom furniture and there was a great mound of broken desks and chairs outside the store shed). For some reason the idea caught on and inspired the children to great heights of dedication and industry. Later in the afternoon instead of the mass exodus to non-stop cricket or swimming, the children mostly opted to stay on site and work on an item for the display. Some painted on desk tops, others chose to do miniature paintings of flowers on chair legs, others carved animals from specially chosen pieces of wood: many of the exhibits were accompanied by a written description. We were allowed to take a selection of extra wood back to school for those children who wanted to do more work. The eventual display was splendid and had provided weeks of work and enjoyment.

There are many strands to Art and Craft and many ways of working them. As we said at the beginning the emphasis is on how not on what. How *does* a child, hold a pair of scissors, draw a straight line, mix the right colour and consistency of paint, print a regular pattern, sew a straight seam and so on.

Make sure you teach them how, then give enough scope for them to choose what — and you are well on the way to worthwhile Art and Craft with your children.

6. Religious Education

In the space allowed it would be impossible to delve very deeply into some of the problems of R.E. in the Primary school. It has become a muddled area and there is still need for a general reappraisal which would affect what goes on in the classroom.

Let's start (to continue the 'first things first' theme of this book) by asking a question: 'What is the purpose of R.E. in the Primary School?' We'll come to an answer in a moment, but first a look at the words Religious Education. What do they mean? What is religious education about? What has it got to do with? It has to do with educating (i.e. helping the children to learn about) religious thoughts, feelings, attitudes and knowledge, and is therefore to do with thought, kindness, courage, self-knowledge and love. It is not (or should not) be to do with forcing God, Jesus, Mohammed or anything else into uncomprehending minds and hearts. Anyway back to the question. If you can answer it with honesty and clear sightedness it will have an enormously helpful bearing on what things you do and how you do them. My answer to the question will not be yours. The purpose for each of us will vary and a whole book could be written on this alone. Since there isn't time for that is it possible in a single sentence to suggest a purpose about which there can be broad general agreement?

I'll try — The purpose of Religious Education in the primary school is so that the children can live and enjoy better lives.

The extent to which it fulfills this purpose depends of course on the quality of religious education which the children receive. Anyway this purpose or goal is rather long term and far off. Are there acceptable stepping stones in the meantime?

These 'stepping stones' may serve as interim goals to help you to organise the content of the children's religious education. But, they should always be leading to the ultimate goal (that the children can live and enjoy better lives), and this shouldn't ever be lost sight of.

Some interim aims might be then

The purpose of religious education is so that the children —

a) can grow in awareness and appreciation of themselves which involves an appreciation of the worth of others

b) deepen and widen their interest in the natural and physical world

c) are helped to grow in courage and kindness

d) come into contact with those questions which are bigger than and beyond their own lives.

We've come so far (and its quite a way) without actually mentioning a God. This has been deliberately done in an attempt to show you how much can be done in Religious Education in the Primary school without bringing in a deity at all. Too much 'religion' (in its narrow sense) — too early, can be counter productive. And, far from linking religion to a way of living and enjoying a better life it is seen as having nothing to do with life at all. Bashing away at the Old and New Testaments *WITHOUT* taking account of the children's interests or home lives probably does more harm than good.

Children start off full of wonder — look at a baby amazed by its fingers and toes or a three year old seeing snow for the first time. Gradually some of the wonder fades as learning and understanding take its place. This is as it should be. Something would be seriously wrong if a 10 year old was still gazing in amazement at his fingers and toes. And yet on consideration the hands and feet are amazing pieces of equipment. You can lead the children to consider these on a more sophisticated level (list possible functions, tasks which would be impossible without them, their design, comparison with other animals etc.), so that they may come again to see them as a source of wonder. Certainly most things (but by no means all) in this world can be 'explained'. But knowledge need not replace wonder. Indeed it can be argued that the more knowledge and understanding you have about something the deeper can be your sense of wonder about it.

So, in your dealings with the children you can, by your attitude and example, maintain and help to deepen their innate sense of wonder about the world and its contents both living and non-living. If you do this you will not be ignoring the children's religious education.

I once had to take a Sunday School class at short notice and with no props other than a booklet which gave an outline plan for a lesson about Noah with a few linked bible readings. This might have been fine if I'd had time to do the necessary preparation. Since I hadn't I abandoned the book and looked around the room for inspiration. Seeing some half withered chrysanthemums in the corner I remembered the astonishment and joy I'd felt on discovering as a 14 year old that all the petals on a dandelion were in fact flowers. While the children were getting the chairs ready I picked some of the chrysanths out of the vase and dished one out to each child. First I removed a 'petal' and asked if anyone knew which part of the plant this was. 'petal' came the unanimous reply. Together we looked at and discussed how in fact it was really a flower with its minute parts tucked neatly inside the tube-like petal. I then asked each child to count the number of flowers on each head. This took several minutes and some recounts were needed. Eventually the final tallies of 130, 138, 140, 141, etc. were entered in their books along with a short account of what we had done.

Now you may say this has as much to do with Botany as R.E., but that in a way is the point. R.E. should have to do with everything. These children seemed genuinely amazed and excited by what they had discovered and when we came to give thanks in prayer for the many wonders of nature they were perhaps better prepared to feel thankful than if they'd simply listened to the story of Noah.

Now, I am not advocating the banning or burning of the Bible and of course the story of Noah has wonderful possibilities for Primary school children. But there is much in the world that can lead the children towards God, much which is nearer their understanding (than the Bible), and which remains for the most part untapped.

One approach then, is through the world and the interest of the child. Is this enough? What about the Theology? Can we ignore it? If we do we exclude the children from huge chunks of human history, experience and activity. Besides the legal requirement for adequate religious provision does not, I think, intend that you stop short of theology.

So, theology then, but what theology? For many of you this will be decided by the circumstances in your school. Although Christianity is still the religion of the majority of people in this country there are many schools in which it is the minority religion. And, there are many more in which there is a cultural and religious mix.

Clearly those of you in schools where there are children of religions other than Christianity have to deal with R.E. in such a way as to include and incorporate those.

Much work has been and is being done to meet the challenges of multi-cultural education. Teachers on the shop floor in multi-cultural schools are in the best position to push forward the frontiers of knowledge about what these challenges are and how best to meet them.

Whether or not you are in a multi-cultural school though it is important that the children have a chance to investigate religious cultures other than their own. The less we know about something the greater is the chance for fear and mistrust to creep into our minds. It is hoped that by encouraging the children to develop a genuine interest in a different religious culture you will help to sow the seeds of tolerance and understanding in them. Also you will help to bring their own religious culture into sharper focus.

It is probably a good idea to embrace more than just the religious aspect of the culture. There are many ways to open up the avenues of interest —

— 'International' events of various kinds — project /theme/Festival

— fashion show — children dress up in clothes from a different culture, others describe the costume as it is displayed

— food tasting — parents invited to cook a national dish to bring into school to be tasted — recipe folder compiled etc.

Those of you who do not have a cultural mix in your school will have to use what you can in the way of books, visual aids, visiting speakers etc., to widen and deepen the children's experience and understanding of cultures other than their own.

Since my experience of R.E. with children has not been within a multi-cultural context but within that of Christianity my theological comments and examples are offered within that context.

The Bible

Bearing in mind the message at the beginning of this chapter is there an effective use to which we can put the Bible in the Primary school? In it there is literature of the very highest order, and of course many wonderful stories. References to these occur in every branch of our culture and the children deserve access to this as part of their heritage. The stories of the Old Testament lend themselves to every aspect of the curriculum — drama, maths, language, art and craft, history and geography. The children enjoy the challenge of things like —

— acting out the story of Jonah (making props for the inside of a whale is particularly enjoyable)

— making a watertight 'Moses' basket

— drawing David and Goliath to scale

— putting the animals into the Ark two by two

— listing necessary provisions for 40 days and 40 nights

— miming the story of the crossing of the Red Sea, and so on.

The children should hear and read the stories of the Bible in words which they can instantly understand. It is important therefore that you use a good modern translation (N.E.B., Good News Bible) *as well as* The King James version which of course has to be included in any worthwhile comprehensive study of the Bible.

Not only will modern translation give the children instant access to the stories, but it may also help them to appreciate the power and beauty of the language of the King James version if it is read either before or in conjunction with it.

The Old Testament

The Old Testament is teeming with stories suitable for primary school children. Obviously you cannot cover them all. Ideally an overall plan should be worked out between the staff so that wasteful repetition is avoided.

If however you are left to your own devices, then select stories which will hold some appeal for your children. While the stories are worthwhile in themselves and there is something to be pondered in each one individually there is a wider context into which the stories can and should be put. The children should be helped to see an overall picture as well as specific bits of it. For example you could select say the story of David and Goliath for its appeal of the mounting excitement, of the build up to the confrontation, and the emotional satisfaction of seeing the mighty giant of force felled by a gentle boy etc.

Enjoy and exploit the story through art, drama, music etc., but also bear the wider context in mind. Either before, during or after the story, sketch in the lead up and the follow up. It needn't be elaborate in fact the simpler the better — 'now remember Israel was a very new monarchy she'd only had one King. That was King Saul and he'd let God down so in a way David was a second chance' etc., etc. Then . . . 'well of course David went on to make a great deal of this second chance and became one of the most impressive kings Israel ever had, so much so that when in future times of national hardship and difficulty the people would long for a king who would be a 'son of David', that is a person who would be like David and who could bring them the same help and guidance,' etc. You may have to read up the background yourself but that shouldn't take up too much time.

At any rate giving a context like this to the stories will at least encourage the children to sense that there *is* a context and not just a rather meaningless collection of disjointed and disconnected people, committing disjointed and disconnected acts.

The New Testament

This tells us the story of Jesus and the struggles of the early christian church. The story of the birth, life and death of Jesus is one surely worth hearing by anybody's standards. Then there are Jesus' own stories and teachings infinitely relevant, infinitely surprising, infinitely worthy of investigation.

The older children, rather than receiving your or someone else's interpretation, should be given the opportunity to 'go back to source' to read a variety of translations so as to interpret the words in their own way. Ask them 'what do *you* think Jesus meant by the parable of the prodigal son, or the words poor in spirit?' Share you opinion (if you have one) of course, but allow them theirs even if they differ from yours. A useful way to investigate is to give two groups of Juniors a parable (or selected passage) to look at in detail and discuss, so as to be able to debate in open forum to the rest of the class what conclusions each group came to about the meaning of the passage.

Be wary of 'flogging the stories to death'; by the time a child has heard the same story a dozen times with the same interpretation, he or she probably stops listening. Also, if the stories have been told since the reception class, there's the added detraction of the stories seeming 'babyish'. So, select from the stories and teachings so that the children are presented with material suited to their age and stage. Resist the temptation to put meaning into every story every time. Allow the children to form their own interpretation sometimes, even if this means no interpretation at all.

Younger children should learn about God and Jesus in terms which are sufficient for their needs and understanding. Simplicity is the key here, and the children's own questions will be a good guide to their needs. Say too little rather than too much, and answer their questions simply but honestly, e.g.

Child   What is God like?

Teacher   I don't really know but I think he's very kind. What do *you* think he's like?

Child   I think he's like clouds.

Teacher   Perhaps he is. Shall we draw some clouds?

Often the child is not seeking a profound answer just one sufficient for that moment.

A profound or elaborate explanation will often be interpreted literally by a child or in a way he or she can understand. For instance it is not much help to tell a child that God always hears and answers our prayers if that child then prays for a bike and doesn't get one. In this case it would be no consolation for the child to be told that God knows what is best for us better than we do ourselves. Answer their questions in terms that they can understand, using words they are familiar with, and examples from their daily lives.

The message of Jesus should be handled with equal sensitivity and honesty with children at all stages of the Primary school. His is a message of forgiveness, hope and love with as many second chances as you care to take. But it isn't a magic code to be cracked by singing hymns or reciting prayers. He said it was good to be good. He didn't say it was easy. We would be misleading the children if we pretended otherwise.

Most of the content outlined in this chapter can and ought to be tackled whether you believe in God or not. Whether you believe that Jesus is the Son of God is a separate question from whether or not you should teach the children about Jesus. Naturally you cannot be expected to tell the children that He is the Son of God if you do not believe this to be true. This would be dishonest and unhelpful. Nevertheless you cannot avoid the question — 'Is there a God who exists whether we believe Him to or not?'

Your answer to this question will determine many things. Let us hope that it does not stop you from allowing the children to ask the question. The question will be present in a variety of forms in many of your children. Do not cheat them of an honest reply. Make it clear though when you state your case that they realize it is YOUR case. You have a responsibility here for dealing with vulnerable minds and hearts. Your influence may be greater than you realize. Treat this responsibility with respect. Faith apart, nobody has yet proved anything. Yours is not the right to tell the children what is SO, only what you believe. There is a world of difference between the two.

Those of you who are convinced one way or the other have not the right to be convinced *on behalf* of other people There are many things which can be done to enhance the child's religious education and which will not go against your conscience. The child's ultimate decision on religious matters will be made, based on what his or her own unique self makes of the various influences from home, school, peers, relatives and friends. Probably the less you deliberately set out to influence the child the more valuable your influence will be.

On the other hand the widespread belief that by leaving the slate of a child's mind blank he will be more fairly able to make up his own mind in matters religious — 'when the time comes', seems to me based on a false premise. 'When the time comes', unless there is something for him to take up how can he do so? Unless there is something to discard, how can he do so? Your job then, is not to hold back so that the children get nothing, it is to come forward in truth and honesty and give what you can for them to accept, reject, modify or adapt.

Finally what you do, how you act, will probably be much more important than what you say. All the words in the world will mean nothing if your example goes against them. To conclude this chapter then a brief word about Atmosphere and Assemblies.

Atmosphere

One of the suggested means of furthering the children's R.E. is by trying to provide experiences which the children can enjoy, appreciate, contemplate and occasionally be owerawed by. They also need time and space to absorb such experiences, and this is where the right atmosphere comes in. Not an atmosphere of piety or sanctity, but simply one of peace and quiet. There's probably too little peace and quiet these days for anybody's purposes, but certainly for effective R.E. the children should have regular experience of peace and quiet. This can take the form of a minute's silence after a prayer or half an hour's silent reading, or the many variations in between. They may put it to good use or little, make nothing of it — or much. This needn't concern you. Your concern is to see that they get it.

So much for atmosphere in general. What about a specific occasion when the right atmosphere is a vital and integral part of that occasion, for example the morning assembly?

The Assembly

These vary enormously in purpose, format and value. There ought to be staff consultation in order to arrive at an assembly which is best suited to particular needs and circumstances. Should it be the whole school every morning? Who should lead it? How much should the children be encouraged to participate? How can different beliefs be represented and reconciled?

There is a lot to think about (or there should be) and no two schools will arrive at exactly the same outcome. Whatever is the outcome in your school lets hope it does not include the depressing spectacle of rows of children trying to sing 'All things Bright and Beautiful,' with expressions denoting that the very last thing on any mind is anything either bright or beautiful. Lets hope too that it does not become a forum for a voicing of complaints about litter, lateness, unmarked clothing or running in the corridor.

Of course these things are important and have to be dealt with, but if it's imaginative involvement and a deepening of understanding you're after — these won't help to achieve it.

I've never actually seen this in practice but I cannot see why a separate weekly 'business' meeting to deal with things like lost property etc. wouldn't be effective.

Anyway here is a list of starting points for discussion to help you toward the kind of assembly which would be best suited to your own needs.

How far do you think the assembly in your school should:
- be enjoyable to all concerned?
- be a shared experience and responsibility for all members of the school?
- be concerned with spiritual nourishment and growth more so than any *particular* religious beliefs?
- seek to deepen the children's understanding rather than preach at them?
- be living and dynamic rather than dully routine?
- interact at many points with the curriculum and not be isolated from it?
- be concerned with things of abiding worth, courage and kindness of course, but ALSO, work well done, a new skill learned, effort, humble good will, etc?
- be used as an administrative device?
- show examples of beauty from the world of nature, art, music, science?
- acknowledge religious practices from more than one faith and demonstrate these when appropriate and possible?

There is, indeed, a lot to think and talk about. But think and talk you must if you care (as you should) about the childrens' hearts as well as their heads, their spiritual growth as well as their physical growth. Or, their whole selves and not just one bit of them.

7. History and Geography

These labels are probably unhelpful in the Primary school. They suggest a set of learning methods and content which IS HISTORY or IS GEOGRAPHY, and nothing else. In practice there is no such set. This mythical notion of History and Geography 'in a box' contributed to the opinion that really these subjects were unsuitable for the Primary school. Certainly there are aspects of History/Geography which are not suited to the Primary child. But there are many, many aspects which are. Whether you label these History and Geography is immaterial. It is not the label which is important, it is the content.

While these subjects are separate from each other, there is a great deal of common ground between the two. For example:

a) both deal with the actions and movements of people, the reasons for these actions, and the effect of the actions on the physical and human environment;

b) both deal with areas and countries of the world and their inhabitants — in their own right and in the light of how they relate to and impinge upon one another;

c) both involve the use of the basic skills of reading, writing, counting, measuring and calculation. And both can employ wider skills such as those of Art and Craft and creative writing.

Sometimes it is helpful to see History and Geography as different aspects of the same thing. There are a great many events which are neither just Geography or just History but a combination of both, e.g. Industrial Revolution, Growth of the Cotton Industry in Lancashire, Highland Clearances, Spanish Armada, etc.

When you can, use the common ground to advantage. Where you think it will be worthwhile, point out the significance of the inter-relationship between the Geographical and Historical aspects of a situation or event. Where there is no point in doing this treat each subject separately — e.g. there would be little point in trying to weave much Geography into the story of the beheading of Anne Boleyn.

Nowadays, History and Geography are mostly dealt with through themes of one kind or another. This approach grew from a desire to make them more relevant, interesting and enjoyable for the children. Sometimes this is successful, sometimes it is not. Some dangers are outlined in the chapter on *'Themes'*.

What do you think a child should gain in the Primary school from the study of History?

— some notion of the movement or unfolding of time

— an awareness of the far distant, middle distant and relatively recent past i.e. that the Danes came after the Romans but before the Tudors.

— an understanding of what life was like during at least one period in history — (this understanding can only come about by allowing the child to enter imaginitively into the period i.e. as many facets as possible of the life of the period are covered — clothes, food, cooking methods, transport, laws, population distribution, social attitudes etc.)

— knowledge of a few key figures in history

— the ability to see something of the similarities which exist from age to age, yet also to see the difference between the ages

— an understanding that history can be looked at from more than one point of view

And Geography?

— an understanding of some physical features — hill, mountain, river, stream, valley, coast etc.

— a knowledge of his own town/village and its immediate environment

— some knowledge of his country, its shape, size (in relation to its neighbours and the rest of the world)

— an 'in depth' knowledge of a country or area other than his own

— an understanting of the similarities/differences which exist between countries, and a knowledge of the inter-dependence of countries

— an idea of people's relationship with their environment — how the environment affects people in terms of occupations, clothing, housing and how they in turn affect the environment — farming, irrigation, building, pollution etc.

Obviously there's far too much here to be 'covered' by the time a child leaves Primary school. Even if you do not agree with all of these you will still probably end up with too ambitious a list. Select from it so that the children have time to enjoy and assimilate the work. They'll be better able to take these subjects up properly in the Secondary school if the work of the Primary school has

a) aroused their interest

b) given them some CLEAR ideas (that the Stone Age came before the Vikings) rather than muddled ones which have to unlearned.

Use textbooks to your advantage but beware of slavishly following them through from beginning to end. There are many more bad textbooks around than good ones. Before you give a textbook to the children, examine it with a critical eye. Do not assume that it will do the job it

claims to do. As you look through ask some critical questions
— is the text pitched at a suitable level for your children?
— is the text lively, interesting?
— do the illustrations match the text well?
— is all of the content relevant to your children or could you omit
some part of it?
Read a chapter yourself then ask yourself what you have gained
from that chapter. Look at any questions — do they fit the text? Do
they help to bring out the information you would like your children to
have? All this is not so time consuming as it may seem. It can be done
over a few lunch times or evenings. You will probably enjoy the exercise
(doing it together with a colleague is fun and you can learn a lot from
each other's approach). Time spent in this way will develop in you a
critical approach to textbooks which will in its turn help the children
enormously.

There are no hard and fast rules about what and how you teach
in History and Geography in the Primary school. There may be a school
policy from which you can learn, but mostly you will be left to your
own devices. However you decide to tackle these subjects here are —
i) some questions to ask yourself before you start;
ii) some useful aids;
iii) some points to bear in mind;
iv) some ideas which can be adapted to a wide age range and various
situations.

Questions

a) Have I got a reasonable amount of resource/reference material
before I start? (reference books, pictures, objects of interest, etc.) A
reasonable amount is not quantifiable but anything is better than one
textbook.

b) What knowledge/experience have the children already had here?
Ask the children themselves and previous teachers.

c) What are the main objectives of this piece of work? Do I want
the children to increase their awareness of a different country/period in
history, or do I want them to improve their ability to stick labels on a page?

d) Are there other teachers in the school who plan to undertake
similar work? If so can we collaborate?

Useful Aids

a) Time Line (History)

There are many designs to choose from and you will be able to devise one exactly tailored to your needs and physical surroundings. Here are some ideas which you can copy or adapt:

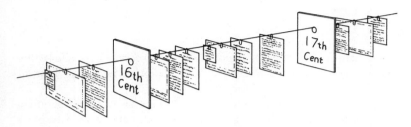

A piece of string is suspended across the classroom. Large paper clips are used to attach date cards of significant events. Centuries or periods are marked off by larger cards.

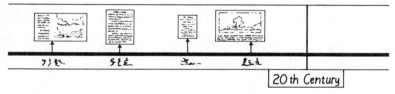

A simple strip of paper (the reverse side of a durable wallpaper works well) attached to the wall. A time line is then painted on, and notable dates are attached to the line.

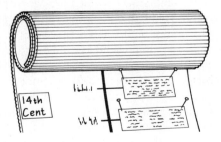

A roll of thick paper — (corrugated card is best since dates of the period in question, can be pinned on for the duration of the project and removed when the time line is 'rolled' to a different period).

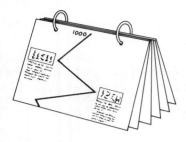

Large leaves of paper bound with ring binders. A large loose-leaf binder makes a durable case if you want the time line to pass into the reference book area.

You can make the line encompass as long or as short a period as you need to suit your purposes. Also there are various ways to block off specific sections of time, e.g. different colour for each century on long strip or different page in large folder. When covering a relatively short span e.g. 100 Years War, be sure to leave some space at either side so that children see the period as part of the whole and not as a chopped off period which is unrelated to anything else.

To be properly efficient the line must be well used. It must be referred to, checked, added to and changed from time to time. To stick up a time line at the beginning of term and then to practically ignore it is a complete waste of time. Unless it is used the children and you will very quickly fail to notice it, and any aid it could have given you will be lost.

b) Globe/World Map

We were told at college never to display a world map in the classroom before the children had reached the age of 8 or 9. This was partly to counteract the old fashioned image of the largely ignored map hanging on the classroom wall. It was also based on the assumption that young children could not comprehend a world map and worse that they might comprehend it wrongly. There is of course some wisdom in this. The walls of an Infant room do not usually accommodate a world map. At this stage there is a more pressing need for wall space to be used for large letters and numbers, pictures and visual aids more suited to the Infant level. Nevertheless a world map and globe should certainly not be barred from the Infant room. In these days of an ever shrinking world children have more contact than ever before with all corners of the globe. Many of them have relatives in Australia, Canada, New Zealand and the U.S.A., and hear of uncles, aunts and grandparents who go to visit these countries. They may even go abroad for holidays themselves. At any rate they are constantly in touch with different countries through the medium of television and radio.

In the light of this personal experience it is an excellent idea to show young children a globe of the world. You will find that they are naturally interested. Essentially this must be conversational exercise. You can hope that some children will pick up and retain accurate and useful information but you cannot expect it at this stage. Try to use as a big a globe as you can find. Talk about the various countries, trace round some of the interesting outlines with your fingers, compare sizes, pronounce some 'strange sounding names' just for the fun of it, trace the source of a river, the journey of a relative, find the source of a postcard and so on. If you link these beginnings of Geography to the children's personal experiences there will be no danger of them being irrelevant; —

'Paul's uncle has sent us this postcard from Africa — shall we try to find Africa on our globe? — here it is, let's see if I can follow its outline with my finger. Paul would you like to follow the outline, etc.'

At this stage a globe is probably more interesting to the children than a flat map, but even these if used in the way outlined above can be used to good effect.

The following aids are useful for both History and Geography and should be part of your 'starting kit' of resource material before you undertake a project.

c) Maps of all kinds

Maps of the underground systems of big cities, of train routes, of city centres, of shopping precincts, street plans, architects plans, historical maps, blank maps on which to show main cities/rivers, road/rail routes, population distribution, also sites of battles, of early settlements, routes of armies, plastic relief maps to show physical features of a region in three dimensions. Collect these when you can, many of them can be had for the asking.

Plastic relief maps are of course expensive and not usually found in the Primary school. You can, with the aid of papier mache make your own 3D models of a region. The accuracy of the model will depend on the age of your children. Younger children will find plenty to talk and think about in the making of a simple hill and valley model. Older children (top juniors) may be able to achieve greater accuracy of proportion and scale.

These topographical models can also be made for the re-enactment of significant battles in a history project. The discussion amongst the children about the height of the hill, the extent of the plain, the position of the army etc., helps them to enter imaginatively into the period so that it comes alive for them.

d) Good Pictures

Again collect these whenever you can. Do not wait until you need a picture for a specific reason — that is when you may not find just what you need. Having found something you like put it in a safe place until you can file it. Keep your pictures in some sort of order so that you do not have to go wading through the whole collection each time you need something. Older children can help to classify. Before you embark on a project have a quick look through your collection and take out anything of special significance to be placed in the resource box for the project.

Some points to bear in mind

a) A great deal of Geography and History is to be found quite easily outside the classroom. Take the children to see geographical aspects of the community, or physical features of the landscape. Visit places of historical interest in the local environment. There is plenty to be found if you look hard enough. At the primary stage you are attempting to fire the children's interest. A visit to a 'real' farm/factory/valley/castle is worth weeks of book work.

b) An important feature of the study of History in the Primary school is that it can allow a child to work for his or herself. It can help children to use reference material in such a way as to build up their own picture. The ability to work for oneself is a vital key to successful learning. This is not always recognised in the Primary school.

c) An important part of the study of Geography in the Primary school is the acquisition of accurate language. At one end of the spectrum will be the infant children with no idea of the difference between a forest and a few trees, (this is understandable especially if their only experience of a forest has been from a storybook where a few trees have been drawn to illustrate a forest). Further up the school you will be concerned with refining ideas of such Geographical terms as — population, mountainous, lowland, coastal, rural, urban, etc. A good way to check a child's understanding of a geographical term is to ask for a description of it in the child's own words. A child can remain under a misapprehension about a term for a long time. An explanation in his or her own words will bring to light any discrepancy of meaning which may have crept in.

d) Make sure that the content of your work here is relevant to the age range of your children. I have seen 7 year olds working on a project on France. They busily collected labels from wine bottles and French foodstuffs, pictures of localised national dress. French flags were drawn and coloured. Various items were stuck neatly into a folder. The children had now 'done' France. All this activity had gone on without the children seeming to sense anything of the Frenchness of France, that it was in any way different from Cornwall, that it was even physically separate from Britain. The project lasted for approximately half a term.

Although there are no hard and fast rules I would say that 'doing France' in this way for half a term would be inappropriate for this stage. France itself is not inappropriate but the approach must be much lighter — find it on a globe/map, talk about how to get there, the Ferry, the Channel — say some French words yes/no/please/thank you (the children will love this), *taste* some French cheese THEN look at the label etc. 'First things first' is as useful a guide when planning the content of your History and Geography projects as it is elsewhere in the curriculum.

Ideas

a) *Drama*

The drama of History brings it alive for us. It adds flesh to the dry bones of facts and dates. Use this important dramatic element in all sorts of ways to help make History come alive for your children.

Conceal a few Infants in a large cardboard box (free for the asking from stores which sell T.V.s, refrigerators etc.) to re-enact the story of the Wooden Horse of Troy.

Work with juniors on words to fit the possible feelings of Henry II when he heard of the death of Thomas à Beckett.

Cook a mock Elizabethan banquet — prepare and write out the menu — dress up to attend the banquet (you can achieve an amazing spread from a few basic items; sausages, bread, fruit etc. plus the will and imagination to turn these into the delectations of a banquet).

Let the children take an active part in re-living History. Let them fight the battles, die the deaths, experience the triumphs, the hardships, the persecutions which make up the real and living fabric of History.

b) *Story Telling*

Before books it was by the telling of stories that History was handed on from age to age. Stories have always been a source of universal enjoyment and learning. Make story telling a prominent feature of your work in History. Tell the story rather than read it when you can. Make your aim pure enjoyment rather than that the children should learn anything. Use a different method if you require them to learn a name or a date. There is an endless fund of stories and the variety is enormous. The stories are applicable to all ages. Look out for well written books which the children can read themselves. Badly written ones abound, and they can have a deadening effect. They can turn children away from History and generally do more harm that good. If in doubt about the quality — read it yourself — are you gripped or do you find your attention wavering? Encourage the children to tell stories aloud in their own words. Two children can sometimes hold the attention of the others better than one. Give them some time for preparation and let them rehearse in private if they want to. This activity is useful on many levels — for the children who tell the story to test their knowledge of the story, for the children who listen to hear a new and fresh interpretation in their own words and also for you, to learn what and how they have understood of what they have heard and read.

c) *Life in Grandma's Day*

It is said that many children do not really have much sense of historical time when they leave the Primary school. This does not mean that therefore Primary History is valueless. Rather it means that the emphasis in Primary History ought to take account of the fact of the children's limited sense of historical time. One way of reaching back in time which does take account of this fact is through the children's personal contacts. Parents, grandparents, elderly friends and relations can provide a real link with the past for the children. Ask them to bring in old photographs, postcards, letters, bus/train tickets, theatre/cinema tickets, gas/electric bills, rent books, pay slips, coats, hats, shoes, old toys, household equipment — anything which will bring the immediate past to life for the children. Using these 'real' objects you can build up a picture of what life was like in your community 50-70 years ago. The list of differences between then and now is staggering.

The children can help to mount displays, use some of the collected objects (with permission of the owner) as props in a play, write descriptions of some of the fashions to be seen on the photos, list buildings which have appeared/disappeared since 19 . . . , describe a journey to school in 19 . . . , list 10 similarities and 10 differences between 19 . . . and now. Some of the older members of the community may like to be invited to come in and talk about an aspect of their childhood to the children. The whole exercise should give the children a real idea of an age which is removed from their own in time, customs, fashions and attitudes, and yet is attached to their own lives by living and graspable links.

d) *Assignment Cards*

These can be used to good effect in Primary History to help the children to work for themselves. To help them in a limited sense to build up their own picture, and to form their own conclusions — ORGANISA-TION is vital. Make it quick and easy for the children to find the required information. Give specific pages of large encyclopaedias. You must thoroughly know the material through which the children will be working. If time allows you can provide exactly what you need by writing some of the reference material yourself. Older juniors experience a great sense of achievement through working for themselves. Once they have grasped the idea they can be left to work responsibly for remarkably long periods of time.

Assignment cards can be used to equally good effect in Geography. There is great scope here for work on the atlas. Initially the aim is simply to accustom the children to using the atlas, to increase their confidence in using it and to enlarge their interest in it. So, make the questions on your cards relatively simple and do not put too many questions on the card otherwise the task will become laborious. Probably 3 or 4 questions is a sufficient number to introduce the children to this kind of work. When you feel that the initial aims have been more or less achieved you can tailor the content of the cards to suit more specific needs.

i) From the map on page X find the name of a city in Scotland.

ii) From the key draw the symbol for railways etc.

Later stages —

i) From the map on page Y find a city on the south coast of Wales.

ii) On which page of the atlas can you find the longest range of mountains in England? Write down the name of this range.

iii) Which of the following countries is an island?

England   Scotland   Ireland   Wales.

The cards can be:

- re-enforcement exercises — content such that it consolidates work already done;
- testing exercises — content made up of questions which are specifically based on recent teaching;

• diagnostic — content such that it will show up any specific difficulties, e.g. difficulty in understanding the key.

If there is not a suitable atlas for your needs, you could make some simple ones.

It is not difficult to make a collection of maps. Indeed the making of a simple atlas is a good and worthwhile activity for older juniors to undertake for themselves.

e) *Treasure trails/maps*

These can be done by large or small groups of children and more than one trail can be followed at the same time. Probably though it is a good idea to introduce the idea to a small group and to follow only one map. In the hall or playground lay out boxes of different shapes to represent buildings, parks, trees etc. 'Hide' a treasure, then draw a map of its location. This can be done by you with the help of say two children. The others follow the map to discover the hidden treasure. The boxes can be rearranged and a new set of map makers chosen. A later development is the plotting of the immediate environment of a map — classroom, corridor, playground etc. Some maps will be easier to follow than others and some will be positively misleading to those who are trying to follow it. This is a good way to illustrate to the children the need for such things as standardization, accuracy of scale, use of common symbols, etc. Do not however at this stage be over fussy about accuracy for its own sake. The main object is to get the children to make maps, to read maps and to enjoy doing so.

f) *Puzzles and Games*

Various kinds of games and puzzles can be made and used to interest the children in different geographical aspects of the world picture. Sometimes the value will lie in the actual making of the game and in these instances the end product can be discarded fairly quickly. At other times the end product will be worth keeping, and therefore more care will be required in the making of the game. Here are some games which can be given a geographical slant:

Snap (numerous categories)

European Countries
World Continents
Areas of Britain
Countries of the World —

bold outline shapes drawn on stout card, name of country printed across

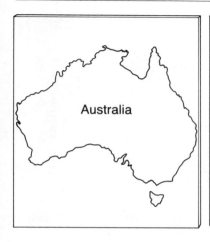

Australia

India

There are variations —

To help keep the noise down. Instead of shouting 'snap' on recognising a matching pair the child holds up a duster or grabs a rubber, which is positioned between the players. There will be disagreements about who grabbed the duster first but no more than there is about who shouted snap — and it is generally quieter. This game can be developed to help the children think of the countries in their world setting. On 'winning' a matching pair the child places one of the pair of countries on an appropriate position on the world map. This map has to be specially drawn to fit the game.

Jig saws —

Chop up maps of various kinds. Stick the pieces on thick card and cover with clear plastic.

On felt or light coloured p.v.c. do an outline drawing of the world or various parts of the world — Europe, Canadian Provinces, Australian states etc., also cut-outs in similar material of countries, provinces, states etc. The children then piece together the various sections of a region to complete the picture.

Painting by Numbers

You will need to supply a box of blank maps with the main physical features sketched in. Number these features and put the key somewhere on the map —

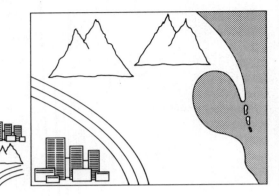

1 city
2 mountain
3 motorway etc.

Instructions can be on separate cards. Paint the cities red, the motorways yellow, the mountains brown, etc.

Quick Quiz Question Cards

Which country do you live in?
Do you live in the north, south, east or west of your town/city/village?
What is the native language of Spain?
Name one country which produces coffee?
Which is the longest river in America?

Two cards paper-clipped or rubber-banded together. One colour for questions, one for answers. The game can be played in pairs — each child answering as many questions as possible, then checking the answers on the answer card, or as a group — one child playing question master — reading the questions and keeping the scores — the others competing against each other. Alternatively the cards can be used by individual children to test their own knowledge. You can make the questions completely random as above, or you can concentrate on a specific area depending on your requirements.

There isn't nor should there be a blue print for the best progression in History/Geography in the Primary school. There is such a vast time and space involved compared to the childrens' direct experience of a few years and miles. It would clearly be unrealistic to set out to give them a 'sense of history' or a firm grasp of geographical concepts. Nevertheless there is worthwhile work to be done to

a) give the children some 'basics'. In History nowadays we do not expect a child to leave the Primary school knowing the names and dates of all the monarchs, battles, treaties, etc., from earliest times to now. But, surely we should try to help them to form some notion that the Normans came *AFTER* the Romans but *BEFORE* the Spanish Armada. Otherwise the vital element of the unfolding of time is ignored.

In Geography we may not expect a child at the top end of the Primary school to know the population of Japan, or the main export of Brazil, surely though we should want him or her to know how to get from home to the local library, what a valley is, what a coast is, which area of the country the school is in *(N.S.E.W.)*, etc.

b) excite their imagination to help them to *START* to contemplate a time and space far larger than anything in their direct experience.

In order to make sure the work *is* worthwhile, ask yourself as you plan the content:

Why? (i.e. what do I want the children to get out of this)

How (i.e. how will the work achieve this end)

and, then as you work through the content with the children note how far the *how* seems to be achieving the *why*.

8. Primary Science

Despite earnest attempts to establish Primary Science in the curriculum it is still not properly established. This is largely because many Primary school teachers lack confidence in this area. They imagine that in order to do justice to the subject they must know the answers to all sorts of scientific questions. This is simply not true. Remember in Primary work a good maxim is 'first things first'. And some of the first and most important elements of Primary Science are well within your grasp to transmit to the children.

What then, are these elements? What constitutes sound scientific method for the Primary school? How can a non-scientist provide effective Primary Science?

The answer is four fold

a) Curiosity

b) Questions —— how best to answer them —— efficient use of reference material/experiment in the spirit of 'lets look and see'

c) Experiment

d) Respect for things both living and non-living.

Curiosity

This is fundamental to a scientific way of looking at things. The wondering why (plus the desire and will to find out) is at the root of most scientific enquiry. Young children are naturally curious but they cannot of course be curious in a vacuum. So first, the environment of the classroom is important, and it should have things in it about which the children can *be* curious. Nothing elaborate is needed, ordinary things like mirrors, magnets, tadpoles, mustard seed, etc., have plenty of curiosity value. Second you can stimulate their curiosity by drawing their attention to condensation on the windows, leaves turning to the light, motes of dust in a shaft of sunlight and so on. You don't have to know the why and wherefores of such phenomena in order to arouse the child's curiosity. Third, and probably most important, you can encourage or discourage the children's curiosity by how you answer their questions.

Questions

These should be encouraged, and you can do this best by receiving the children's questions with attention and interest.

There are three possible responses to a child's question.

a) A direct answer — (what's the normal temperature of human being?)

b) An admission that you do not know, but that the answer could probably be found in x reference book from y member of staff — (what's the most common British bird?)

c) A suggestion for an experiment to find the answer — (what's the boiling point of water?)

There are also responses such as, 'hang on William; see me later about that Diane; not *now* Sara.' While these are sometimes necessary, they do nothing to encourage the child's interest or curiosity.

How you respond will depend on the time and circumstances of the question, but it is important for a child to see that most of his or her questions *can* be answered, otherwise the questions will just stop coming. It is also important that *you* realize when a child needs an answer quickly. If your automatic response is 'look it up' or 'work it out', the child will quickly lose interest.

Ask yourself why the child needs the answer, e.g. when a child asks say 'how many legs has a ladybird?' (a junior could be completing a crossword, an infant could be making a picture), it is better to say six than to tell her to look it up. Depending on the circumstances you could jog her memory and remind her that a ladybird is an insect, but if this doesn't help then *TELL* her. Do not make your answer to every question another hurdle. Your job is to help the children over the many hurdles they will meet. *NOT* to place unnecessary ones in their path.

The following story well illustrates the need for direct answers. A boy of 10 had devised a long and involved scientific problem. He was eagerly working it out in his bedroom. Twice he walked past his father in the sitting room to his mother in the kitchen. He asked her to work out mentally some difficult computation. When he came down a third time the mother asked him why he did not ask his father. 'Oh he'll tell me to work it out' came the reply. For that child, the working out of the whole problem was the important thing. He had therefore gone about achieving this end as quickly and as sensibly as he could. To have held up his progress by making him work out every wretched computation would have dulled his interest rather than sharpen it.

So quick answers then, when necessary. But there are times when a quick answer is not the best response, or even a possible one — if you do not know the answer. When an answer is to be found in a reference book, how can you make sure the child is confident about using it? A child has to be taught how to use reference material, then given a chance to practice. It is not something which comes naturally.

Make up lists of words to be looked up in a given time. The object is to familiarise the children with a dictionary, so speed is more important than the meanings.

Devise work to familiarize the children with reference books. e.g.
- Which chapter (from the contents list) is on Fishing?
- How many pages are in the index?
- What does the key on page x show?
- On what page of the index can you find the word Astronomy etc.

To use reference books properly requires enthusiasm, patience, the knowledge of the alphabet, the knowledge and understanding of a contents list, an index, a key, the awareness that most reference books contain their own keys located at the front of the book. These things are important. Clearly, if a child spends half a morning or even half an hour struggling to find a reference to something, then first things have not come first. There will be times when the best help you can give will be to look up the reference for the child. When you have the energy you can give further help by 'thinking aloud' — 'right Meteor — that could be in the X encyclopaedia under 'M' or in the Y book of information under Astonomy, now lets have a look in the index, ah yes, meteor pp — and — , etc.' Naturally you will not have the time or the energy to do this often, but even once or twice will be better than never.

At any rate before a child is asked to 'look up' anything take a few seconds to check that a) he knows *where* i.e. in which book, and b) *how*, i.e. what are the possible headings to look up. This will not be necessary when you know your children well. Even then, though, it is a good idea to check up from time to time on their reference skills, to see that they are making as efficient use as possible of the material.

Naturally they will be useful in areas other than Primary science, but they are crucial here if a child is to maintain interest because they allow the child to get on and find out for herself. Without them the child could waste time hanging around waiting for your assistance and runs the risk of losing interest altogether.

A third possible response to a child's question (e.g. 'What happens to the sugar in your tea?') is a suggestion that she 'try and see,' or —

Experiment

An experiment will not always be the result of a child's question. Sometimes it will be initiated by you. Whatever the reason for the experiment use it — to show the children something about scientific method — first, the question, then the hypothesis (or guess), then the testing to see, and then occasionally something approaching a conclusion. You can show the importance of *close* and *detailed observation, imagination, accurate recording*. You want the children to see an experiment as a possible way of proving something. They should also realize that without care the experiment can be useless. i.e. *attention to detail* is important as slip shod work could ruin an experiment. Up to a point you can allow the children to conduct their own experiments. Here you will supervise more than participate. Allow the children to make mistakes, i.e. do not correct every single mistake in order to save the experiments. A child often stands to learn more when things go wrong than when everything runs smoothly.

Expensive equipment is NOT necessary. Indeed there is a lot to be said for avoiding the use of sophisticated equipment. It can distance the children from what is actually happening. By the same token there is much to be said for the children making their own simple apparatus.

There is often much to be learned about an experiment in the actual making of the apparatus. Also it is possible that if you use ordinary household items to make apparatus, the children will be more likely to see science as in and of the world and not something which is separate and apart from it.

There are plenty of books around from which you can make up your own list of basic requirements for the making of simple equipment. Go to the library or to a good bookshop and look through a selection of science books for young children. You will find the same experiments crop up again and again. It is not difficult to equip your classroom with the necessary basic requirements to conduct a wide range of experiments.

Sometimes an experiment can arise out of an unlikely starting point. I once told my class of 10/11 year olds of an incident which had occurred during the previous weekend.

A member of my family had called around tea time. Having made some tea I put a tea cosy on the pot and placed the pot beside the fire. A comment was made that beside a fire, tea cosies were pointless. I mentioned the incident in passing to the children on Monday morning. One child suggested that we might do an experiment to find out whether tea cosies were pointless beside a fire. Luckily it was an old school and we had a covered solid fuel fire in the classroom. The experiment went as follows:

- Two identical teapots were found.
- A tea bag was placed in each.
- An equal amount of boiling water was poured into each pot.
- One pot was covered by a tea cosy, the other left uncovered.
- Each pot was placed beside the fire in the classroom.
- One hour later the temperature was taken of the tea in each pot.
- It was discovered that the tea in the covered pot was significantly hotter than that in the uncovered pot.

During the general discussion which followed the experiment it was suggested that the tea would probably be drunk in less than an hour and therefore the conclusion (that tea cosies had a useful function even beside a fire) could be wrong. Some children repeated the experiment the following day and reduced the cooling period to half an hour. The difference in heat loss between the two pots was less significant but still measurable. The children went on to discover the point at which the difference in heat loss between the two pots would be too slight to be measurable.

The whole thing generated a great deal of discussion and interest. We encountered the difficulties involved when setting up an experiment with a control, i.e. that two similar teapots would not do and that they had to be as near identical as possible. We looked briefly at heat loss and retention — made a small collection of good and poor conductors of heat. We noted everyday objects which were based on a similar heat retaining principle to the tea cosy — (duvet, lagged hot water tanks, quilted anoraks). All of this falls squarely into the realm of science, all is well within the childrens' interest range, and at no point is the work beyond the capabilities of any Primary school teacher.

Another starting point is to use easy instant experiments to direct the childrens' minds to the what and why of such questions as: What happens —

- when a lump of ice is left in a saucer in the classroom
- when a spoonful of water is dropped on to a piece of glass/a piece of blotting paper
- when a spoonful of sugar is stirred into a glass of water
- when a crisp biscuit is left on a plate in the classroom overnight
- when a wet sock is left on a warm radiator overnight
- when a shallow basin of water is left in the classroom for a week
- when a piece of bread is left in an airtight container for a week.

These can be developed in as much depth as your circumstances allow. Try not to let things grind to a halt just because you do not know the answer to why cakes and biscuits should not be stored in the same tin/why a penny looks bigger underwater/why an electro magnet will lift more hair clips when more current is added . . . . You can easily find out the answers to these questions — ask member of staff, your family and friends. This way you will be learning alongside the children and be less likely to make assumptions about what and how they understand and therefore be very well placed to give them the kind of help they need.

Where can you look for help if you do not yourself instantly see the potential science in things around you? One answer is in science text-books for the Primary school. BUT THESE MUST BE USED WITH CARE. Slavishly following a course in a textbook can be as unhelpful to the children's scientific development as doing no science at all. So, use books by all means but pick and choose from them to suit your children. Do not start or end a lesson at a given point just because the book says so. Add extra information and omit some sections so that the book fits you rather than the other way round.

A lot of accessible science can be found in the perhaps unlikely source of old fashioned encyclopaedias. *Wonder Book of Knowledge for Children, The World's Wonders, The World of Children* are the kind of titles to look for. They can be picked up at jumble sales, secondhand book shops even the school attic. Although the pedantic tone of some of these books may be off-putting at first it is offset by the unsophisticated approach to the science which makes it that much easier to understand and extract. So if you find the modern books rather daunting in their sophistication, it might be worthwhile for you to try and find some of these older books which adopt a gentler approach.

Living Things

The traditional 'Nature Study' is no stranger to the Primary school curriculum. Perhaps because of this it ought to be scrutinised afresh and looked at in the light of Primary Science. It is good that young children should have an opportunity to become familiar with and learn about plants and animals. It is desirable also that this learning should produce more than a vague notion of the plant and animal kingdom.

Use the same approach to the study of living things as you would to other areas of Primary Science, i.e. —

a) *Question*

The children will have their own questions — encourage and extend these — point out features of living things in such a way as to encourage the children to question why there are — hairs on the leaf of a fox glove/prickles on a holly leaf/bright spots of colour at the base of a tulip petal/whiskers on a cat, etc. In the same way point out such things as the lightness of a feather/the marking on the skin of a mackerel/the oil seed rape growing in fields/the lightness of thistle down/buoyancy of the outer skin of a coconut/the wings on sycamore fruits, etc. The questions can be answered in whatever depth you deem to be appropriate but an important part of any answer will be —

b) *Observation*

As far as the Primary school is concerned this is probably more important in the study of living things than it is in other areas of Primary Science. This is especially true when dealing with animals. The children can, almost by observation alone, find out about such things as

— the locomotion of a snail/caterpillar/earthworm/gold fish
— the diet of a sparrow/thrush/robin/blackbird
— the life cycle of a frog/butterfly, etc.
— the colour of buttercups/daisies/forget-me-nots etc.

— the shape of a guinea pig/rabbit/hamster etc.

— minute detail (with the aid of a magnifying glass) about the scale of a fish/bark of a tree/feather of a bird/fossil of a shell, etc. In a rich and varied programme of Primary Science the children will experience all of these. The emphasis, though, should be on allowing them to experience the thrill of observing natural form. It should not be on teaching formalised knowledge about botanical or zoological structure.

One way to help the children to observe closely is to make some question sheets. These can be on isolated objects e.g.

Sea shell/daffodil/geranium/walnut/apple/rabbit/snail

Or you can make sheets to accompany a specific project. In either case make the questions *specific* e.g.

What is the approximate length of this flower?

What colour are the petals?

Draw the shape of one of the petals.

NOT

What do you notice about this flower?

Some questions of a general nature will be necessary. These will allow the child to put his own point of view and also show you how he sees a certain thing. Nevertheless these questions ought to be kept to a minimum, (say one of two per sheet).

c) *Experiment*

This is not the place to go into a debate about the pros and cons of vivisection. It is though the place to say quite unequivocally that the work you do with living things should increase rather than diminish the children's respect for these things. The growth of respect for things other than ourselves is gradual and long term. That is, it is not naturally present in small children. This was graphically displayed to me when I discovered my 2 year old happily chomping her way through a live slug she'd found in the garden, and when I overheard one of my 9 year olds yelling 'you rotten bugger' to a classmate who'd just stamped on a bee 'for fun' — (the dilemma was whether first to respond to the 'bad language' or to the act of wanton cruelty. I hope I did the right thing.)

Education should foster the growth of respect for things other than ourselves. So, start by *telling* the children you think this respect *is* a good thing, then be *very* careful about what you DO to animals. Do not experiment with them unless you are sure of your ground. Part of your work in Primary Science is to foster in the children a healthy respect for forms of life other than their own. It is easy for a child to become so caught up with his experiment that he forgets he is dealing with living creatures.

I once experienced of a project on Wasps and Bees. It started off well, gained momentum and became the vehicle for some excellent work from two boys of average ability. Suddenly things seemed to go 'over the top'. Wasps and bees were being caught and killed in an unacceptable almost cruel fashion to serve the latest experiment. The fault was mine. I was so pleased to see the boys involved with and deriving such pleasure from their work that I let the project go beyond the point of its natural conclusion. I ought to have stepped in and helped the boys to bring the project to a close before the experimenting for its own sake took over from any real interest in wasps and bees.

In your work with living things in Primary Science it is good that you transmit the idea of science as a constructive rather than destructive force, though of course it would be dishonest not to admit that it has been destructive. It is good that through science the children may glimpse something of the unfathomably rich and complex fabric of life which covers the earth. And, that they move towards an appreciation of the interdependance of all things, towards a respect for the ecological balance of nature, (but without becoming obsessive about it). Nature is bountiful and is well equipped to cope with the odd bunch of buttercups being picked, or the single twig of lambs' tails being gathered. It is the fullscale *disregard* for her which upsets the balance.

It is good too that you transmit an unsentimental view of nature and its living things. A kitten playing with a ball of wool may delight the onlooker but the extension of this is the cat killing the bird. Living things kill each other (man more than most). Survival is a struggle and living things are usually produced in sufficient numbers to accommodate predatory killing on an enormous scale. The harsh facts of nature are as true as her beauty, and as such should be made available to the children.

So, living and non-living things will make up your content in Primary Science. What though are the important concerns? First the method. A rough plan for what you might follow during the year is a good idea but what it *is* doesn't matter. Aim to teach the children the scientific method (questioning/observing/testing/checking before attempting an conclusion) as an *approach*. Second, be prepared at any time to set aside your background plan in order to let the children's interests and enthusiasms lead you to scientific discoveries which are fresh, interesting and illuminating to the children.

The bias in this section has been towards Juniors because this is the area where most of the difficulty lies. Infants on the whole (and of course their teachers) cope very well. For the children at this stage life is a mixture of myth and reality, science and magic. They see motes of dust lit up in a ray of sunlight as 'crumbs dancing in the sun' — or their breath on a cold day as 'making pictures in the air'. For them it is enough that the steam is 'pushing up the lid of the kettle', air pressure and density don't come into it. Nor should they. The younger the child the more one has to be dictated *by* the child. This is as true in Primary Science as anywhere else. So, only give infants as much science as they seem to want/need. Again, the best guide here will be their questions and general conversations.

If a child of 5 or 6 asks 'why does that cork float' it is often enough to say 'because corks like to float' rather than 'because it displaces a volume of water which is heavier than itself'. Hand in hand of course with the simple explanation goes the provision of, in the case of this example, a large quantity of objects which will demonstrate to the child the whole floating/sinking spectrum. This is so that the child is coaxed onwards to the point (maybe years later) at which a scientific explanation will be understood. Naturally if a child seems unsatisfied with your explanation ('Corks can't *like*', she may reply), then you have to go a step further e.g. 'Well it's hard to explain, the cork pushes some water out of the way and the water tries to get back to its own place, it pushes back against the cork and keeps it afloat.'

The point is that the answers should be adequate for the child's needs. It isn't a matter of watering anything down. It is a matter of giving an answer which will best serve the child's development. That is, an answer which will satisfy the child for the moment but which will at the same time allow him or her to move on to further questions.

9.   Physical Education

Motivation will not be a problem here. Most (though not all, children thoroughly enjoy P.E. in the Primary school. Your task really will be to squeeze the maximum benefit out of it for the children. You can do this if you treat P.E. seriously. Some of you may be tempted to see P.E. as a way of letting the children romp around to 'let off steam'.

The traditional view was that P.E. had only a limited effect on the child's well being, i.e. his physical well being was affected only in the narrowest sense. This view has now largely been rejected. Physical education is now understood to have a valuable contribution to make to the child's all-round development. Alongside the change in attitude has developed a change in content. As well as the traditional gymnastics, jumping, climbing, throwing, catching, team games, etc., there are now many more avenues of physical education open to Primary school children e.g.

Movement/Dance

Where the children are encouraged to use their bodies as a means of self expression. Part of the aim here is to increase a child's awareness of his or her own body — its potential and its limitations, the range and quality of movement of which the body is capable.

There is a lot to be learned from the experts here. If you feel inclined in this direction, seek out and take advantage of any in service courses which may be on offer, (or out service ones for that matter). From such courses you stand to gain on the level of your own personal development and therefore also on the level of what you can bring to the children.

Formal Dancing (country or folk)

This affords a different experience but an equally valuable one. It requires a skillful touch to achieve the correct balance for primary children. Not so formal that you drive out the fun but formal enough so that the children do actually learn the dance. They ought to learn the dance so that they can do it almost automatically. Once this is achieved they will really be able to enjoy the dancing and also attend to things like grace and poise.

I remember a reasonably successful way of introducing country dancing from a school in Hertfordshire. Each Friday for 20 minutes before the afternoon session started, the whole school had an open invitation to come to dance in the hall. Usually the deputy head led the dancing and organised the music but the head and other members of staff took over when necessary. Almost one third of the children turned up regularly but not always the same third. The age range was from 5 to 11 and usually 4 or 5 members of staff turned up to help out. The whole thing was completely voluntary and some weeks were more successful than others. On the whole it was well worth doing. By the time the younger children were old enough to learn some of the dances in class time, they had absorbed enough idea of the dance to make their teacher's job that much easier.

Swimming

The opportunities for Primary school children to learn to swim have greatly increased over the past two decades. But by no means all children can swim by the time they leave Primary school. All children should learn to swim while they are at Primary school. Not only as a necessary part of 'equipment for life', but also because of the wider experience which swimming can offer, e.g. the challenge to come to terms with a new and totally different environment, the sense of achievement on learning to swim, the increased self confidence etc. Take what steps you can to ensure that your children avail themselves of every possible opportunity. The younger the child the more likely he will be to greet the water without inhibition. Some years ago a local Primary school raised funds for an indoor pool to be housed in an unused classroom. The head of a nearby nursery school heard of it and lost no time in negotiating a weekly slot for her 4 year olds. There are usually too few swimming pools for the number of children who need them. Occasionally though there are pools which are under used. It is worthwhile to enquire into every possibility. If you feel strongly enough about it and where it would be viable, you could even launch an appeal for a small swimming pool in your own school.

Volleyball/Netball/Football/Gymnastics

These give the children the experience of exerting their skills not only for personal pleasure but also to serve a team. Gymnastics is slightly different in that usually the team is secondary to personal endeavour. In the others 'the team' and personal endeavour should merge into one. Where there are school teams, the children have the added bonus of meeting others from different schools, visiting these schools, and playing hosts in return.

Tennis

Since this is a favourtie of mine I wish I could have included it in the above list. The great pity is that our junior children do not have more access to tennis courts and coaching than they do at present. Many children never hold a tennis racket till they reach Secondary school, and even then very often the access to courts and coaching is pretty limited. It is such a missed opportunity, not only to find potential talent but also to provide some children with a source of pleasure and fulfillment in their adult lives.

The Unwilling Athletes

What about the children who do not take to physical exertion? Their reasons are various: they feel that they cannot perform well; they do not feel in tune with their bodies and are awkward and embarrassed by them; physical exercise is not enjoyed at home; or, they simply don't like it. For these children P.E. can come to be associated with feelings of shame and humiliation: never 'getting it right'; always coming last/missing the ball/letting the team down, and so on. The older the child the greater the suffering. Coercion will do nothing to incline a child towards the pleasures of physical exertion. It is almost certain to have the opposite effect. A sensitivity towards those children is required. Try to assess the reasons for the dislike of gymnastics/field games/dance or whatever. Let them opt out occasionally ('those of you who have chosen not to play rounders this afternoon can bring your work to the field and work by me/take your work into the hall where Mrs X will keep an eye on you'). It alleviates the strain for them and it can lessen their resistance no end.

It isn't possible to let them opt out all the time of course. Besides in the Primary school very often the children are *still deciding* whether or not they like this or that — 'I used to hate team games in Mrs A's class but I really enjoy them now'. So try an occasional shift of emphasis, let the child try the same thing from a different angle, e.g. Ann loathes the gym but likes ball games in the playground.

Teacher

> 'we won't have all the apparatus out in the gym today only the ropes and climbing frame, and the small balls. We'll see how many different games we can invent using the small balls.'

Groans from the rest of the class probably but for once Ann has a chance to enjoy the gym. The wider range of content will perhaps help more children to find some aspect of P.E. which appeals to them.

Another encouragement for the non athlete is a P.E. content in which the best is NOT always a foregone conclusion. Occasionally therefore devise games in which athletic skill is not the main advantage, e.g. games based on

> Tug 'o War where strength is the advantage

Egg & Spoon where balance and patience matter most

Obstacle where the small and deft have the advantage

. . . and so on.

Having done all you can to entice the children towards P.E. and to eliminate possible barriers for them, you should remember that for some, physical exertion is simply not enjoyable. In their case there are no mental blocks to remove and coercion as a means of changing their attitude is a waste of time. The best you can do for these children is to reduce the amount of compulsory P.E. but at the same time keep an eye open for new ploys to tempt them in.

The Natural Athletes

These deserve the chance to develop their talents as far as possible, and to receive just praise in sporting events of various kinds. Where individual competition is the aim (in order to find the 'best') there is something to be said for voluntary participation. I'm not sure of the wisdom or kindness of causing stress to a child by forcing him to run/swim/play in a competition in which he *knows* he will be among the last/bottom/worst.

Nevertheless the athletes deserve due praise. Some schools perhaps unwittingly deny their children such praise. These schools, in an attempt to eliminate 'competition', have abandoned the traditional sports day for an all winners no losers 'Fun day/event'. The races are all obstacle or novel in some way and every child receives a prize.

The first such event I witnessed had been advertised as a 'Sports Day', I expected the usual run of events. Noting that there were no flat races on the programme I asked the person sitting next to me (a mother of one of the children) if there were to be any. 'No', came the disgruntled reply, 'running's the only blooming thing David's good at and they've gone and cut it out.' She was right to be disgruntled. Her child was being denied his (perhaps only) chance to 'shine', and to do something really well. Yes, it's always the same few who win the flat races but being good at something isn't a disgrace to be hidden away. It is something to be enjoyed, celebrated and shared. It shouldn't be overrated either, but it certainly shouldn't be denied.

Competition is a perfectly natural impulse and as such it can be used to excellent effect in education. It is the misuse of competition (when it is introduced at the wrong time for the wrong reasons) which causes the harm, not the competition itself.

Discipline

This is worth special consideration in the light of P.E. in the gym because the children will be more than normally excited and noisy, and there will be an added safety risk.

Make a rule that whenever the children enter the gym they practise some simple exercise — deep breathing/relaxing and contracting various muscles/ankle circling, etc. Whatever the exercise it must be done either sitting or lying down. You may be delayed for some reasons — to round up stragglers or to talk to a member of staff. It is necessary that children know what to do while they wait for you, otherwise things could very quickly degenerate into chaos. Chaos which you will have to sort out. Many teachers insist that the children sit down and do nothing while they wait. This is fine from a safety point of view but not from the point of view of P.E.

Give the children a signal at which they must stop instantly. The signal is unimportant (whistle, hand clap, voice command), the instant they stop is the important thing. Take the trouble to spend time and energy on achieving this. Nothing will wear you out quicker than having to shout stop half a dozen times in a rising crescendo — nor will it help your control, and control is essential in the gym.

Go over the safety aspects in the gym from time to time (these will vary from school to school. This need not take more than a few minutes but it is important. Do not wait for an accident to occur to remind the children of the safety rules.

If you find that things tend to disintegrate towards the end, change tactics and take what steps you can to bring the lesson calmly to a close. One way is to give the children responsibility for putting away equipment. Make a feature of how well it can be done. You can have all the children watching while one group puts away one lot of equipment then a different group puts away another, etc. Another idea is to give the children something to do when they have finished — exercises like the ones already mentioned, or mental exercises — 'when you have finished lie down and see how many parts of the body/outdoor sports/indoor sports/famous football or tennis players/pieces of sports equipment etc. you can think of and name OR, is it possible to empty your mind? See how long you can think of absolutely nothing. You may be able to allow the children to return to the classroom to get dressed as and when they are ready, i.e. without waiting for everyone else to be ready, but you will have to know you children very well before you do this.

Responsibility for Equipment

Apart from its use as an aid to discipline it is good that children should be given responsibility for equipment. They should know where and how things are stored. It is in a general sense part of their Physical Education. I once taught Infants in a school which had previously been a secondary school. Consequently most of the equipment in the gym was too heavy for the Infants to lift. Nevertheless I was unhappy that my children were denied any participation whatsoever. Some older juniors put out the equipment at the beginning of the week and since the gym was not used for anything else the equipment stayed out for most of the week. I had a word with the older children and arranged that on my gym days they would put out only the most cumbersome equipment. This left my children to put out the small apparatus as required. Being able to participate more fully increases the experience for the children. A great deal of learning potential is lost if everything is done for them. Besides, the children love being involved. The more they can participate in aspects of school routine the more they will feel relaxed and at home, and the better able they will be therefore to give of their best.

Clothing (see also Health Education)

From the very beginning the children ought to change out of day clothes into suitable light clothing. Where possible working in bare feet ought to be encouraged. Otherwise well fitting plimsolls should be worn. For some reception children, changing for gym is a traumatic ordeal. You may encounter tears and tantrums at the prospect of having to part with their clothes and shoes. It is possible that these children associate their clothes with comfort and protection. Sometimes you can indulge them until you have gained their confidence enough to be able to coax them into dressing properly for P.E. Sometimes a brisk approach is better — 'come along now off with this jumper, now your shoes'. It can happen that the longer you indulge a child the greater the eventual trauma becomes. You will be the best judge of the appropriate course of action for a particular child.

There is an obvious link between P.E. and Health Education of which good use could be made, and yet it is often neglected. There is a reason for changing clothes/working in bare feet etc. You probably shouldn't take up the children's actual P.E. time with talk and chalk, pen and book, but at least give regular reminders. A quick mention while they are changing or a few words at the end of a lesson will be better than nothing. The connection between physical exertion and, heart rate, rate of breathing, perspiration, muscle tone, etc., may gradually emerge so that the children will see one thing as part of the other and vice versa. Physical education is crucial to a well balanced curriculum. It can have such a positive effect on the children's well being that it indirectly improves their work in other areas of the curriculum. First though, it is important in its own right. Recreation and leisure are now a feature of more people's lives than they have ever been before. P.E. presents a marvellous opportunity to encourage children to want to take exercise in their own leisure time. It can offer examples of enjoyable and worthwhile recreational pursuits. It can foster the idea that good exercise usually goes with good health. It can, like Drama, help to extend the range and variety of social groups within the class. It can therefore improve the quality of social harmony between the children, and give individual children a greater capacity for tolerance and understanding.

10. Health Education

This used to be a relatively simple matter of 'health and hygiene', but with the earlier maturation of children and the greater awareness generally of health matters, health education is now somewhat more complicated. Some areas are 'easier' than others —
— Dental Care/Road Safety are fairly straightforward
— Diet/Exercise/Rest are less straightforward, bound up as they are with home attitudes and influence
— Smoking/Drugs and Alcohol are further compounded by the teacher sometimes having to adopt a hypocritical stance
— Sex Education is probably the most contentious area of all. It has to be evolved from a consensus of opinion of home/school staff/head teacher and individual class teacher. Its success will largely depend on the harmony of purpose achieved by these separate groups.
Another strand to the complexity is the unanswerable question of how much responsibility the school should take for health education. Can't we reasonably expect the home to deal with this? The question is unanswerable in that there are as many answers as there are schools, homes and children.
Finally what IS health education? So much of it could reasonably be expected to be covered by other areas of the curriculum (P.E., Science

(human biology), basic hygiene). But what we can reasonably expect doesn't necessarily happen. Clearly health education is not a simple matter. Nevertheless it is an important one. Because of this, strategies have to be worked out which will complement what the child receives (or doesn't receive) from home, and other areas of the curriculum. But *WHAT* strategies? This so much depends on particular circumstances that fixed strategies are impossible. The following ideas therefore are offered not as strategies in themselves but as means by which you can arrive at your own strategies. Even if there is (as there ought to be) a coherent policy on health education throughout the school, you will still have to work out a content and approach to meet the needs of your own children.

The content is roughly divided into 3 kinds of health education
a) Spontaneous
b) Habit Forming
c) Attitude Forming (which sometimes means attitude bending).

Spontaneous

This will arise (with infants and juniors alike) from such things as a cut finger, a blister, a visit to or from the dentist, a yawn, dirty fingernails, badly fitting shoes, a road accident. It will be valuable because it can be seen by the children to be coming from and concerned with their daily lives. There is a danger that health education as a 'subject on the curriculum' will be seen as a thing apart. The children may find it interesting but will see no connection between it and their daily behaviour. Like the child who had worked for an afternoon on a Road Safety project. On leaving the school to go home he was seen to dash straight off the pavement and across the road without a glance to right or left. How much you can make of isolated incidents will depend on the moment. It could be a five minute talk following a minor classroom accident, or a whole afternoon following a road crash outside school, or an hour following a child's visit to the dentist. Sometimes of course it will be nothing at all. Spontaneous work like this has an important role to play in making health education relevant to the children, so do not neglect it, and try to make use of it whenever you can.

Habit Forming (dental/physical hygiene, general safety, road safety, diet)

This is more important with infants than with juniors. It is also easier. Juniors too though need constant routine reminders to keep their noses clean, to cut their finger nails, about how to carry or hold a knife/pair of scissors, etc. It is desirable that children acquire HABITS of healthy living. A habit is an action which is done, automatically i.e. without much thought. You can help your children to acquire habits
— of cleanliness
— of giving due care and attention (when handling knives, scissors, electric plugs, hot water, etc.)
— of sensible eating, etc.
Regularity and frequency of practise are vital here. Daily attention needs to be drawn and daily practice given to details of hygiene and safety. The best way to do this is to be automatic about the habits yourself. Children with dirty hands/fingernails can be sent/helped to clean them depending on the age of the child. This must be done *NOT* with any overtones of displeasure or of value judgement. Treat it rather as something which has to be done and has been overlooked, i.e. make as *little* of it as possible, but do give it daily attention or half the effectiveness will be lost. There is nothing to be gained by having a hue and cry from time to time about habits which need *PERSISTENT* encouragement.
Whilst on a working party for the Schools Council I did a project on dental hygiene with a class of 5/6 year olds. Each child was given an individual 'dental pack', we borrowed beakers from the kitchen and each child had a small mirror. For the duration of the project, every afternoon before we started work we had a short teeth cleaning ritual. Having watched me clean my teeth the children then set to work while I went round and commented on various aspects of teeth cleaning. I had full time help in the classroom with the distribution of beakers, water etc., and the whole operation probably took about 10 minutes. The project lasted a few weeks — not long enough for the novelty to wear off — and the novelty probably helped as much as anything. Nevertheless the effectiveness of that one strand of the project (of the doing rather than knowing), was demonstrated again and again. The children were forever checking the inside of their own and each others mouths, parents came and asked what sort of toothbrush they ought to buy, carrots and apples were brought in to eat at milk time. On could *feel* the interest in and awareness of teeth. Whether the project had any long lasting effect is

doubtful since it was short. The tale is recounted merely to demonstrate the effectiveness of: *doing* rather than listening; of activity rather than knowledge in the acquisition of a habit. A child can know perfectly well *why* he ought to brush his teeth last thing at night. This won't necessarily make him do it.

Habits of sensible diet and exercise can be fostered at school. They can also be hindered or simply ignored. Are your children given a piece of apple or carrot at the end of their lunch? Are they encouraged to rinse their mouth with water? What do they eat at break time? How would you react to a school tuck shop which SOLD chocolate bars and crisps at break time to swell school funds? Do you know when your children go to bed at night? Do you care? Do the children know you are interested and what do YOU think would be a reasonable hour?

The formation of habits which are likely to foster good health are a vital part of health education. In order to help the children here you need patience, energy, hard work and persistence. It isn't easy but without it you will halve the effectiveness of anything else you do in health education.

Attitude Forming/Bending (smoking, alcohol, drugs, diet, exercise)

This will take up relatively little time in the Infant room since more immediate health education will be the primary concern. It is probably wiser to encourage a child to be interested in/take a pride in personal hygiene and appearance before taking up time with the hazards of smoking. The two are not mutually exclusive but one does come before the other. A child who is genuinely interested in his health and well being, is less likely to see the attractions of smoking than one who has little or no idea about what constitutes good and bad health. Nevertheless attitudes start early, and your influence will matter here. One small gesture can be made against smoking. That is the removal of cigarette packets from the junk modelling collection. It may seem a miniscule detail but it does give cigarettes negative rather than positive associations ('thank you but we'll throw the cigarette packets away. We don't collect these, because we think cigarettes are harmful' or words to that effect). There seems to be something not quite right about a health education programme which aims to warn of the dangers of smoking and yet allows cigarette packets to make up part of the children's educational equipment.

The approach towards attitude forming with Juniors can be two sided. One based on the gathering of factual information, and the other on looking at how advertising tries to influence attitudes. The children can gather information about the amount of money spent on cigarettes/alcohol in one month/year, and suggest ways they think the money could be better spent. They can gather information about lung disease, the harmful effects of alcohol/drugs, various experts (doctors, social workers, ex addicts) can come to talk to the children and answer their questions. Adverts from magazines (for chocolates, cigarettes, alcohol) can be collected for analysis and discussion. The use of humour is probably as effective as anything at this stage. The children can use drama to portray cigarette smokers in a ridiculous light. Let them copy well known adverts and add their own words.

Come to M. . . . . . . country   . . . and learn to smoke like a fool

Drama is the most effective way for them to engage imaginatively with the problems faced by people owing to an abuse of alcohol/drugs. Let them make up plays to perform to the rest of the class on stories based on the destructive force of drug/alcohol addiction.

Obviously these are sensitive areas and no good will come of pretending otherwise. The children know very well that millions of people (perhaps including you) find tobacco and/or alcohol good/desirable. Are you going to admit this to them? Should you? No easy answers. Probably a relatively light, matter of fact approach is best suited to the Primary school. Mostly these things are on the fringes of the children's experience. There are plenty of areas of health education which are well within the children's experience, and these should take precedence over areas which are less central.

Finally, where attitudes are involved, so too is the home. Whatever you do musn't create a conflict within the child between home and school. Home is the dominating influence. School is less important. Acknowledge this fact and work towards some kind of harmony with the home influence, however different the attitude there may be from your own. This may not be easy but it's the surest way to make a positive contribution to the child's health education.

Sex Education

People tend to get very worked up about the question of what (if anything) and how the school should do about sex education. At one extreme are those who feel that this is the sacrosanct responsibility of the home and should not be touched on by any one outside the home. At the other are those who not only feel that the school has a clear responsibility here but that it is better placed than the home to deal with sex education in a dispassionate way. On one hand it isn't really good enough to say that the home *should* take the responsibility and therefore the school *needn't*, when the evidence suggests that so many homes simply *don't* take the responsibility. On the other hand the 'how' of sex education is a long term thing, and, it's success so much depends on the quality of the relationship between teacher and pupils that some schools are much better equipped than others. Some overstep the mark, others came nowhere near it. It is hard to get the right balance. And yet if you seriously claim to be interested in and care about your children's all round development, long term as well as short term, their well being in the future as well as now, then you must take some responsibility for their sex education. This may mean in some cases that you recognise how well the home is coping and therefore you play a minor role. It may mean you have to play a much greater role. It should always mean that you answer the children's questions simply and honestly.

Either (ideally) together with the rest of the staff or by yourself you will consider many things —

— that it is the parent's job to teach this BUT — clearly many parents do not do the job

— that it is simply a matter of explaining the biological facts with accurate technical details and names

— that it is not possible to ignore the human factor i.e. the emotional and social aspects

— that other issues can arise — illegitimacy, contraception, abortion, and is it fair to thrust any or all of these on a primary school teacher?

— that it is a fact that increasing numbers of children reach puberty before they leave the primary school

— and so on.

There are no easy answers, and no one method to deal with all situations. The question of how best to deal with sex education requires careful thought and deep consideration. It is easy to get things wrong. The faults are usually those of degree. That is, the subject is made too much of, and children are worrying themselves about things before they have the emotional maturity to cope with them. Far from lifting a web of confusion from the children's minds this over inflated approach will add to their confusion and perplexity.

The approach where the subject is made *too little of* is equally confusing and unhelpful. I once saw an example of this in a school of 200 children (5-11 years). The top two classes were shown a non self-explanatory film and then vigorously discouraged from asking further questions. It was as if an unpleasant, embarrassing business had to be dealt with, then swept under the carpet as soon as possible.

Some people argue that one way to cope with the problem is to introduce sex education before children become sexually self-conscious. This is fine up to a point but there are difficulties:

a) the age at which a child becomes self conscious about sex, varies enormously

b) information which is inappropriate to a child's stage of development will simply be discarded.

I once witnessed an attempt at sex education with Infants which was unsatisfactory because of a lack of skill in matching material to age range. The attempt came under the umbrella of 'Curriculum Development' and was done in the spirit of experiment rather than from any conviction that this was how the subject should be tackled. Nevertheless it does demonstrate point b) above.

A film had been made of a group of Infants *'Having Babies'*. The children were playing in the Wendy House and several of them had teddies or dolls stuffed inside their vests. One child when interviewed on the film about where her 'Baby' had come from said 'from my bagina', a misnomer greeted with much mirth from the assembled audience of teachers. It was not clear what the aims of the experiment were or indeed whether or not there were any aims. If the aim was to help children to understand where babies come from — it failed. As was demonstrated several weeks later when the same children were hearing about Angela's new baby (Angela was a member of the class)

'And where did Angela's baby come from' asked the teacher.

'From the hospital' came the reply.

'Yes, but how did Angela's mummy get the baby in hospital?'

'From the doctor' came another reply.

The teacher in charge of the experiment had good enough intentions, but her approach was muddled and she assumed too much on behalf of the children. Information which is not clearly relevant or immediately usable will very quickly be discarded.

In general, when dealing with the sensitive areas of sex education do not thrust information upon the children. They are usually the best judges of their level of interest. The number and type of questions they ask will give you a good indication of how much information is required. Too much too soon will be misconceived, quickly forgotten, or both. There is something to be said for placing human reproduction in a wider context. That is by having small mammals (hamsters, mice, rabbits) in the classroom/school. The children can see them produce and rear babies etc., and learn about sex in a natural way. But while this can be a helpful approach it cannot be a *substitute* for human reproduction which because it *is* human, has its own particular complexities. It is probably true that rural children who live among animals have an advantage here over their urban counterparts. In general though, the children will not be helped to come to terms with their own sexual development simply by having seen baby rabbits born and reared.

Junior children are well on the way to becoming sexually selfconscious and no amount of relaxation will enable you to get rid of this completely. Indeed, there would be cause for concern if you did. Still, there's not much point in trying to go through a lesson which is punctuated with giggles, snorts, blushes, embarrassed shuffles and so on. What can you do to reduce the children's self consciousness?

i) The first thing to do is to look at your relationship with them. Is it open and relaxed, based on mutual respect and co-operation? If so, your problems will be halved. If not perhaps you should sort out first things first. At any rate there are some 'defusing' measures which can be taken e.g. Before you use books, slides, film strips etc., note in advance points of possible embarrassed amusement so that you are prepared to deal with them if they arise.

ii) Co-operate with another member of staff so that you can withdraw groups of children for instruction. This will reduce the tension for them *and* the effect of inveterate gigglers and the like on the whole class. Also you can suit material more accurately to a particular group of children.

iii) As a preamble to human reproduction look briefly at the reproduction of single celled organisms (like the amoeba) to focus the children's attention more on the reproductive aspect than the sexual one.

iv) Go into the fascinating detail of sexual reproduction, e.g. the vast number of sperms (millions in one ejaculation) produced, and the fact that only one can fertilize the egg; how, when one sperm has penetrated the egg it triggers off the formation of a membrane around the egg so that no other sperms can enter; how a baby girl is born containing all the eggs she will ever have (several hundred thousand) but that most of them disintegrate, etc. Miniscule detail of this kind has a way of engaging the children's minds so that any embarrassment they might have felt is swept aside by their interest.

v) Show that in this respect humans are the same as every other living organism, i.e. that like produces like

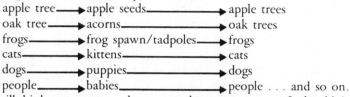

You will think up your own ploys to get the message across. It shouldn't be so clinical that it seems to the children to have nothing to do with them at all. Nor should it be so heavy handed or unbearably embarrassing that their development here is hindered rather than helped.

During the course of the children's sex education it will emerge that although sexual intercourse is the means by which human beings (among other higher animals) reproduce their species, it doesn't always result in reproduction. This can lead to the emotional and social aspects (contraception, abortion, promiscuity). The extent to which you go into these aspects will vary from school to school and indeed class to class. Mostly though these things are on the fringes of Primary children's experience and not central to it. By the time the children leave the primary school, they should have a clear idea of HOW human reproduction occurs. It is probably enough for them to be aware that there ARE emotional and social aspects without necessarily understanding these in depth.

Finally a practical consideration. Many girls start to menstruate whilst still at primary school. Top junior girls therefore should know where to get the necessary equipment and where to and how to dispose of it. It may be an unsettling or even bewildering business for some girls. By removing the practical problems you will help them in a small way to come to terms with this aspect of their sexual development.

Here we leave the content of the curriculum, though the list could go on. I hope you haven't read it all at one sitting. That would be enough to put anybody off. I said at the beginning that the content here is neither comprehensive nor prescriptive. A curriculum is not a static thing (otherwise the children would still be adding pounds, shillings and pence, and measuring in poles, chains and furlongs). It is a living thing to serve the needs of living children. To be successful it must change from time to time to meet new demands, but not so that everything is in a constant state of flux. Just enough so that adjustments/improvements which should and could be made, ARE made.

To begin with though do not be too hard on yourself. Keep things simple and do not crowd in too much. Organise your priorities in the light of your inclinations, the children's needs and the school's demands. Do consider yourself first so that you are in a position to be of most help to the children. A lack of organisation or a taking on of too much could lead to you feeling like a frazzled wreck at the end of each day. This will be no good to anybody. So, in order to serve the children best, consider your needs/inclinations as a priority.

There has been much talk recently about the 'delivered' curriculum. The use of the word delivered in connection with the curriculum I find curious. Apart from the images of bakers vans and the like which it conjures up, the word has unfortunate connotations which do not reflect the best Primary school practice. Once you have, like the postman say 'delivered the goods', then you job is over. Whether the goods are opened or even picked up is not really your concern. This is not the spirit of good Primary practice today. The word 'offer' would come nearer the spirit of good practise in present day primaries. It implies that you want what you offer to be taken up, and further that if it isn't taken up you will seek out something else to offer which will. That is, there is constant striving to match the material to the child (*not* the other way round) so that effective education can take place. The idea of a 'delivered' curriculum with its 'take it or leave it' connotations could set us back fifty years or more.

1. Important Concerns

This chapter deals with some areas which are not in the curriculum as such, but which have a bearing on its quality and how you make it work.

1. Remedial Education

Remedial children —— for want of a better label, (others like 'children with learning difficulties', 'backward', 'slow readers' etc. are no better. No one label can ever be fully satisfactory to describe such a disparate group) often suffer a double disadvantage. First, they suffer a learning disadvantage through no fault of their own. Second, they receive an education which compounds their disadvantage instead of one which reduces it.

The whole area needs more attention than it gets. These children need to a greater extent than their non-remedial counterparts gifted teachers, stimulating resources and patient attention. They very rarely get this.

The material given to these children must be seen to lessen whatever difficulty they have. Otherwise school for them must seem as an ever more puzzling maze, in an ever increasing fog. Often they are lumped together and dished out with the same 'remedy' regardless of individual problems. Rather like giving a patient with a broken leg the same treatment as one with a headache/cut finger/sore throat, etc.

Generally speaking this vitally important area is not given due recognition in the Primary school. Yet this is where most good could be done. The earlier a learning difficulty can be identified the easier it should be to give appropriate help. Of course in one sense the problem of remedial children is less acute in the Primary than in the Secondary school, and therefore it is easier to ignore. Because of the younger age group and the freer organization of the Primary school, the children's problems can go undetected. In many schools the children drift along in the stream without any serious attempt being made to assess individual problems or to arrive at satisfactory ways to meet these. This is a grave mistake. To wait until the size of the problem forces the issue is wrong. More emphasis on remedial education in the Primary school would probably mean fewer children would *need* it in the Secondary school.

The word *remedial* implies that there is something to be remedied. It might be expected that the remedy would be related to the problem. This is rarely the case. As we have said, children are labelled remedial (or a variety of other descriptons) and lumped together as a homogeneous group. The fact that their learning difficulties spring from widely different sources is seldom taken into account. The fact that not enough is known about learning difficulties in children is not taken into account either.

There is a widespread assumption that children will learn if
a) you make the steps small enough, and
b) you make them repeat the work often enough.

There is some sense in this. Children who are slow learners will probably benefit from being presented with slightly smaller learning steps, and also from the opportunity to repeat and consolidate their work more often than average/fast learners. The trouble is that the assumption is often taken too far — the steps become too small, the repetition too great. Remedial children are given exercises the point of which is so infinitesimal that it disappears. The work appears to be pointless to the children, bearing no relation to their everyday life. Boredom sets in, negative attitudes to themselves, their problems with their work and their ability are deepened. Clearly this kind of 'help' worsens the plight of slow learners.

All children, but more especially children with learning difficulties, require work which is attractive and interesting. More important it should be work which can be seen in the context of their everyday lives. To chop work up into dry unrelated particles is to compound a child's learning difficulties.

Children can either be removed to receive remedial help or the remedial teacher can come into the classroom. There are pros and cons for both arrangements depending on the school and the personalities involved. It is ideal when the class teacher can cope with her own remedial children but this is not always possible. Whatever arrangement is used it is of the utmost importance that it in no way adds to the feeling of stigma or inferiority which slow learners so often suffer. This is not to suggest that a pretence of any kind is put forward to the children. Such a thing would be dishonest and in any case would be unhelpful. Nevertheless there are steps which can be taken to ensure that a slow learner has no cause to feel doubly hard done by. For example, make sure that a child does not miss anything of particular enjoyment/value (T.V., gym, art and craft, film) in order to receive remedial help.

In order to give a child the best possible help the remedial teacher should know as much as possible about the child. It will probably be up to the class teacher to talk to the remedial teacher about the child and his or her circumstances, and to offer information of a general nature. The fuller the picture the class teacher can paint the better so that the remedial teacher may be able to diagnose more accurately the child's particular problem.

There are schools in which there is no provision of any kind for remedial work. There is no teacher with special responsibilities, the problem of children with learning difficulties is not recognised as such and the difficulties of the children are largely ignored. No matter how heavy the workload is (and it can be back breaking), the class teacher should try to do better than this for these children. Their needs are just as important as those of the abler children. Because the needs of the less able are more difficult to a) ascertain and b) satisfy this does not mean that these needs can be ignored.

The term 'remedial' has been used here to describe those children who for different reasons show learning difficulties. A child may be simply a slow learner which is not really a difficulty at all. These children should be allowed to go at their own pace and enjoy as much sense of achievement as their abler counterparts. After all for one child to add 69 and 87 and get the answer right will *BE* a real achievement, for another it will be as natural as breathing.

The problem may be more complicated. Many remedial children suffer from emotional disturbances, a malfunction of the sensory motor organs, or deprivation of one kind or another.

Remedial education is seen here as a means of *counteracting* any influence which may contribute to a child's learning difficulties, and as a way of compensating for deficiencies in the child's home or personal life. Finally it is seen as a way of doing a job thoroughly and well.

The assumption often is that children who cannot read, write, add or whatever to an 'average' standard are either lazy, not interested, disobedient, uncooperative, that is — culpable in some way. More often than not such an assumption is false. These children probably want to read, write, count etc., with the best of their fellows. And, that they can't is more of a problem and worry to them than we realise.

So, it is a question of accurately assessing the problem then giving the *RIGHT* kind of help.

Years ago I had a child in my class who had an original, lively and inventive mind. He could rig up a pulley in the classroom, set up an electrical circuit so that when he opened his desk a light went on inside. His reading and writing were not up to standard though, and he had been deemed 'remedial'. The remedy in his case was to go off to the library twice a week with other remedial children from around the school. There under the guidance of the remedial teacher he would work from a book entitled 'Reading to some Purpose'. The title was ironic. As far as John could see he seemed to be reading for no purpose at all other than to practise putting capitals and full stops at the beginning/ends of sentences. Much better would have been to use his interests (electric circuits, elementary physics, animals), and gear some questions around these to encourage him to write. John's work was not improved by his remedial help. At best it was a waste of time; at worst it put him off even more the very things it was supposed to help, i.e. his reading and writing.

I once gave a talk to some remedial teachers. The thrust of my argument (or question since I wanted them to give the answer) was 'Isn't good practice in Remedial Education similar to good general Primary practice in mainstream work, only MORE SO? That is *more* attention to the child, *more* one to one between child and teacher, *more* scope for creative work and play, *more* attempts to bring the outside world into the classroom and so on.

I explained at some length why I thought such practice might be especially useful for remedial children.

During the discussion after the talk one teacher said that 'Your method' (whatever that meant) may be fine for normal children but that it wouldn't 'do for him'. He had a very 'difficult' boy of nine or so, who just *could not* count. 'You lay out 20 bricks on the desk, one time he'll count 1, 2, 3, and so on up to twenty with no problems, the next time he'll count 18, 21 anything but 20.'

I was somewhat nonplussed and made some noises in reply about how very difficult it must be, etc. I should have said that perhaps the child had not had sufficient practise in one to one correspondence. Give such a child activities which *provide* this practice (give him a pile of pennies and a slot to put them through, counting as he goes; take him out to the playground and let him grasp the railings one by one as he counts to twenty, let him shake alternate hands with you as you count 1, 2, 3; put 20 big hoops on the floor of the hall and let him place a classmate one by one in a hoop as he counts to 20 and so on) and nine times out of ten there will be a visible improvement in the child's ability. There is no argument for saying that such work is too 'babyish' for a nine year old. A nine year old who cannot count to 20 has a problem. Anything which can be seen to help him to master his difficulty will not be scoffed at. Besides, seeing that you are more concerned about helping him than shaming him, he will be more concerned about meeting you half way than about being insulted by babyish work.

So in the light of existing circumstances in your school what can you do to realize maximum potential?

The following questions are offered as a starting point from which you can sketch out your plan for doing this. They are completely random and no preconceived plans lie behind them.

- Is there a policy for remedial education throughout your school?
- How many children in your care would you say need special help?
- Is there a remedial teacher in your school?
- Does she have any special knowledge of the subject?
- Is the remedial group reviewed throughout the year so that children can return to a normal timetable if this is considered best?
- Is there an effort made to screen children for learning difficulties at an early age (say 6–7½)?
- Is there an attempt made to treat children individually or in groups with similar difficulties?
- Are the children removed for remedial help? Is this the best arrangement?
- Do you work with the remedial teacher? Does she have a plan of work for each child?
- Could you swap places with the remedial teacher occasionally so that she takes your class while you work with the remedial children?
- Who decides which children are in need of remedial help?
- Do you have access to material specially written for remedial purposes?
- Is there consultation with parents about a child's learning difficulties?
- Are your children ever deprived of subjects which they especially enjoy in order to receive remedial help?
- Have you looked at the textbooks/printed material which the children use? It is suitably matched to the particular learning difficulty?
- Have you ever devised work which attempted to match a child's learning difficulty?

- Is there a stigma attached to remedial learning in your school? If so can you do anything to counteract this?
- In the everyday work of the classroom are the children grouped according to ability?
- Do you make any provision for mixed ability learning i.e. when children of different intellectual capacities can work together (and learn from each other) on a project which requires a variety of skills?
- Do you show the children that you are interested in the work they do with the remedial teacher?

The questions are intended to help you not to undermine you. No one could answer all the questions satisfactorily. Do not be surprised/disappointed if your answers present a somewhat bleak picture. You cannot be expected to be on top of everything all the time. Besides the task of giving Remedial Education its due attention is outside your immediate responsibility.

Nevertheless you will be in direct contact with children who display learning difficulties. The quality and suitabilty of remedial help which these children receive could depend entirely on you.

2. Tests and Testing

These are useful up to a point but they ought not to assume too much importance in the Primary school. A test can help you in various ways e.g.

a) to assess the work you have been doing, i.e. to test yourself
b) to find out how much the children know
c) to find out how much they do not know
d) to check that your own standards are reliable (this will involve the use of standardized tests).

It is important that you know what you want of a test (even if it is a mixture of things). No test can be as well suited to the children as that which you devise yourself. Every child should have the opportunity to show himself — and you — how much he *does* know as well as how much he does not know. Therefore devise your own tests tailored to fit the work, the children and the needs of the moment.

The quality and usefulness of a test depends to a large extent on how the results are interpreted. There are two ways in which the results can mislead. They can lead us to think that a child understands MORE than he does — the fact that a child can write $4 + 5 =$ 　$\boxed{9}$　 and fill in the box correctly does not tell us a lot about his understanding of 4, 5 or 9, the fact that he can write, 'Edinburgh is the capital city of Scotland' does not tell us a lot about his understanding of Edinburgh, Scotland, the word capital or the word city. They can lead us to think that a child understands LESS than he does — the fact that a child does not fill in the $5 + 4 = \square$ box does not necessarily mean that he does not understand that $5 + 4 = 9$ (i.e. asked to add $5 + 4$ using rods and beads he could). It could just mean that he cannot formalize his understanding.

This is an extreme view and in the main the results of tests probably give a reasonably accurate picture. Nevertheless it is a narrow, one dimensional picture. This leads us to the second way in which the results of a test can mislead.

They can lead us to think that the results of a test(s) give us a full picture of the child. The fact that a child does well/poorly in class tests is a comparatively *small* piece of information about that child. The results will be less misleading and more valid when they are set in the context of your own assessment which is based on daily contact with the child.

The usefulness of the test as a teaching device will be greatly increased if you vary the content and format of the tests you use.
e.g. Spelling
    a) teacher reads words aloud, children write down the spelling
    b) teacher reads a list of words explaining the meaning where necessary, say — great, gate, wait, mate, late, bait, — then children are asked to write down the words which have a similar spelling
    c) teacher reads a list of words through then gives clues — children write down the answer to the clues —
       'large or big' — (great)
       'you can do this for a bus' — (wait)
       'fishermen use this' — (bait)
    d) children given lists of words and devise crosswords for each other.
Variety of this kind is essential not only to give everyone a chance to show what they can do, but also to help to deepen understanding about this or that aspect of learning. A child may instantly know that $8 \times 4 = 32$ yet spends ages working out how many chairlegs there are in a group of 8 chairs, OR — spell 'threw' correctly in a test of 'ew' words but write threwe, throu, thru (or whatever) in different circumstances. A child has not actually learned something until *he or she can use it in a variety of situations and recognise it as the same thing.*

Varying your tests also means that you will allow as many children as possible to do well. There are some children who will never do well in a written academic test yet who may do very well in a practical test. So include practical tests (mend a broken toy, repair a torn book, arrange a display of natural items — feathers, stones, flowers, or machine parts — nuts, bolts, screws); and pose practical problems in a test — on a camping trip, if you had no food container, how could you keep food dry and safe from animals? What would you use instead of a raincoat to keep yourself dry during a rainstorm? How would you light your house if electricity was cut off? How could you measure the length and breadth of a window frame without a measuring tape or ruler? What preparations would you make if you knew that the water supply was to be cut off for 24 hours?

Tests like this can bring to light talents which would never emerge in a straightforward academic test. Many children leave the primary school never having done well in any test. This is a poor reflection on the school and not surprisingly these are usually the children who have a low opinion of their achievements and a negative attitude towards school. Include different types of tests therefore so that it isn't the same top few who are always rewarded. Generally speaking they have reward and motivation enough. Much as you will enjoy your high-flyers and much as you *should* praise them, it will do them no harm to step aside once in a while to let others shine. And, it could do the others a whole lot of good.

Another way to make the test more useful is to split the children into ability groups for tests. Not only can the test be better tailored to suit a particular group, but more children also have a chance to experience that sense of achievement (*and* encouragement) which comes from doing well in a test.

Standardised Tests (to tell you such things as a child's reading age or mental age)

These are useful to reassure you about your own standards but do not be too much in awe of them. When such a test is being administered the children will be quick to sense an atmosphere of tension. Many of them under such conditions will become tense themselves. Tension will not help a child to give of his best, and you will not achieve as accurate a result as you might have done.

On the other hand it is important that these tests are administered strictly according to their instructions otherwise the result will be somewhat invalidated. It is advisable to use more than one test (you rarely get an identical result from two different tests and sometimes the discrepancy is surprising) in order to get a more balanced view. Also of course, for general purposes, place the result of a such a test in the *context of your own assessment of the child.* The judicious use of the test can be a most valuable teaching aid. The view that the use of the test in the Primary school is almost pointless and even harmful is unnecessarily extreme. Provided that you do not set too much store by the results, nor take up too much time with them you can use tests to good advantage. Besides, the children love the excitement which a test can bring. Also, a test helps to concentrate the mind and 'fix' things which otherwise might remain out of focus.

3. Discipline

As was said in Chapter 2, good discipline is important. This doesn't mean that the children have to be treated like square-bashing zombies. Nor that conformity through fear should rule the day. It means that you and the children should feel relaxed and at ease with each other. Also that there is a sense of order and harmony in the classroom rather than one of chaos and anarchy. Where there is no good discipline there is probably no good anything else. There are two kinds: that which is imposed from without and that which comes from within (self discipline). Both are necessary to the smooth running of a primary school classroom though one is more important than the other.

One of the phrases which sticks in my mind from college and which has been borne out by experience is 'expect respect'. That is *assume* that the children *will* respect you. Then, of course work to earn it.

The children will not try to please you if they don't respect you, nor if:

a) they don't *know* what pleases you. *Tell* them what you expect (and why) in the way of good behaviour

b) they don't *care* whether you are pleased or not. They are more likely to care if first you show that *you* care about *them*

c) they are bored. Material which engages their minds and imaginations leaves them no time (or inclination) for mischief.

Having been out of the classroom for some years I had to go back into one recently to test some material for a maths textbook. The book was intended to be used with top juniors (10's and 11's), and I went round to the local middle school to explain what I was doing and to ask if I could 'borrow' a class for an hour. When I got to the school some days later I found that I had been given a 4th year class (13 year olds). The next hour turned out to be something of an ordeal. To start with I was nervous at being in front of a class again *and* acutely aware that the material I had for them was pitched at a much younger age level. Anyway things started well enough, I explained the what and why of the lesson and the children set to work on the material — a page of music in which the children had to 'find the maths' by answering ten questions. After a while a restlessness began to grow. Silly questions were asked, pencils were dropped, broken, replaced, comments were made to me ('This isn't maths miss this is music'), and to each other ('Come on dodo, give's that rubber'). I stopped them once or twice to keep things from disintegrating completely but I was really only containing the situation and was enormously relieved to hear the bell ring for break. The children were probably just as relieved, they were in the top stream for maths and were generally intelligent, co-operative and motivated. But here was a strange teacher who seemed a little nervous — an irresistable signal for them to play the fool and test me out. The main reason though for the breakdown of the lesson was the unsuitable material on which they were working.

Sometimes, then, it's the material's fault more than yours, but *you* suffer the problems of a breakdown in classroom order. Avoid such problems therefore by checking through material before you dish it out to the children.

d) they feel unduly restricted.

I remember when I was around 9 or 10 our teacher saying (it must have been in desperation) 'Right, hands behind your backs, you can all jolly well sit still until the bell goes. Not one movement or sound from anyone.'

Now I was the least rebellious 9 year old imaginable but for some reasons I could NOT respond to this dictum. I brought a hand from behind my back towards my throat.

'SANDRA! out here' she pointed to the front of the classroom.

'Did you *hear* me, I said not *one* movement didn't I? What were you doing?'

'I think I felt a pain in my throat,' I lied.

To her credit (and my relief) she didn't quite manage to hide an involuntary smile. I think I was sent back to my seat with a verbal admonishment to keep my hands *behind* my back.

There's no point in *asking* for trouble. On the whole children are reasonable beings and will take a resonable amount of restriction. If the restriction becomes unreasonable one or two are bound to resent it and cause trouble.

Self Discipline

This is the discipline worth striving for. In the long run it is this one which will bring the greatest benefits to the children in their adult lives.

To help the children towards self discipline you must

a) believe it is possible (i.e. that the children *can* indeed behave responsibly — from the reception class onwards)

b) show them by your actions that you believe this. Let them see that you expect them to behave responsibly (because you believe they can) and, to a large extent, they will. Give them responsibility for jobs around the classroom and school: small (watering the plants/feeding the fish) as well as big (marking the register, counting the lunch numbers, putting on the record player, displaying the songs/hymns for assembly). Occasionally, let them do things *their* way — whether it be to dress themselves/make their *own* greetings cards/make and design their *own* books. The increased confidence which comes from doing a job absolutely unaided is worth the back to front tights, upside down birthday card, back to front book etc. The very fact that you allow them to do these things will help to develop their independence which in turn will help towards responsible behaviour.

c) give them a share in the running of the classroom/school. As well as fulfilling the function of b) above this makes them aware that things actually have to BE run (i.e. that things don't run themselves). After a month of checking the scissors every night, a child will be more inclined to put the scissors back in their proper place as well as to pick up a stray pair from the floor instead of stepping on or over them.

Children's behaviour is largely a reflection of our expectations. The more you show that you believe they *can* be trusted to behave responsibly the more they will.

One morning during my second year in teaching I was 15 minutes late for school (having abandoned a petrol-less car and run the remaining 2 miles). I was somewhat frazzled when I got to school (not least because of an authoritarian Infants Mistress who treated probationary teachers as slightly superior infants, and expected us to be in school at least half an hour before the children) I rushed in to my class of 45 six year olds expecting her to be there. To my surprise there was no sign of an adult in the classroom but a quiet buzz of activity was evident. The children were busy at this and that, some were building towers with Cuisenaire Rods, others were drawing, others reading etc. So intent were they on their various activities that they hardly noticed my appearance.

The school was a 1000 strong primary and the routine of coming in from the playground, undressing, going into the classroom was so well organised that it had become almost automatic.

On asking whether Miss M had been in I was told she hadn't. 'Who set you to work?' I asked. 'Just us' came the reply. Still incredulous I said 'but who said to take the rods out?' 'Oh well you weren't here so we thought we could have some busy time' (our term for their own time when they could do what they liked). I went through to the teacher next door expecting some more information — she hadn't even realized that I wasn't in school.

Children can attain self reliance and responsibility IF YOU ENCOURAGE AND ALLOW THEM TO. Too often they are not given the chance to become responsible.

Naturally they will let you down sometimes. Their better selves will not always be in command. When this happens don't undo things by adopting an air of 'I told you so' or 'I knew you couldn't be trusted' etc. By all means let then know that you are disappointed and even angry (if you are) but don't slip into destructive comments. There's a world of difference between 'I thought you could be *trusted*' and 'I *knew* you couldn't be trusted'.

A sense of responsibility has to grow in a child. It is not 'there' in infancy any more than it suddenly 'appears' at puberty. It develops with practice. Generally speaking, children are not given enough practice to develop responsibly.

Moral Development

The development of self discipline is linked to a growing sense of right and wrong. This brings us to Moral Development. Like most developments this is a gradual process. In the Primary school the issues are on the whole fairly straightforward. It is clear to see and easy to demonstrate that cruelty and stealing are bad/harmful/hurtful — therefore wrong, and that truthfulness and kindness are good/helpful — therefore right.

There is a growth line here as there is in mental and physical development. Your job is to encourage movement along the line as you do in other areas of development. We do not expect a child to run before he can walk or read before he can talk. Similarly we ought not to expect too much too soon from a child in the way of moral development. Sometimes the desire to eat a sweet or own a marble overcomes any sense of right and wrong about stealing. And, a fear of recrimination can be a stronger motive than a love of truth.

Kindness and understanding will teach more about right and wrong than anger and retribution will. Also your example will be worth a thousand sermons. Punishment can be an aid to moral development or it can be simply punitive. Ask yourself what you want the punishment to do:

— make the child think about his actions?

— deter him from repeating them?

— make him feel ashamed?

— alienate him?

— give yourself or another child the satisfaction of revenge, etc?

Naturally you will not always get it right. There are many times when a split second decision is called for and of course you'll make some mistakes. Children if truly cared for are astonishingly forgiving. So, don't worry about the odd mistake. Apologise when you can though, it helps a lot and besides it is only courtesy.

My son, at 8 years old, was taken out of his line in assembly one morning to sit by a teacher because he had been 'squashed'. When assembly was over the teacher unthinkingly sent him back to his classroom. (The rest of his class stayed on for hymn practice.) Back in the classroom his own teacher asked why he was there. 'Miss E sent me back' he said. 'You must have been naughty Tom, you can copy out this morning's hymn from the hymn book in your best handwriting. I shall ask Miss E about this at playtime.' Even the most spirited of children (and he was one of these) can feel too inhibited to explain a misunderstanding, and Tom set to work.

This was bad enough but after playtime insult was added to injury, 'You can leave that now Tom I've had a word with Miss E. She only moved you because you were squashed.' '*Then*, she threw my best handwriting in the bin' Tom reported indignantly. I explained that everybody makes mistakes — even teachers. Nevertheless a 'Sorry' here would have made a big difference to Tom.

Though the majority of your work here is straightforward, there will be many 'grey areas', personal relationships, children being 'left out' or made fun of, children cheating, etc. Sorting out the rights or wrongs, or degrees of blame in these areas will not always be easy. It requires a sensitivity of approach, but you can only do your best. You will be most effective though when the children realize that you are sincerely concerned for the best interests of all of them. And, naturally, for them to realize this you have to BE sincerely concerned.

Honesty helps a lot. I once had to umpire a game of cricket (the rules of which I had only the haziest notion) with some eleven year olds. Ten minutes into the game a fracas occurred about some infringement or other, which I hadn't actually seen. I could have made an arbitrary decision in favour of one side or the other but each side was so evidently convinced that it was right. I explained that I hadn't seen the incident and so didn't really know who was right but if they agreed I could toss a coin to decide then at least the game could continue. They agreed, the coin was tossed and the game continued. One or two of the children may have been put out and obviously this is not recommended as a proper way to umpire. Nonetheless on the whole they seemed to realize I was trying to do the best I could for everybody and at the end of the afternoon a lot of pleasure seemed to have been had by all.

Again the best kind of teaching here is by example. How can a child grow in goodness who hardly ever sees it? By being discourteous to the children you will teach them to be the same, and vice versa. And a courtesy based on a caring concern for others, is not a million miles from moral development.

4. Parental co-operation

The fashionable phrase these days is parental involvement. I have purposely avoided using it because I think there are too many misconceptions about what it actually means. And, it seems to me that parental co-operation is what we should be after. First, it is less open to misconception, and second it is nearer to what good, on-going primary practice should be about, towards the end of the 20th Century. We'll come to that presently, but first a look at some of the misconceptions about parental involvement:

a) That it is new. Good practice for the past 20-30 years (and longer in the case of Infant schools) has always sought the involvement of the parents in their children's education. That it is spreading is good. It is perhaps a mistake though to put it across as something new (the findings of recent experiments in parental involvement back up what good practitioners have known all along). It would be more convincing to say to the unconverted that the move to increase parental co-operation stems from a desire to spread that which has been demonstrated to be effective over a number of years. Then at least the instant and automatic mistrust of 'the new' would be eliminated.

b) That it means something specific — it doesn't. Parental interest and co-operation can be manifested in many different ways, from serving tea at a school function to listening to their own child read.

c) That it means parents should be involved in the running of the school (this in itself is unhelpfully vague and open to any number of interpretations.) In well run schools there is no question of the professionals ducking out of this responsibility. And, the parents are on the whole well enough pleased with how the school is run anyway without seeing any *need* to 'become involved' (other than in a supportive capacity) in this.

The first job of a staff then is to see that the school IS well run so that the parents have no cause for complaint. Staff have to see that the school is run for the well-being of its members both present *and* future, i.e. they have to take perhaps a longer term view than parents do. Naturally, parents' suggestions are to be welcomed and treated seriously. At the same time they have to be thought of in terms of the whole school and years to come, not just in terms of one class or one year.

d) That the statutory parents on a school's governing body/provision of a parent's room/statements from the head that parents are welcome at any time, etc., NECESSARILY means that the school is sincerely concerned to court the parents co-operation. Outward signs are easy and yes they are better than nothing. But, they cannot be a substitute for the real effort which is needed, if you are to show the parents that you seek and welcome them as partners in their children's education.

e) That it means involvement in the children's *general* education (as if they weren't involved up to the hilt in this already. Whether the school approves or not of the parent's effect on the children doesn't alter the fact they *have* an effect and a much deeper and longer lasting one than the school.) It really means involvement in the child's school education.

f) That parents who are not involved in the school sense, i.e. who are not seen at the school every day, watering the plants, cooking with groups of children, listening to children read or whatever, are NOT helping their children as much as those who *are* doing these things.

g) That parents *want* to be actively involved in their childrens' school education. Most parents are very happy to let the school do the job for which it is well equipped (so long at it is seen to *do* the job). For one thing many of them have jobs of their own to attend to. For another they want to get on and live their own lives whether or not this entails paid employment. An acquaintance once told me of the new head of his son's school who was very keen on 'giving the parents a piece of the action'. He sent a questionnaire round to parents asking them what kind of maths they would like their children to learn. 'I hadn't the least notion what maths I wanted him taught' said Jeremy, 'so long as they did a decent job. I thought it was *his* business to decide such things. I've more than enough decisions to worry about as it is.' This head probably had the best of intentions but, besides sloughing off a certain amount of responsibiity, he was taking parental involvement to a ridiculous extreme and certainly out of the realms of common sense.

h) That teachers have to be accountable to the parents *before* the children. Your first duty and accountability is to the children. Sometimes this can cause conflict with a parent. May main experience of this is having to explain to parents that because x is not on the same reading/maths book as Y, doesn't mean he is lazy, stupid or slow and that 'pushing' him would NOT be the right thing to do. If, against your better judgement, you 'push' a child because of parental pressure, then your priorities are wrong. Yes, we must listen to and learn from the parents. They are experts in matters concerning their own child. But we must also listen to and learn from the child. The two do not always teach the same lesson.

These then are some misconceptions about parental involvement. Parental co-operation would be nearer to good practice because it is more easily attainable by all parents. It has a simple message — 'A working together in a common cause to a common end'. This can be done in a variety of ways — by transmitting positive attitudes about the school to the child, by backing up the school's policy on handwriting, homework, number work, etc., buying raffle tickets, coming to meetings, washing towels, serving at jumble sales, helping in the classroom, etc. — All these things are equally co-operative. A co-operative endeavour allows each bit (in this case home/school) to be separate but complimentary. It suggests a *merging* of the influences of home and school so that the child is educated in the round as it were. Parental co-operation will *encompass* parental involvement (for some parents), without making the other parents feel out on a limb or not up to scratch.

Involvement on the other hand has to be seen to be believed as it were, (can a parent claim to be involved if all she does is to buy raffle tickets for the school bazaar?). One definition of the word is actually 'complicated affair'. It is not necessary for a parent to be involved in his/her child's school education. Co-operation is enough. This brings us to a crucial point i.e. co-operation with what? Anything? Does school just because it IS school know best at all times? Obviously not. The onus is on the school to impress the parents with its seriousness of purpose, and its high hopes and expectations for, and of, the children. *Then* to look for co-operation. NOT to look for it before deserving it. If you let your parents see that you are completing your end of the bargain thoroughly, and well, you will have no problems of a lack of co-operation nor of destructive interference which so often stems from fear and anxiety on the part of the parents.

Those schools where specific strategies have been worked out to encourage real parental involvement in the life of the school have had a large measure of success (due, as much as anything to the good will and dedication of the staff). But generally speaking, if parents are to become a permanent feature (i.e. one which doesn't vanish once the novelty has worn off), the strategies will have to be less specific. Welcome those parents who want to become involved, but offer the same spirit of welcome, whenever you have the chance, to those who do *not* want to.

Recent experiments to involve parents in the early stages of their children's reading have had encouraging results. That there could be any doubt that parental involvement in their child's reading could be anything but beneficial was somewhat surprising to me. In the school where I started teaching 20 years ago this was taken for granted, as indeed it was in the school where I learnt to read 35 year ago. It was natural a) to expect parents to be interested in their children's school work, and b) thought to be sensible to capitalize on this interest and enlist the parents help, and c) assume that the two sided approach could only help the child.
Once the child could read the first book in the main reading scheme (28 words) it could be *taken home*. A great deal was made of this event (Tanya can take her book *home* today/Well done Alan I think you will be able to take your book home by Friday) so that it was a real milestone on the road to reading, and gave the children something to work towards. After this the book went home more or less daily with the page number (up to which the child had read) written on a marker. The parent heard 1 or 2 pages, or the same page again if the child was not ready to go on, and entered the new page on the marker. This isn't offered as THE way to tackle early reading, and indeed there was a lot wrong with the

system. Nevertheless it was highly successful, and it demonstrated the common sense of enlisting the parents help as agents in their children's learning. Reading lends itself particularly well to this kind of treatment, but a great deal of early number work could easily (and on the whole isn't) be helped in a similar way.

Your job will be easier and more enjoyable if you have the backing and support of the parents. Mutual trust and understanding between parent and teacher must only be good for the child. From time to time though, a parent may need to be reassured that you are doing a decent job, and that the child is making the most of his or her time in school. This is especially so when

i) children first start school

ii) children move to a new teacher

iii) new ways of working are introduced

iv) re-organisation of any kind takes place

v) a child is going through a 'difficult phase'

vi) the parents themselves are suffering from some kind of trauma.

Take the time and trouble to give this reassurance when it is needed. It could save weeks of anxiety for a parent. Naturally parents are interested in what goes on in school in relation to their children. Yet many have only the vaguest notion about this, and are intimidated by the school and its workings. To a certain extent this is inevitable, but there is still huge room for improvement. I myself still feel somewhat of an 'outsider' when I go into my sons' schools. This, despite the fact that I've had ten years in the classroom, and that one of the schools is 'welcoming, open and friendly', indicates just how much onus is on the school to put the parents at ease. Onus too to put them in the picture about their children's work. I really know very little about the work my children do day by day. Of course I could go to the schools and ask, but I am very reluctant to take up a busy teachers' time when I have no real cause for concern — only a wish that I had more idea of what was going on.

The more confidence the parents have in you the more they will be happy to leave you to the job for which you have been trained. Most parents are happy to do this anyway, but one or two anxious parents can start off a mood of growing dissatisfaction. You would be wise to allay such anxieties before they become a problem.

It seems to me that, in England at any rate, a neglected point of contact between home and school is homework. Regular homework can be an ideal vehicle to help the parents to become involved in their children's school education. The work should be varied and relatively easy. The sessions should be short (5-10 minutes for Infants; 20-30 minutes for Juniors), and regular so that the child becomes used to the rhythm of working at home. A hit and miss, once in a while type homework, means that the child has to 'gear up' mentally each time, simply in order to face the task. This is a burden and a chore, and does little if any good. Handled in the right way, homework has a lot to offer to the dialogue between home and school, e.g.

a) It forms a link between home and school.

b) It informs the parents about what work the child is actually doing.

c) It can bring to light the child's misunderstandings, which the parents should be encouraged to come to discuss with you.

d) It may mean more work for you, but this is offset by the advantage to the child — and therefore to you too. Besides, and organised programme of homework helps *you* to be more organised about your work generally.

e) It helps the child to form habits of 'working at home'.

f) It helps to break down the image of home/school as representing completely separate and distinct entities and functions.

While it is desirable that parents should feel that they have open access to the school, they should not be allowed to undermine your position within the classroom. Some heads allow (even encourage) a situation to arise in which the work of the classroom and the school generally is disrupted because of too much parental intervention. Teachers should be accountable to parents but not too accountable. You must be allowed to make professional decisions without recourse to the parents. This means of course that you must be able to MAKE professional decisions AND back them up with reasons. If you can do this you are in a strong position to insist on a reasonable amount of professional autonomy.

Parents help in the classroom has its pros and cons. Usually it is valuable but sometimes it can be a nuisance and more trouble than it is worth. A colleague of mine went through a very unhappy patch in her school when 'parents in the classroom' became the mark of enlightened teaching methods. My colleague was an excellent teacher but worked best without parents in classroom. She especially objected to feeling that the staff had been manipulated on this matter. She remained inflexible, and hers was the only classroom into which parents did not go (to hear children read, help water the plants, clean the paints, or whatever). Over the weeks she began to feel that perhaps she was not such a good teacher as the rest of the staff who had, (some reluctantly), opened their doors to the parents willy nilly. Her classroom work probably suffered and therefore the children were the ultimate losers. It is a pity to allow things to get out of hand in this way. Common sense and a genuine concern for the children will help to organise parental help in a manner which is satisfactory to all concerned.

Parents should be interested and even to a certain extent involved in the work of their children in school. Nevertheless their contribution to their children's education is more important outside the school. As we've already said, those parents who have time and energy to spare for the school are to be welcomed and thanked, but those who do not show an inclination to become involved are not to be condemned. The attitude I heard expressed at a recent meeting of a local P.T.A. — that it's always the same willing few who show up when there's work to be done — doesn't really help anyone. The majority of parents are happy to leave their children in the capable hands of a professional, if the hands are seen to *BE* capable and the staff to *BE* professional.

Most of the responsibility for the relationship between home and school lies with the head. He/she will set the tone of the school and ultimately make most of the decisions regarding policy. Nevertheless you will have many ways in which you can foster good relations yourself.

Direct Contact

Those of you with infant children have a special responsibility here as well as a wonderful opportunity. You will see much more of the parents than the rest of the staff. The younger the child the greater (usually) is the parental interest. Capitalize on this interest whenever you can. When the parents come to collect the children you could mention in passing any event of interest concerning a particular child, 'John fed the goldfish/tied his own shoelaces/worked hard on his writing today — didn't you John?' Little exchanges like this will help a parent to see that you take a personal interest in the child and their confidence in you and the school generally will be increased. If on the other hand a parent picks up the impression that you have no real interest in her or her child, she may well start to feel anxious about her child's development in school. Those of you with older children will not have so much direct contact, but you are still in some part responsible for the parent's impression and assessment of the school. Make good use of the contact you do have. If a parent comes into your room to see you, give a greeting or acknowledgement of some kind even if you are busy with something.

I have seen parents having to stand unacknowledged by a teacher while she finished the register, collected lunch money or whatever. This is really plain bad manners. A few words ('Hello Mrs X. I'll be with you in a moment,' or even a *glance* of acknowledgement) couldn't seriously interrupt proceedings whatever they were. To display a lack of something so basic as common courtesy will do nothing to increase the parent's assessment of you or the school.

Try to get your parents names right. These may not always match the child's name. A small detail but in public relations details matter. Keep the parents informed as much as possible about what is happening. The children are not always the most reliable messengers. When a message has to be conveyed with dates and times write a note rather than rely on word of mouth. A further reminder say two days before the event is also useful, and appreciated by the parents.

Finally, when you do write a letter to the parents, make it a proper one. There seems to be a peculiar habit amongst school teachers to end a letter with a typed version of their name instead of a proper signature. This has a distancing effect. A personal signature not only helps to make the letter more personal, but also more normal and 'of the world' rather than peculiar and 'of the school'.

An extra touch can be added by addressing the parents personally — 'Dear Mrs Martin, Mr Singh, Mr and Mrs White' etc. has an instant effect never achieved by 'Dear Parents.' I know it's asking a lot, and not every letter could be like this. Nevertheless, it's this kind of detail which helps to strengthen the parents regard for your commitment to them and their children.

Indirect Contact (Public Relations)

For many parents the child will be the measure of his teacher. The child who is happy at school, interested in his work, who himself shows a high regard for his teacher, is more likely to encourage his parents to hold the teacher in the same high regard. On the other hand, the child who is unhappy at school, bored/frustrated/confused by his work and shows no regard for his teacher, is hardly a good advert for you at the school. You have the opportunity to influence the children so that their attitude towards school becomes more positive or less positive. Parents will see/sense this influence. Children are notoriously non-committal about what goes on in school, but they do sometimes repeat a phrase or statement which can tell the parent a great deal about the teacher. e.g.

I listened to two three year olds talking in my kitchen as they drew with chalk on a blackboard.

1st child
'Are we allowed to scribble here?'

2nd child
'Yes my mummy lets us scribble'.

1st child
'We're not allowed to scribble at nursery, we've got to draw properly.'

My own son reported from his own (very formal) nursery — 'Mummy, Miss F doesn't let boys play in the Wendy house. Why doesn't she? Daddies live in houses don't they?'

My younger son reported from his (very informal) nursery school — 'I made a sword today from a twig in the playground but when it was clearing up time my teacher told me to throw it in the bin. Why did she tell me to do that mummy? It was my best sword.'

Before I left the house to go to my seven year old's open evening he was reminding me what to look for in his books.

'There's one page I don't like, I wish teachers wouldn't put round circles and crosses on, only ticks. Mrs M, she's made a mess of my book. I could have easily done the wrong ones again.

A six year old to his mother — 'Mrs X said my writing was terrible and I had to do it all over again. I did it nice the next time and then she said it was worse than the first time and it wasn't.'

A mother to an eight year old who had taken an envelope with two interesting foreign stanmps — 'What did Mr Y say about the stamps?' 'He told me to put them on the cupboard and we'd look at them later but he never asked for them again so I just took them home.'

A mother to a ten year old who had been given a piece of coral from an uncle — 'Why don't you take that in to show Mrs — ?' 'NO, Mum. She's not interested in that kind of thing.'

A friend's seven year old complained

'I can't finish this book tonight Mummy'.
'Why not?'
'Mrs H has to go to the big cupboard in the hall for a new one'.

'Well that's all right'.

'No it isn't. The last time she said 'don't read books so fast Juliette' '.

The intention behind the reporting of these exchanges is not to make you frightened to say anything. It is to make you aware that sometimes the things you say will be reported to the parents from a child's point of view, and therefore take on quite a different complexion. Also the parent sees the child and his needs as much more central than you can (with 25 others to consider). Therefore what happens/doesn't happen to the child during the course of the school day is perhaps seen as more important than it actually is. It will be helpful for you to bear this in mind when dealing with an irate parent of one kind or another.

As well as the things you say to a child the things you do will form part of the parents assessment of you.
e.g. if a child grazes his hand/breaks a shoelace/tears his trousers/loses her gloves
do you — ignore the incident as much as you can?
      — make things worse by scolding the child?
      — diminish the child's panic?
      — do what you can to solve the problem?
Nobody expects you to be a saint, and there will be times when you will rant and rave over a minor issue (sometime to good effect). Nevertheless a child who reports that his shoe has been flopping up and down all day because of a broken lace will present a different picture of his teacher than the child who shows that some effort (even a piece of string) has been made to rectify the problem.

The school is assessed in all sorts of ways e.g. *the litter problem* — is it horrendous, ignored or dealt with; *a visitor's first impression* — is it a welcome smile from child and adult, or a secretary's irritated response implying that visitors are decidedly unwelcome at all times; *The garden* — is it cared for and pleasing to look at or unkempt and ugly. Many of these are outside your immediate influence but it will do no harm to think about them, and could even spur you on to action when an opportunity arises.

It comes down to a calibre of caring. Sloppy standards are not impressive on any level. If you care about the children, and have their interests at heart, it will be obvious to the parents and will come across in all kinds of ways. Not the least of these will be your apparent pleasure and satisfaction in the job. For it should go without saying that the more you put into the job, the more you'll get out of it.

At a harvest festival recently I noticed that the children were all in stocking feet (the staff were in ordinary outdoor shoes) in order to preserve the surface of the floor. This was necessary since the hall also doubled as a gym. Nevertheless to see the children (9-13 year olds) shuffling about in stocking feet was not impressive. The image conjured up was of prisoner of war camps. How much more impressive it would have been to see the children in gym shoes or even special 'hall shoes' made or knitted by themselves.

Schools are in the uniquely vulnerable position of having been experienced in some way or other by most of the population. Other professions have a reasonable amount of protection from the slings and arrows of the outside world, because of a lack of knowledge about what is actually involved in say plumbing, publishing or pig farming. Some years ago I went for an annual contact lens check-up. I spent a total of four minutes in the optician's chair. During this time *one* lens was taken out, glanced at, cleaned and put back. The other could have been scratched, chipped, even non-existent for all the optician knew or bothered to discover. For this 'check-up' I paid the princely sum of £9.50. I calculate this as £142.50 per hour (minus a few pounds for overheads, etc.). Without going into debates about the fairness or otherwise of teachers' financial remuneration, it seems that something is not quite right here. And certainly one witnessed a job not well done. Of course the role of the teacher excites the general imagination to a far greater degree than does the role of the opthalmic optician. Still, if one were able to turn the searchlamp back towards the myriad faultfinders, for example to the politician's own profession, the academic's own achievement, the supermarket manager's own service, the road mender's own skill, the doctor's own decisions etc., the faults would I'm sure be no less, and in some cases far greater than those found when the lamp is upon the teaching profession. Nevertheless, because people have had some experience of schools, many of them feel that they can and must *pronounce* about how schools should/should not be run, what teachers should/should not be doing etc. There isn't an aspect of school life, from school milk to examinations, which is free from a welter of *uninformed* advice. In many respects it is good that such interest is shown but you should keep comments in perspective. YOU know more about the ins and outs/pros and cons of vertical grouping, integrated studies, discipline, handwriting policy, etc. IN YOUR SCHOOL than anyone from outside the school.

Ignore the comments which clearly stem from a lack of understanding (these can come from the so called quality newspapers as well as the shopkeeper down the road), and get on and do the job you are well equipped to do. Enlighten such comments when it is appropriate, and when you have energy to spare, but don't waste your energy. When asked by a friend of mine what this book was about I said Primary education.

'Oh yes the stuff of articles in the Manchester Guardian' he quipped. 'It's difficult to keep up with the fads, first it's this then it's that.'

Fads are absolutely NOT what Primary education is about. Certainly there have been experiments in method and content but these are relatively superficial. Primary education (among other things) is about a steady and consistent improvement in quality. This has been demonstrated over the last half century or more. An achievement all the more remarkable when you consider the sometimes overwhelming odds. And, an achievement which is due in large measure to the steadfast commitment of the single teacher on the shop floor, to serve the children well and to do a decent job.

There it is then, *Primary First* or First things First; get it right at the beginning and you'll halve potential difficulties. Get the first button wrong and you'll never be properly buttoned up.

You have chosen an immensely enjoyable and rewarding career. A small number may have chosen unwisely. It is hoped that they will realize before too long and seek out something which will be better suited to their talents and inclinations. Most of you will go on to deepen and increase your experience and skill. Many opportunities will present themselves. Some of them you will have to miss. Do not miss them all.

There are many paths to heaven and many ways to be a good teacher. If this book helps at all to make you become in your own way a better teacher, it will have served its purpose.

Index